Teaching Hemingway and the Natural World

TEACHING HEMINGWAY
Mark P. Ott, Editor
Susan F. Beegel, Founding Editor

Teaching Hemingway's *The Sun Also Rises*
EDITED BY PETER L. HAYS

Teaching Hemingway's *A Farewell to Arms*
EDITED BY LISA TYLER

Teaching Hemingway and Modernism
EDITED BY JOSEPH FRUSCIONE

Teaching Hemingway and War
EDITED BY ALEX VERNON

Teaching Hemingway and Gender
EDITED BY VERNA KALE

Teaching Hemingway and the Natural World
EDITED BY KEVIN MAIER

Teaching Hemingway and the Natural World

Edited by Kevin Maier

The Kent State University Press   Kent, Ohio

© 2018 by The Kent State University Press, Kent, Ohio 44242
All rights reserved
Library of Congress Catalog Card Number 2017016132
ISBN 978-1-60635-318-9
Manufactured in the United States of America

Library of Congress Cataloging-in-Publication Data
Names: Maier, Kevin, editor.
Title: Teaching Hemingway and the natural world / edited by Kevin Maier.
Description: Kent, Ohio : The Kent State University Press, c2018. | Series: Teaching Hemingway | Includes bibliographical references and index.
Identifiers: LCCN 2017016132 (print) | LCCN 2017031205 (ebook) | ISBN 9781631012846 (ePub) | ISBN 9781631012853 (ePDF) | ISBN 9781606353189 (pbk. : alk. paper)
Subjects: LCSH: Hemingway, Ernest, 1899-1961--Study and teaching. | Nature in literature.
Classification: LCC PS3515.E37 (ebook) | LCC PS3515.E37 Z6983 2018 (print) | DDC 813/.52--dc23
LC record available at https://lccn.loc.gov/2017016132

Contents

Foreword
    MARK P. OTT   vii

Introduction
    KEVIN MAIER   1

Part One: Michigan

"Nick trailed his hand in the water": Understanding the Importance of Landscape in *In Our Time*
    ELLEN ANDREWS KNODT   11

On Familiar Ground: Intimate Geographies and Assumptions of Place in Hemingway's Nick Adams Stories
    LAURA GRUBER GODFREY   20

"Summer People, Some Are Not": Seasonal Visitors, Cottage-ing, and the Exoticism of Hemingway's Michigan
    JEFFREY HERLIHY-MERA   35

Organic Space and Time: Using Henri Bergson to Explain Nick Adams's Intuition of the World in "Big Two-Hearted River"
    SCOTT ORTOLANO   45

A Darwinian Reading of "Big Two-Hearted River": The Re-enchantment of Nick Adams?
    MICHAEL KIM ROOS   57

It's All About a Perfect Drift: Reading the Fishing Metaphor in "Big Two-Hearted River"
    LARRY GRIMES   72

Part Two: Gulf Stream

Not Against Nature: Hemingway, Fishing, and the Cramp of an Environmental Ethic
    RICK VAN NOY AND DAN WOODS   89

Man or Fish?: An Ecocritical Reading of *The Old Man and the Sea*
    ALLEN C. JONES   102

The Sea Has Many Voices: A Maritime Studies Experience of *The Old Man and the Sea*
    SUSAN F. BEEGEL   114

Part Three: Africa

"Shootism" Versus "Sport" in Hemingway's "Macomber"
    GARY HARRINGTON   129

Pity and the Beasts: Teaching Hemingway's Stories via Sympathy for Animals
    RYAN HEDIGER   141

Teaching the Conflicts in "The Snows of Kilimanjaro"
    SEAN MILLIGAN   152

Part Four: Europe

"I hated to Leave France": The Geography and Terrain of Hemingway's *The Sun Also Rises*
    DONALD A. DAIKER   163

A Few Practical Things: *Death in the Afternoon* and Hemingway's Natural Pedagogy
    ROSS K. TANGEDAL   178

Part Five: The Transatlantic Hemingway Text

Flashbacks and the Trials of Hemingway's War Veterans: Healing in the Natural World
    ROBERT MCPARLAND   195

Skiing with Papa: Teaching Hemingway in the Backcountry Snow
    SCOTT KNICKERBOCKER   206

Appendix   213
Works Cited   220
Selected Bibliography   231
Contributors   233
Index   237

Foreword

Mark P. Ott

How should the work of Ernest Hemingway be taught in the twenty-first century? Although the "culture wars" of the 1980s and 1990s have faded, Hemingway's place in the curriculum continues to inspire discussion among writers and scholars about the lasting value of his work. To readers of this volume, his life and writing remain vital, meaningful, and still culturally resonant for today's students.

Books in the Teaching Hemingway series build on the excellent work of founding series editor Susan F. Beegel, who guided into publication the first two volumes of this series, *Teaching Hemingway's* A Farewell to Arms, edited by Lisa Tyler (2008), and *Teaching Hemingway's* The Sun Also Rises, edited by Peter L. Hays (2008). In an effort to continue to be useful to instructors and professors—from high schools, community colleges, and universities—the newest volumes in this series are organized thematically, rather than around a single text. This shift attempts to open up Hemingway's work to more interdisciplinary strategies of instruction through divergent theories, fresh juxtapositions, ethical inquiries, and often employing emergent technology to explore media beyond the text.

Kevin Maier's *Teaching Hemingway and the Natural World* speaks to issues that continue to be of intense interest to students and scholars today: How did Hemingway engage the natural world? Did he see animals—marlin, trout, big game, bulls—as creatures to be conquered? Or, as a fisherman, hunter, and aficionado of the bullfight, was he trying to connect with an inner primal state, a spiritual brother? The expertise and insight Maier brings to his highly regarded, wide-ranging scholarship on such topics as environmental rhetoric, hunting, fishing, and tourism is manifest throughout this volume. These diverse essays exploring Hemingway's fiction through the lens of the natural world will revise our understanding not only of Hemingway but of hunting, bullfighting, skiing, fishing, tourism, landscape, the literary marketplace, popular culture, and men's studies. Indeed, this volume demonstrates that not only is Hemingway's work being taught in more thoughtful, creative, and innovative ways in today's classrooms and lecture halls than every before, but scholars are now extending the classroom and taking the Hemingway text to trout streams, ski slopes, and fiestas around the world.

Introduction

Kevin Maier

Ernest Hemingway is a writer we often associate with particular places and animals: Michigan's Upper Peninsula, Spain's countryside, East Africa's game reserves, Cuba's blue water, and Idaho's sagebrush all come to mind. We can also easily picture the iconic images of Hemingway with fly rod bent by hefty trout, with bulls charging matadors in the background, or of the famous author proudly posing with trophy lions, marlin, and a whole menagerie of western American game animals. As Robert E. Fleming once put it—updating Gertrude Stein's famous quip that Hemingway looked like a modern and smelled of museums—Hemingway "was also a hunter, fisherman, and naturalist who smelled of libraries" (1). Hemingway indeed read widely in natural history and science, as well as the literature of field sports. This lifelong interest in the natural world and its inhabitants manifests itself in Hemingway's writing in myriad ways. To be sure, from the trout Nick Adams carefully releases to Santiago's marlin, from Robert Jordan's "heart beating against the pine needle floor of the forest" to Colonel Cantwell's beloved Italian duck marshes, and from African savannahs to the Gulf Stream, animals and environments are central to Hemingway's work and life.

Since its origins, Hemingway scholarship has been marked by a robust treatment of these animals and environments. Malcolm Cowley's introduction to *The Portable Hemingway* focused on the fishing of "Big Two-Hearted River," for example. Similarly, Phillip Young's famous "code-hero" hypothesis arguably hinges on an understanding of hunting culture's rules of engagement for the natural world. In both these instances, and in much of the early scholarship, however, Hemingway's representations of the natural world are mined for how they explain male psychology more than for how they suggest a particular relationship to the natural world or its inhabitants. While these representations often served as background for broader arguments related to more human-centered matters in early scholarship, more contemporary critics have opted to treat animals and environments directly. Fleming's 1999 collection *Hemingway and the Natural World* offers an excellent foundation, but with the rapid emergence of environmental literary studies in the last two decades much work remains.

This collection aims not only to advance scholarship on Hemingway's relationship to the natural world but also to facilitate bringing this scholarship to the classroom. Indeed, the goal of the *Teaching Hemingway* series is to present collections of essays on various approaches to teaching emergent themes in Hemingway's major works to a variety of students in secondary schools and at the undergraduate and graduate levels. The goal of this particular volume of the series is to explore how teaching Hemingway might help shed light on broader questions about the human relationship to the nonhuman world. Organized geographically, each section that follows features two or three essays about Hemingway's favorite places.

Despite our association of Hemingway with particular places and with the natural world more generally, his work is not often featured as part of the broader conversations about environmental literature. As the first two essays in the collection eloquently suggest, one potential reason for this gap might be explained by the way Hemingway represents environments. Indeed, in the first texts to be firmly established as canonical environmental literature—Aldo Leopold's *Sand County Almanac* or Rachel Carson's *Silent Spring*, for example—verisimilitude and scientific accuracy of descriptions characterize the representations of environments; Hemingway's environments are often much more obliquely presented. This is odd, of course, because truth and precision are certainly hallmarks of Hemingway's ethos and style, but they do not necessarily characterize his rendering of landscape. Ellen Knodt helps her students arrive at this conclusion by linking Hemingway's landscapes to Paul Cézanne's cubist visual rhetoric. Unlike canonical environmental literature, Knodt's essay suggests, Hemingway's landscapes are suggestive rather than descriptive, presented in juxtaposition rather than logical or rational sequences. Knodt concludes that Hemingway's landscapes are "something more" than a typical argument in favor of an intense connection to landscape through precise and accurate description. Laura Gruber Godfrey picks up where Knodt leaves off. Noting a similar lack of precise descriptive landscape detail in the Nick Adams stories, Godfrey amplifies Knodt's argument by suggesting that Hemingway's "words are not merely arranged to make us see these places, but more so to make us think that we are seeing them *again*" (22). Godfrey specifically asks her students to seek out largely absent landscape details to make this claim, their absence helping students see that Hemingway's style, in his early Michigan-based fiction especially, evokes the sense that we are in conversation with a "storyteller with whom we share a deep well of geographical knowledge and understanding" (25). Godfrey focuses on "Three-Day Blow" and "Summer People," suggesting that landscape details that lie below the iceberg in Hemingway's work help convey an intimate relationship to place.

Focusing on his approach to teaching "Summer People," Jeffry Herlihy-Mera cautions us to avoid a too narrowly focused celebration of Hemingway's depictions of the natural world, offering several smart ways to bring issues of social class and tourism into our discussions of his fiction. Drawing on his unique perspective of teaching Hemingway in Puerto Rico, Herlihy-Mera and his students help us remember that Hemingway and his characters are in fact well-to-do visitors to the beautifully depicted Michigan landscapes, and this culture of privilege informs their interactions in significant ways.

To kick off the next cluster of Michigan-oriented essays, all of which focus primarily on the oft-anthologized story "Big Two-Hearted River," Scott Ortolano, like Knodt and Godfrey, also turns to Hemingway's "aesthetics of omission" in his descriptions of the environment, finding elements of Henri Bergson's philosophical tenets instead of traces of cubism or a rhetorical style that privileges intimacy. In Ortolano's approach to teaching "Big Two-Hearted River," students' close readings are enhanced by an introduction to Bergson's philosophy, which helps them arrive at the conclusion that the story "provides a method of discovering existential fulfillment within the changing environments of 'modern' America" (47). Michael Kim Roos also addresses the existential in his contribution, but instead of suggesting that Nick finds meaning in the Bergsonian "flow of life," Roos suggests Hemingway "infused the story with evolutionary details" to portray Nick as engaged in a struggle to understand more fully his place in a Darwinian natural world indifferent to the individual organism's finitude. Roos's astute historical reading is accented by careful attention to textual detail in a way that students might emulate. In contrast to Ortolano and Roos's philosophical and theoretical approaches to the famous story, Larry Grimes's essay rounds out this this section with what we might call a "grounded" reading of "Big Two-Hearted River." Grimes asks his students to actually get outside to camp or fish in conjunction with reading the story, but more importantly he reads the story through a Thoreauvian lens, asking us to think of it in the tradition of Transcendental nature writing rather than the predominant critical convention of reading the story's fishing as Nick's effort to control his postwar emotions. For Grimes, in other words, the trauma of Nick's war experiences, which scholars have long argued are central to understanding the story, are less important than the subsequent immersion in the natural world.

All six of the essays in the first section of the book remind us that Hemingway indeed thought carefully about the natural world, helping us as teachers find ways to bring these ideas into our classroom discussions. In fact, this disproportionately large first section suggests that these early short stories might prove to be the best vehicle for bringing Hemingway into the conversation of a literature and environment course, just as they might help highlight a broader argument about nature's nation in an American Literature survey.

The next section develops similar arguments, though the essays broaden the scope beyond Michigan. Rick Van Noy and Dan Woods help us move from the Upper Peninsula to Cuba, as their contribution makes a similar argument to Grimes, again noting that "Big Two-Hearted River" should be read to suggest that Nick finds balance and a deeper connection to the natural world through his fishing. Van Noy and Woods extend this reading to *Old Man and the Sea*, working throughout their essay to counter the conventional approach of reading Hemingway as presenting the theme of "man against nature." More specifically, they argue that his texts suggest instead that important lessons are learned through immersion in the natural world. This attention to the contrarian "theme" of man versus nature suggests another potential reason we don't often read or teach Hemingway in relation to environmental issues: his perceived domination of the landscape. Working against the idea that Hemingway and his characters only see the natural world anthropocentrically, Van Noy and Woods find a nascent or proto-environmentalist ethic in their reading of *The Old Man and the Sea*. Similarly, Allen Jones offers a thorough overview of the various ecocritical arguments surrounding the famous book, concluding by narrowing his focus to the novel's final scene to make a compelling case that we ought to read the book environmentally, such that it "expands our understanding of the world and our place in it as scholars and citizens of an increasingly fragile environment" (103).

Susan F. Beegel's eloquent essay presents a grounded and historicist conclusion to this section, offering several compelling ways for teachers to contextualize the maritime history so central to *Old Man and the Sea*. Drawing on her experience teaching the novel as part of a Literature of the Sea course designed for students engaged in a broader maritime education program, Beegel provides several practical suggestions for syllabus plans, classroom exercises, and how to bring comparative historical details to discussions of the novel. Her persuasive claim is that to understand the book we need to "explore the relationship between the writer and his subject, the natural world" (124). To understand this novel's depiction of the nonhuman, Beegel reminds us, it is helpful to try to see the sea through Santiago's boat-level eyes—or, as she puts it, "to understand the fisherman we must study the fish." While this perspective is perhaps best gained through experiential and interdisciplinary education, one can also elucidate this history with image-heavy "slide lectures" and good comparative approaches.

In a series of seminal essays, Beegel has long argued that we should consider Hemingway's relationship to nature; her scholarly approach always carefully historicist, she asks us to avoid anachronism, to attend to the particular, and to be attentive close readers. Teachers would do well to read her important essay "Eye and Heart: Hemingway's Education as a Naturalist" in *A Historical Guide to Ernest Hemingway*. While Beegel finds evidence of a naturalist in Hemingway's life and work, the prevailing attitude among environmental critics has long held that Hemingway's exuberant hunting—both in his life and in his texts—exacted such a bloody toll on the natural world that linking him to the naturalist traditions seems, simply, contradictory. Glen A. Love made this claim most emphatically in his 1987 essay, "Hemingway's Indian Virtues: An Ecological Reconsideration." In a single footnote, Love offers a devastating catalog of animals killed by Hemingway to suggest that, despite his gestures toward something we might recognize as an ethic of care, Hemingway typically "adopt[ed] an aggressive and isolated individualism which wars against those natural manifestations he claims to love" (203). As Love notes, Hemingway's "body count" was never higher than in Africa. The three essays in the next section engage this hunting, finding ways to help us teach Hemingway and his work without dismissing his engagement with the natural world entirely.

Following Beegel's scholarly lead, Gary Harrington turns to the historical, in this case, Hemingway's *Esquire* essays, to offer a compelling reading of the "The Short Happy Life of Francis Macomber." In Harrington's analysis, ideas about hunting presented in the nonfiction essays serve to alter the way we might shift our sympathies between the fictional story's two main characters, and in particular their respective engagements with the natural world. In the following essay, Ryan Hediger asks us to think of the lion as a character deserving of reader's sympathy, noting that the famous story explicitly encourages us to see the situation from the lion's perspective. Hediger highlights the pedagogical efficacy of asking students to identify with animals, extending his reading beyond "The Short Happy Life of Francis Macomber" to suggest the ways in which the approach helps us engage other stories, but in particular "The Africa Story" from *Garden of Eden*. In the final essay in this section, Sean Milligan takes up the symbolism of African landscapes and animals more directly, suggesting that a productive way to teach "The Snows of Kilimanjaro" is to focus on the conflicts. Milligan indeed begins with a thorough and useful introduction to this pedagogical tactic made famous by Gerald Graff, offering helpful overviews of the key tensions in the ways critics have treated these symbolic landscapes in the story over the years. Taken together, these three essays point to ways that the original assessment of Hemingway as a "game hog" might do a disservice to the author's larger engagement with the natural world, arguing that attending to hunting in a proper historical context with careful attentive close readings might in fact enliven classroom discussions.

In the first essay in the next section focusing on Hemingway's work set in European contexts, Donald Daiker turns from conflicts to contrasts, suggesting the efficacy of teaching *The Sun Also Rises* in terms of its various geographies. For Daiker, mapping the novel's physical geography against its emotional geography allows us to better follow Jake's "journeys from dangerous to safe terrains" (174). Ross Tangedal, meanwhile, argues that we might read Hemingway's neglected first bullfighting book, *Death in the Afternoon*, as a representation of Hemingway's writerly pedagogy. His essay focuses, as he puts it, "on key pedagogical factors within Hemingway's text, how he uses the natural landscape of Spain, the cultural epoch of bullfighting, the technical confidence of *aficion*, and a critical eye on writing *teach* his readers" (181). Even if we aren't assigning *Death in the Afternoon*, Tangendal's ideas offer a compelling way to think about Hemingway's rhetorical tactics. Moreover, Daiker and Tangendal's essays remind us that, for Hemingway, there is more to Europe than cafés and parties—even if he is linked to Europe's predominantly urban landscapes, it is important to remember that Hemingway keys in on more natural environments, too.

While the last two essays in the book defy easy geographic classification, they both read Hemingway's work with an eye toward helping readers understand our relationship to the natural world. Robert McParland recounts his experiences teaching Hemingway to American veterans to ask whether stories about war and, in particular, subsequent renewal in the natural world might help both veterans and nonveterans understand the horrific experiences of soldiers. Scott Knickerbocker, meanwhile, recounts his experience of teaching Hemingway's writing about skiing—"Cross Country Snow" in particular—to enhance an experiential environmental education course. Knickerbocker offers a defense of close reading as a pedagogical tactic, suggesting that reading Hemingway attentively in different contexts can lead to an ecological awareness.

Although the essays in the collection adopt a wide range of disciplinary approaches and treat a wide range of texts, they all share an interest in bringing greater awareness to Hemingway's writing about the natural world. They remind us, moreover, that classroom discussions of Hemingway's writing about particular places and animals sheds light not only on human concerns but on the broader concerns of the natural world, too.

Works Cited

Beegel, Susan F. "Eye and Heart: Hemingway's Education as a Naturalist." *A Historical Guide to Ernest Hemingway.* Ed. Linda Wagner-Martin. New York: Oxford UP, 2000. 53–92.

Fleming, Robert. "Introduction." *Hemingway and the Natural World.* Ed. Robert Fleming. Moscow: U of Idaho P, 1999.

Love, Glen A. "Hemingway's Indian Virtues: An Ecological Reconsideration." *Western American Literature* 22 (1987): 201–14.

Part One

Michigan

"Nick trailed his hand in the water"

Understanding the Importance of Landscape in *In Our Time*

Ellen Andrews Knodt

Undergraduate students unfamiliar with Ernest Hemingway's fiction are often puzzled by his short stories. Students complain that "nothing happens" in a story like "Big Two-Hearted River." Accustomed to reading for plot, students overlook Hemingway's use of landscapes to convey meaning. They assign discussion of landscape to that literary term "setting," which means little more to them than the place and time of a story. As a result, they often miss a story's complexity. Even acquainting them with Hemingway's famous iceberg metaphor doesn't fully bring their attention to landscape. In order for students to understand the complexity of these stories, they need to slow down their reading and consider the descriptions of landscapes the foreground, rather than merely the background of the story. But how can we bring the importance of landscape to our students? I have found that three approaches have helped students to appreciate Hemingway's descriptions of landscapes in these early stories.

First, to open up students' appreciation of Hemingway's landscapes, we can link his writing to the art of painting, which he acknowledges as an important influence. His writing apprenticeship in Paris included his fascination with Impressionist painters, particularly the work of Paul Cézanne. In the excised portion of "Big Two-Hearted River," printed posthumously as "On Writing," Hemingway writes, "He wanted to write like Cezanne painted. . . . He, Nick, wanted to write about country so it would be there like Cezanne had done it in painting" (*Nick Adams Stories* 247). His affinity for landscape was evident from the beginning of his career as he writes to Edward J. O'Brien in 1924 about his *In Our Time* stories: "What I've been doing is trying to do country so you don't remember the words after you read it but actually have the country. It is hard because to do it you have to see the country all complete all the time you write and not just have a romantic feeling about it. It is swell fun" (*Letters* 154). At the end of his life, as he wrote his posthumously published memoir *A Moveable Feast* (1964), Hemingway remembers trying to get the landscapes depicted in his earliest stories in such detail that the readers could experience it as he did: "Some days it went so well that you could make the country so that you could walk into it through the timber to come out into the clearing and work up to the high ground and see the hills beyond the arm of the lake" (91). Since most students have little or no knowledge of Cézanne, these connections still will not mean much to them. What does Hemingway mean that he wants to write the way Cézanne painted?

So that students may begin to have a visual understanding of Hemingway's comments, I distribute postcards depicting Cézanne landscapes to my students and ask them to study what they see. (Instructors could use images from the internet, but I like the students to "possess" their own Cézanne landscapes.) We discuss the images on the postcards, taking note of Cézanne's blank spaces, colors, geometric forms and layers, and anything else students notice. Students realize that Cézanne's landscapes are not photographic realism but impressions built up by colors and shapes that emerge as an image of a mountain, a house in the woods, or a beach on the seacoast. Theodore L. Gaillard Jr. points out how Cézanne "would intentionally leave small areas of the canvas blank . . . causing viewers to fill in spaces with preconscious constructs" (67).

Once students are acquainted with Cézanne's art, a second approach introduces them to scholars' explanations of ways that Hemingway's landscapes mean more than they may at first appear to mean. One such scholar, Emily Stipes Watts explains in her landmark study *Ernest Hemingway and the Arts* (1971) that in Hemingway's fiction "elements of literature and painting had, at times, become blended in such a way as to suggest a single idea of art" (xii). This single art, combining the visual and the verbal, accomplishes a great deal in a compact space. Landscape in Hemingway's works, according to Watts, "although realistically described, still represents something more, some metaphysical or emotional or symbolic expression of the artist himself" (42–43). In similar terms, these landscapes are examples of what Carlos Baker calls a "double vision," combining the realistic and symbolic (292).

Watts explains further the connection Hemingway often creates between landscape and character: "Hemingway often sketched in only enough landscape so that the reader is aware of the immediate physical relationship between nature and the fictional character" (29). This use of landscape to comment on a character's situation conveys far more than the mere setting of a story or novel, as according to Watts, "On one level, Hemingway was employing a technique of imagist poetry in creating these scenes. That is, he was isolating and describing a specific image as precisely as possible. The carefully chosen words of physical description are made to stand for the emotional or intellectual significance" (48).

Agreeing with Watts, Gaillard directly asserts that Cézanne's art "deeply influenced Hemingway's writing as seen in Hemingway's use of the blank-canvas power of the implied but unspoken, [the] meticulous placement of emotionally colored words and images . . . [which] would force us to focus on highly descriptive detail whose imagery . . . would come to vibrate with symbolic meaning" (67). Remembering his early comments on Cézanne, Hemingway again expressed his debt to the painter in *A Moveable Feast*: "I was learning something from the painting of Cezanne . . . to make the stories have the dimensions that I was trying to put in to them. I was learning very much from him but I was not articulate enough to explain it to anyone. Besides it was a secret" (13). According to H. R. Stoneback, Hemingway himself "nailed the secret" in a manuscript marginal note: "Make the emotion with the country."

After students are aware of the connection of Hemingway to Cézanne, and scholars' discussions of the importance of landscape to meaning in Hemingway's stories, they read the stories assigned and are urged to write in their journals about the Cézanne landscapes on their postcards and the landscapes in the stories. Two stories assigned that illustrate connections between landscape and meaning are "Indian Camp" and "Big Two-Hearted River," each of which involves interpretations that depend on landscape.

Examining specific scenes in "Indian Camp," an early story in *In Our Time*, shows the connection between nature and a fictional character. The story is framed by a boat trip on a lake to and from the Indian camp. Students are asked to focus on the description of the first boat trip. In the beginning of the story, the emphasis is on the boats and the Indians' rowing; the sounds ("Nick heard the oarlocks of the other boat"); the technique of rowing ("quick choppy strokes"); and the weather ("mist," "cold on the water"). But there is no direct connection between Nick and the water, and there is little emotional content, except "Nick lay back with his father's arm around him" (*Complete Short Stories* 67). (For an extensive analysis of this and other scenes in "Indian Camp," please see Robert Paul Lamb, *The Hemingway Short Story*, 3–83.)

At the end of the story, after Dr. Adams performs a jackknife caesarean and the Indian husband commits suicide, the return trip by boat is quite different.

Michael Reynolds calls such scenes "echo scenes in which Hemingway will run the same scene past the reader twice. However, on the second run the emphasis of the scene will have shifted slightly so that the reader is invited to make a comparison between the two scenes" (245). The second boat trip occurs after Nick and his father talk as they walk back to the lake, and the father apologizes for what the young boy has witnessed ("I'm terribly sorry I brought you along, Nickie.... It was an awful mess to put you through" [69]). Nick asks several questions about birth and death to which his father replies, concluding with Nick's question, "Is dying hard, Daddy?" and his father's reply "No, I think it's pretty easy, Nick. It all depends" (70).

Our class discusses what differences the students notice between the first and second boat trips. The final two paragraphs of the story focus on the return boat trip on the lake, with the father rowing instead of the Indians and with Nick alone in the stern. Instead of nighttime, this time it is a new dawn: "The sun was coming up over the hills." And this time, "A bass jumped, making a circle in the water," showing the life-giving property of the lake. But perhaps to my mind, even more significant is Nick's physical action, quite typical for a young boy: "Nick trailed his hand in the water. It felt warm in the sharp chill of the morning." Nick has direct contact with the water, which he finds warm, comforting in the chill. Its warmth is reassuring. This brief physical moment, sparsely described, is enough to produce a profound emotional effect on young Nick, for it is followed by the famous last sentence of the story: "In the early morning *on the lake* [emphasis added] sitting in the stern of the boat with his father rowing, he felt quite sure that he would never die" (70).

Students (and critics) vary in their interpretations of Nick's final thought, but this focus on the character and landscape solidifies the importance of Hemingway's natural descriptions. The ending of the published story is enigmatic, relying on the physical description of Nick's contact with the water, in Watts's words, "to stand for the emotional or intellectual significance" (48).

While some readers see his conviction as mere bravado (DeFalco 32), I believe Nick has a genuine epiphany, brought on by his direct contact with the warm, life-affirming water. I agree with Paul Smith's conclusion that "What Nick feels is not a lie" and that "[we can't] invoke any truth conditions to deny the boy's feelings" ("Who Wrote" 148; see also Waldhorn 54–55). While the other conditions of being in the boat with his father may contribute to his feeling, the immediate cause may be his actual contact with nature. Juxtaposing Nick's contact with the water with his new assurance that he would never die—without stating a connection between the physical act and the psychological state of mind—is part of Hemingway's modernist craft. As Paul Smith comments, "What is unconventional [in a Hemingway story] and so inscribes his fiction as modernist, is that the scenes often are juxtaposed with little transition and less logic to effect or explain their sequence or rationale" ("Introduction" 8). Building students' awareness of the importance of Hemingway's landscapes through his desire to blend both visual and verbal art allows students to read more closely, to slow down their reading and notice what is going on even in the shadows of a story.

A frequently anthologized *In Our Time* story that focuses most intensely on landscape is "Big Two-Hearted River." This story often perplexes students because, as mentioned, little "happens." So many readers have commented on the images of the river and its inhabitants—"the trout keeping themselves steady in the current" (*Complete Short Stories* 163), the river "clear and smoothly fast in the early morning" (173)—and on the symbolism of the river and the swamp. But I wish to focus on a moment that I think has been largely overlooked, a moment that is significant because it describes Nick's entering the river, an act he has been so carefully preparing for.

From the beginning of the story, readers have been treated to accounts of Nick's connections to the landscape of northern Michigan. We learn of his hike from Seney through the burned-over country with the river running through it (163–65); of Nick's return to this scene after a long absence, "It was a long time since Nick had looked into a stream and seen trout. They were very satisfactory" (163); of Nick's plan "to hit the river as far upstream as he could go in one day's walking" (165); and, finally, "At the edge of the meadow flowed the river. Nick was glad to get to the river" (166). After Nick's hike, he prepares his camp, cooks his dinner, makes "the coffee according to Hopkins," and goes to sleep, even though "His mind was starting to work. He knew he could choke it because he was tired enough" (169). As Brøgger says of Nick, he is "a man who needs to feel in control of his environment" (26). In Part I of the story, my students sense Nick's attempt to stay composed, to maintain an emotional balance. They notice lines like "He had not been unhappy all day" (167) and "He knew he could choke it" (169). Students who have read more of *In Our Time* associate Nick's comments with his possible return from World War I. But while the story is often anthologized without any context of war, students feel that Nick is trying to get over something: some students mention in their journals that it could be a breakup of a relationship. Part II of the story continues Nick's careful preparations for fishing in the river by carefully gathering grasshoppers for bait (173–74); making buckwheat flapjacks for breakfast, which, though, "he was too hurried to eat breakfast . . . he knew he must" (173); and assembling all of his fishing equipment: "Nick felt awkward and professionally happy with all his equipment hanging from him" (175).

Finally, the moment comes when Nick "stepped into the stream. It was a shock. . . . The water was a rising cold shock" (175). Of course, anyone who has stepped into a northern stream realizes the accuracy of the physical description of the cold water. But I suggest that more is indicated here—as Watts says, "The carefully chosen words of physical description are made to stand for the emotional or intellectual significance" (48). The repetition of the word "shock" indicates Nick's abruptly being shaken out of his carefully controlled actions of making camp and preparing to fish, leading to a lasting change in Nick. This is the moment in the story when Nick is no longer able to control his environment. Indeed, what follows are a series of challenges: "the current sucked against his legs . . . the gravel slid under his shoes" (175); the hooking and letting go of the small trout; wading deeper and deeper in the water from "over his knees" (175) to "up his thighs sharply and coldly" (176); his hooking the huge trout, which breaks the line and is "a power not to be held." The loss of the trout temporarily overwhelms Nick: "The thrill had been too much. He felt, vaguely, a little sick, as though it would be better to sit down" (177). Nick "climbed out onto the meadow. . . . He went over and sat on the logs. He did not want to rush his sensations any." After sitting on the logs, smoking a cigarette, and observing the landscape "light glittering, big water smooth rocks, cedars along the bank and white birches, the logs warm in the sun, smooth to sit on, without bark, gray to the touch [note the synesthesia]; slowly the feeling of disappointment left him. . . . It was all right now." Nick's emotional reaction to losing the trout seems exaggerated to many students, which prompts discussions of why his emotional reaction was so strong. What does Nick's desire not to "rush his sensations" mean? Why does he need to be in control, and when his control is shattered, why does he feel "a little sick"? Students realize that there is a connection between Nick's psyche and his reaction to the natural world. They sense his emotional instability after he receives the shock of entering the cold stream and loses a big trout in a battle that he could not control. But they see how Nick reestablishes an emotional balance as he sits on the log and contemplates the natural scene: it really is "all right now" (177).

Following his return to fishing, Nick now fishes both successfully and unsuccessfully, but he does not react emotionally when he loses another fish "in the leaves and branches" of a beech tree that "hung down into the water" (178). Though this incident could be seen as similar in emotional complexity,

Nick's reaction seems very matter-of-fact: "The line was caught. Nick pulled hard and the trout was off. He reeled in and holding the hook in his hand, walked down the stream" (178–79). He truly does seem to be "all right now," having adjusted to the "shock" of the real natural world. With "two big trout alive in the water" in his sack, the fishing over for the day, Nick sits on the hollow log and eats his sandwiches. As he does so, "watching the river," he observes where "the river narrowed and went into a swamp" (179).

This last part of "Big Two-Hearted River" is Nick's realistic assessment of fishing the swamp, which he recognizes as too complicated for him at this time: "He felt a reaction against deep wading with the water deepening up under his armpits [note the increase in the water's depth], to hook big trout in places impossible to land them." But as he goes back to camp, he thinks, "There were plenty of days coming when he could fish the swamp" (180). Nick needed to face the real challenge of a world he couldn't control ("a power not to be held" [177]) in order to regain his equilibrium. His hiking and camping were still under his control, but the moment he steps into the stream, he feels "the rising cold shock" of reality. The cold river is the catalyst of his change.

A Hemingway letter to Robert McAlmon in 1924 about writing "Big Two-Hearted River" reveals a connection between landscape and epiphany using the same word "shock." He tells McAlmon that he is cutting the original ending of the story (the pages posthumously published and cited above as "On Writing" in the *Nick Adams Stories*):

> I have decided that all that mental conversation in the long fishing story is the shit and have cut it all out. The last nine pages. The story was i[n]terrupted you know just when I was going good and I could never get back into it and finish it. I got a hell of a shock when I realized how bad it was and *that shocked me back into the river again* [emphasis added] and I've finished it off the way it ought to have been all along. Just the straight fishing. (*Letters* 170)

Hemingway's shock of recognition at rereading his draft of "Big Two-Hearted River" and his decision to cut out the "mental conversation" and get back into the river may parallel Nick's shock of stepping into the stream of reality.

In these early stories, Hemingway developed a technique that he was to return to in later fiction. In "Hills Like White Elephants" (1926), another frequently anthologized story, the opening paragraph sweeps the reader over the dry landscape on one side of railroad tracks where "there was no shade," and a bit later in this very short story, the reader learns "Across, on the other side, were fields of grain and trees along the banks of the Ebro" (*Complete Short Stories* 213). Students now aware of Hemingway's craft and interest in landscape as containing emotional or symbolic content will not fail to recognize the contrast and ask, at least, "What is going on here?" Though there are other clues to the meaning of the discussion between the man and the girl, Jig, in this story, descriptions of dry and fertile landscapes play an important role. Perhaps such attention to detail in Hemingway's short stories will prepare readers for moments in Hemingway's novels when landscape speaks to more than just the setting of the story. For example, as I argue in the case in *The Sun Also Rises* (1926), Jake dives deep in the ocean at San Sebastian and surfaces from his deep dive with a decision that we are not fully aware of until the end of the novel when he answers Brett's assertion that "we could have had such a damned good time together" by saying, "Isn't it pretty to think so?" (247). Jake's response suggests their love may never have had much of a chance. In *A Farewell to Arms* (1929), Hemingway's evocative beginning chapter describing the landscape "in the fall when the rains came . . . and all the country wet and brown and dead with the autumn" (4) lets readers know that the war and perhaps the fortunes of the soldier Frederic Henry are not going well.

Hemingway's intense connection to landscape allows him to paint a verbal picture that enables the reader to "walk into" the country (*Moveable Feast* 91), but the picture "still represents something more" (Watts 42–43), and that "something" in these works is that landscape carries with it essential clues to the meaning of the fiction.

Works Cited

Baker, Carlos. *Hemingway: The Writer as Artist*. Princeton, NJ: Princeton UP, 1963.
Brøgger, Frederik Chr. "Whose Nature? Differing Narrative Perspectives in Hemingway's 'Big Two-Hearted River.'" *Hemingway and the Natural World*. Ed. Robert Fleming. Moscow: U of Idaho P, 1999. 19–29.
DeFalco, Joseph. *The Hero in Hemingway's Short Stories*. Pittsburgh: U of Pittsburgh P, 1963.
Gaillard, Theodore L., Jr. "Hemingway's Debt to Cezanne: New Perspectives." *Twentieth Century Literature* 45.1 (Spring 1999): 65–78.
Hemingway, Ernest. *The Complete Short Stories of Ernest Hemingway: The Finca Vigía Edition*. New York: Scribner's, 1998.
———. *The Letters of Ernest Hemingway: Volume 2 (1923–1925)*. Ed. Sandra Spanier, Albert J. DeFazio III, and Robert Trogdon. Cambridge: Cambridge UP, 2013.
———. *A Moveable Feast*. New York: Charles Scribner's Sons, 1964.
———. *Nick Adams Stories*. New York: Charles Scribner's Sons, 1972.

Knodt, Ellen Andrews. "Diving Deep: Jake's Moment of Truth at San Sebastian." *The Hemingway Review* 17.1 (Fall 1997): 28–37.
Lamb, Robert Paul. *The Hemingway Short Story*. Baton Rouge: Louisiana State UP, 2013.
Reynolds, Michael. *Hemingway's First War: The Making of* A Farewell to Arms. Princeton, NJ: Princeton UP, 1976.
Smith, Paul. "Introduction: Hemingway and the Practical Reader." *New Essays on Hemingway's Short Fiction*. Ed. Paul Smith. Cambridge: Cambridge UP, 1998. 1–18.
———. *A Reader's Guide to the Short Stories of Ernest Hemingway*. Boston: G. K. Hall, 1989.
———. "Who Wrote Hemingway's *In Our Time?*" *Hemingway Repossessed*. Ed. Kenneth Rosen. Westport, CT: Praeger, 1994. 143–50.
Stoneback, H. R. Interview by Allie Baker. "Pilgrimage, Poetry and Song: An Interview with H. R. Stoneback." *The Hemingway Project*. 21 July 2015. <http://www.thehemingwayproject.com/pilgrimage-poetry-and-song-an-interview-with-h-r-stoneback/>.
Waldhorn, Arthur. *A Reader's Guide to Ernest Hemingway*. New York: Farrar, 1972.
Watts, Emily Stipes. *Ernest Hemingway and the Arts*. Urbana: U of Illinois P, 1971.

On Familiar Ground

Intimate Geographies and Assumptions of Place in Hemingway's Nick Adams Stories

Laura Gruber Godfrey

"Does he ever spend any time indoors?" The question was funny and meant to be so; it was asked in class by a student after we had spent three class sessions reading Ernest Hemingway's Michigan Nick Adams stories. But it also deserves serious consideration. One of the greatest satisfactions in reading Hemingway's Michigan fiction is that in many of these stories, we do get to spend a lot of time outside, and I often ask students to examine closely Hemingway's methods of narrating landscape and geography. On that day we were talking about the second paragraph from "The Three-Day Blow," a story first published in the 1925 fiction collection *In Our Time:* "The road came out of the orchard on the top of the hill. There was the cottage, the porch bare, smoke coming from the chimney. In back were the garage, the chicken coop and the second-growth timber like a hedge against the woods behind. The big trees swayed far over in the wind as he watched. It was the first of the autumn storms" (39).

Though much of "The Three-Day Blow" does take place "indoors," I first asked my students to describe what kind of fruit grew in the orchard. This led to confused looks; they all assumed they had overlooked this information and turned to search for it in the text. They found it: in the first paragraph of the story, Hemingway does tell us that "The rain stopped as Nick turned into the road that went up through the orchard. The fruit had been picked and the fall wind blew through the bare trees. Nick stopped and picked up a Wagner apple from beside the road, shiny in the brown grass from the rain. He put the apple in the pocket of his Mackinaw coat" (39). So we know that the time of year is fall, after the apple harvest is done and the trees are "bare"; we know at least one variety of apple grown in the orchard—Wagner—and we know that the weather is growing colder (Nick is wearing a Mackinaw coat). Next I asked the class whether the cottage in the story was painted and, if so, what color? This time they tried and failed to discover the answer. I then asked what kind of trees were swaying in the wind, but then I told them not to bother looking; Hemingway's writing, it seemed, was here lacking in the kind of details one might expect to find in a descriptive narrative. For some reason, Hemingway appears not to care whether the cottage is white or gray; as for the swaying trees, one of the only things he tells us about them is that they are "big." (A reader familiar with logging landscapes might recognize the distinction between the swaying "big" trees of the woods and the smaller "second-growth" trees, but many readers would not know the difference.) My students were surprised at how little pictorial or explanatory information was included in this part of Hemingway's story. It seemed to contradict everything they had learned about good writing. Here was a writer famous for his ability to depict landscapes, writing about a geography he had known since infancy; but how were they supposed to picture the scene if Hemingway provided them few visual details with which to construct it?

The visual information in this passage is generalized and colorless, quite different from the kind of specific geographic detail evident elsewhere in the Nick Adams stories such as "The End of Something" or "Big Two-Hearted River." Scholars have long taken notice of this occasional characteristic of Hemingway's narrative style. Walter J. Ong once described the technique as creating the illusion of intimacy; *A Farewell to Arms,* Ong said, was structured "Not [as] presentation, but recall." Of the introductory passage from that novel, Ong writes that "What description there is comes in the guise of pointing in verbal gestures, recalling humdrum, familiar details" (13). And of the first paragraphs of "The Three-Day Blow," Ron Berman notes that "the *route tournante* comes over a hill to a particular terrain. Getting there, we see the scene—but in a delimited way.... The usual descriptives are not there. There are no colors.... There is form but no draftsmanship.... this passage is about perception not place" (271).

Both Berman and Ong see Hemingway's narratives as concerned more with psychological effect than with mimetic accuracy in describing place. But I think this and similar passages are about both perception and place. Hemingway's narrator takes a stance from which particular, familiar objects are both simultaneously being seen and being remembered, even though no change in the narrative point of view is recorded. It is precisely this shift to the landscape of memory that so many contemporary students find difficult to appreciate or follow: they often have trouble orienting themselves spatially in the narratives. The words are not merely arranged to make us see these places, but more so to make us think that we are seeing them again. Hemingway's language, in effect, evokes a geography being remembered not only by the narrative voice but by readers themselves. Even for readers who have no personal knowledge of the northern Michigan geography from which Hemingway draws in these stories, the mental picture we construct of the countryside nevertheless seems familiar; it has the distinct quality of something that is remembered or that we recognize, as if after long absence. We feel, as Ong expresses it, that we are nevertheless "on familiar ground" (13).

This essay discusses some of the earliest examples of this technique—what I call Hemingway's narrative assumptions of place—specifically within the stories "Summer People" and "The Three-Day Blow." I aim to describe the way Hemingway transforms conventional descriptions of geography and the natural world into scaffolding for remembering the scenes. Hemingway himself, writing many of these early Nick Adams stories while living abroad, was in fact remembering this geography, steeped in nostalgia, while composing them. Michael Reynolds notes that "the lake, always his real home, was never far below the surface of his mind. He missed it terribly" (251). The sparse geographical details Hemingway gives to readers in these stories are highly personalized and laden with import and history; these two stories in particular, composed very early in Hemingway's career, can certainly be seen as narratives that mark his interest in the "'that always absent something else' . . . [which] finds residence, among other places, in the interstices, in the spaces between the presentation of one fact and the next, in the paratactical ordering of sensations" (qtd. in Knight 58). In particular, in this short fiction the "absent something else" is much of the pictorial or illustrative geographic detail readers often expect to find in works of literature (and that can be found elsewhere in Hemingway's own writing). Once students are made aware of the way Hemingway narrates landscape and geography *as* memory—both Nick's memory and the collective reader's own memory—they can share the extraordinary and intimate relationship to place that is the cornerstone of Hemingway's early fiction. And perhaps they can begin to reconnect themselves to the places of their own lives.

When I teach these early Nick Adams stories to my students, I am teaching them as much about humans' relationships to place as I am teaching them about literary analysis. Increasingly, I have begun to wonder whether my students are paying less and less attention to the physical environments in which they live.

There are likely a number of reasons for this, but predominant among those reasons seems to be the allure of virtual environments in their lives. With the digital universe available to them at the swipe of a fingertip, and with it the promise of unending entertainment and distraction, paying attention to where they are happens less frequently. The stink of fresh asphalt, the hum of air conditioning in a classroom, the yellow-green of quaking aspens in the spring, derelict buildings, cracked sidewalks, forested hillsides: the complexity, the beauty, the ugliness, and even the mundaneness of the places through which they pass each day are too often left unobserved. What happens, I wonder, if some of our students are becoming outsiders in the places that they call home? What happens when we stop paying attention to where we are—what is being lost?

To direct students toward possible answers to those questions, I turn to Hemingway's writing. It is in the earliest Nick Adams stories that we are able to find evidence of the developing style of selective geographical omission that would become synonymous with Hemingway's writing as his career progressed. The opening sentences of Hemingway's 1929 novel *A Farewell to Arms* illustrate the technique; in those now-famous lines, painstakingly revised multiple times, Hemingway writes: "In the late summer of that year we lived in a house in a village that looked across the river and the plain to the mountains. In the bed of the river there were pebbles and boulders, dry and white in the sun, and the water was clear and swiftly moving and blue in the channels. Troops went by the house and down the road and the dust they raised powdered the leaves of the trees" (3).

Hemingway's narrative immerses readers in a place with which they instantly feel a deep sense of shared memory. It is a masterfully written piece of scenic description, but the descriptors are oddly abstract and indistinct, and much is left out of the picture. Ong pinpoints the specific ways that these seemingly generic descriptions nevertheless invite the reader to be "companion-in-arms" with the writer, going on to explain that "the reader—every reader—is being cast in the role of a close companion of the writer" (3). Particularly noticeable is the way that the deictic expressions identifying time and place—"late summer," "a house in a village" nearby to "the river," "the plain," and "the mountains"—do little at first to locate a reader in relation to a particular time or setting. This initial lack of orientation is particularly evident in the narrator's use of the first-person plural pronoun: "In the late summer of that year we lived in a house in a village that looked across the river and the plain to the mountains." "We?" a reader might ask. Who is "we?" The pronoun implies a relationship that the narrator does not explain; it seems almost as if we have been dropped into a narrative already in progress. Yet for that reason, it is a relationship that can seem openly familiarizing for a reader, evoking longing and reminiscence. Ong's astute portrayal of the technique bears mentioning here: "'The late summer of that year,' the reader begins. What year? The reader gathers that there is no need to say. 'Across the river.' What river? The reader apparently is supposed to know. 'And the plain.' What plain? '*The* plain'—remember? 'To the mountains.' What mountains? Do I have to tell you? Of course not. *The* mountains—*those* mountains we know" (3). The scene lacks "thick" or highly detailed description of a landscape, but generations of readers have responded to Hemingway's imagined scene as if it were seared into their "mental retina" (Scarry 49). Hemingway accomplishes this remarkable intimacy here, primarily, by creating an illusion of the narrator and the readers' shared memory of the terrain.

A *Farewell to Arms* was published in 1929, the work of a mature narrative stylist/artist. But "Summer People" and "The Three-Day Blow" induce much the same sense of shared geographical memory on the part of the reader. One of the strengths of Hemingway's early writing about places is that his accounts derive from actual landscapes he knew, and knew thoroughly, near his family's cottage on the shores of Walloon Lake in northern Michigan. Readers are simply informed about Nick Adams or his experiences: in the stories, numerous instances of "referential innuendo" (Fludernik 161) create the sensation of familiarity with local geography. As is the case with the introductory paragraph of *A Farewell to Arms,* the technique evokes an intimate—though illusory—connection between readers and the narrative "consciousnesses" in the fiction. This implicit feeling of remembered experience is evoked primarily by means of definite, familiarizing articles—"*the* garage," "*the* big trees"—by occasional deictic language that gives readers the illusion of a shared experiential perspective: "there was the cottage, [there was] the porch bare, [there was] smoke coming out of the chimney." The narrative voice focalizes our perspective on the terrain so that we are, so to speak, "always already" acquainted with it, as are Nick Adams and Frederic Henry.

The narrative techniques Hemingway utilizes in "Summer People" and "The Three-Day Blow" illuminate the ways that geography and memory tie together; they show the ways that a sensitive observer of and participant in a place can remember that place aloud for others. They reveal some of Hemingway's earliest explorations into what would become a cornerstone of his style and his aesthetic: reminding readers, as Philip Melling puts it, of Hemingway's belief that "a writer's duty is to explore the histories that precede his arrival.

Landscapes... bring histories to life" (46). In much of his writing, Hemingway uses his powers of observation of place not only to "remember" for readers the natural histories of any given landscape, but also to remind them of the (often hidden) human forces behind the topography; indeed, pure nature that is untouched by humans often seems less interesting to Hemingway than the ways in which the nonhuman, "natural" world and the human world intermingle. These interests reflect Hemingway's increasing attention to rendering, in his prose, what is essentially the "cultural geography" of a place (Godfrey 49). Melling goes on to describe a June 1922 piece for the *Toronto Daily Star* in which Hemingway, depicting the Rhône valley, "begins to ponder the absorbent properties of the earth and the hidden imprints left by others. He sees a landscape in a state of change" (46). In other words, for Hemingway as an observer of landscape and geography and as a writer himself, what cannot be seen is as essential as what can be seen. This "hiddenness" described by Melling (46) is, of course, a stylistic hallmark of Hemingway's writing, an aesthetic expressed by the "iceberg theory" that he later articulated more explicitly in *Death in the Afternoon*. But that same principle of "hiddenness"—in particular "hidden" or barely suggested geographical details—seems to have been on Hemingway's mind when he crafted some of his earliest short fiction.

The Nick Adams stories communicate, quite powerfully, the way that the interiority of Hemingway's Nick is entwined with this character's boyhood geographies. Nick's geography *is* him. Among the many stylistic achievements of Hemingway's early short stories—notable for their economy of language and their almost elegiac depictions of a beloved set of landscapes—"The Three-Day Blow" and "Summer People" show Nick, as a character, to be a body moving through places: as a body so naturally and unquestionably rooted in a physical landscape that physical details of that place become a secondary and, ultimately, an unnecessary concern. For practiced readers of Hemingway's fiction, this narrative stance evokes the sense that we are engaging in conversation with a storyteller with whom we share a deep well of geographical knowledge and understanding.

Recognizing the presence of this technique is a revelation for my students, as it was for me when I realized what Hemingway had accomplished. When I first visited northern Michigan and saw the places that inspired Hemingway's early fiction, I was astonished. I realized that for years I had had the distinct sense that I knew the country well, but in actuality it looked nothing like I had imagined. What I had created in my reader's mind, instead, was a vague and indeterminate image of place, yet a highly specific feeling of a relationship with place. Not surprisingly, I was shocked at seeing the green and lush terrain of northern Michigan for the first time, having imagined it in black and white for over a decade. My students are similarly baffled when, after we discuss the Nick Adams stories, I show them pictures of the vibrant blues and greens of Hemingway's Michigan countryside. They come to find that while reading these narratives, they, too, have been coerced into imagining the geographies in all their full, complex detail (with no such knowledge actually existing). In these earliest Nick Adams stories, Hemingway's narrator assumes that our intimate and detailed understanding of these same Michigan landscapes is a foregone conclusion. Nick's geography belongs to him and, simultaneously, to us.

These narrative assumptions are central to "Summer People," one of Hemingway's earliest Nick Adams stories. When the piece was first published in 1972 as part of *The Nick Adams Stories*, collection editor Philip Young noted that the original manuscript of the story reveals how early in Hemingway's career it was composed: "the manuscript shows repeated vacillation on the protagonist's name. Nick, Hemingway writes, and crosses it out; Allan the same; Wemedge, which becomes here as before Nick's nickname, the same; again and finally Nick, all the way through" (15). While Hemingway at the outset of his fiction career may have shown uncertainty about choosing a final name for his character, he shows no such hesitation in what will become a consistent technique for his fiction. A depiction of the nearly seamless fusion between the human and the geographical, a narrative in which Nick's places are as much a part of his inner life as they are rooted to his daily physical experiences. Although it is impossible to determine exactly Hemingway's intentions for the structure and content of the story, because his original, unpublished manuscript draft was altered significantly upon its posthumous 1972 publication (Seitz 3), we nevertheless can examine the story's narrative perspective as an early example of Hemingway's interest in human geographies with the reader positioned as insider.

The opening paragraph of "Summer People" introduces Nick as a young man who is utterly comfortable in his natural environment:

> Halfway down the gravel road from Hortons Bay, the town, to the lake there was a spring. The water came up in a tile sunk beside the road, lipping over the cracked edge of the tile and flowing away through the close growing mint into the swamp. In the dark Nick put his arm down into the spring but could not hold it there because of the cold. He felt the featherings of the sand spouting up from the spring cones at the bottom against his fingers. Nick thought, I wish I could

put all of myself in there. I bet that would fix me. He pulled his arm out and sat down at the edge of the road. It was a hot night. (*Complete Short Stories* 496)

There are some remarkable narrative elements in this passage. The narrator's stance includes noticeable assumptions about place. Hemingway generally situates readers with respect to the terrain as if they already knew it. For example, he notes that "halfway down the gravel road from Hortons Bay, the town, to the lake there was a spring." In this sentence the narrator clarifies that he is talking about Hortons Bay, *the town* [emphasis mine], in order to distinguish it from (presumably) Hortons Bay, the body of water. Why, one might ask, does the narrator break up the lovely rhythm of that crucial introductory sentence—the phrases are almost cadenced—to specify that he is talking about a town rather than some other entity? The clarification seems to be addressed to someone "on the inside," so to speak. That is to say, the only way this awkward bit of narratorial periphrasis makes sense is to assume that the person to whom the narrative is addressed already knows of the potential for referential ambiguity, someone who is aware that some confusion between the two, the town and the bay, might be possible; it makes "the reader a recaller of shared experience" (Ong 15).

The narrative voice here also makes mention that "there was a spring" halfway down this road. This is a linguistic construction consistent with what some narratologists call a story's "triggering anecdote" (Almond). It provides information that is unknown to the reader but which is essential to understanding the story, as a fairy tale might begin, for example, "Once upon a time there was a little old woman who lived by a river." Presumably Hemingway was here concerned to provide readers with a coherent context for the action to come; the use of the indefinite article—"*a* spring" (emphasis mine)—signals this intention. But almost everything else in the paragraph's setting seems to presuppose a narrator who shares knowledge of the geography with readers: our attention is directed "down *the* gravel road" to "*the* lake" (emphasis mine). Similarly, in the paragraph that directly follows, we are led "down the road through the trees [where Nick] could see the white of the Bean house on its piles over the water" (496). Again, Hemingway feels no need to clarify ambiguities about place for his readers here; we are made to feel as connected to this terrain and its history as is Nick himself. If we are unaware that the Bean house existed, or if we know nothing of the Bean family who lives there, such geographical clarifications are considered unimportant here. The narrative voice excludes almost any sense that readers are outsiders to these places, instead placing us in the delicate position of being insiders and outsiders simultaneously. Teachers can draw attention to this technique by asking students how they give directions for places they know well. When we think through this navigational process, most of us realize that the better we know a place, the more difficult it is to orient outsiders in it. I am thinking in particular, as I write, of a recent trip to a small, remote town in north-central Montana. When I asked the hotel front desk clerk for directions to a historic monument, he leaned back, looked up in the air, and after a long pause said something like 'Oh, well, you'll want to turn right where the Verizon Building *used* to be."

The difference between Hemingway's narrative voice and that of a more conventional third-person narrator is similar to what Gerard Genette refers to in his distinction between kinds of narrative "focalization" or "*perception*[s] *that* [orient] *the report*[ing]" of information in a story. Genette's analysis of what he calls the "internally focalized" (qtd. in Fleischman 217) perspective seems closest to Hemingway's technique in this passage. Suzanne Fleischmann, characterizing Genette's distinctions, writes that "with internal focalization, the narrator is also a character and says only what that character knows or can perceive" (218). This is the case as well in "Summer People," where a third-person omniscient narrative morphs into free-indirect discourse, an experimental mixture of third- and first-person perspectives. In sections of Nick's internal monologues, for example, the shifts in point of view are abrupt and yet neither destabilizing nor incoherent: "Odgar would kill himself, Nick thought, if he knew it. I wonder how he'd kill himself." Later Hemingway writes that Nick "walked down the road, past the car and the big warehouse on the left where apples and potatoes were loaded onto the boats in the fall, past the white-painted Bean house where they danced by lantern light sometimes on the hard-wood floor, out on the dock to where they were swimming" (*Complete Short Stories* 497). In the depiction of this northern Michigan geography, we learn about Nick's long history within these places, and his emotional attachment to them, but the information is presented in a manner suited to a person already familiar with the landscapes and events that are being described. In both passages the personal, temporal, and spatial deictics—note, for example, the way the story combines complex relationships between pronouns, times, and places—evoke a pattern that blends enactment with memory. The narrative voice at times seems to belong wholly to Nick, at other times to some organizing narratological principle or consciousness outside of Nick. The narrative voice does not speak only of what Nick knows or perceives; he (it?) speaks sometimes of things as perceived from the point of view of someone who knows already what Nick knows.

The narrative voice in these stories is an amalgam, combining the personal knowledge and experiences of Nick with the focalizing perspective of someone conscious of the action. The voice does not belong wholly either to the central character or to an implied authorial consciousness. The technique is one Hemingway would use throughout his career, though its effects differ from one text to another (Brøgger 23). In "Summer People," the narrative voice and the internally focalized voices know the natural environments and the things that have taken place on these landscapes, and they know them so thoroughly, that explanatory or minute details are deemed unnecessary. In other instances Hemingway experiments with more complex focalizations and for different purposes. Matthew J. Bolton notices, for example, in the second interchapter vignette of the 1930 edition of *In Our Time*, that "The officer [who is narrating] is recalling his own memory of the evacuation, but his pronouns shift from 'you' to 'I' and then back to 'you.' Casting his own story into the second person is an act of displacement, a foisting off onto the listener of the traumatic scenes that the officer admits returned to him unbidden" (52). The difference is that in "Summer People" the various focalizations are not strategies for "displacing" trauma, but instead are invitations to imagine a shared geographical memory.

"The Three-Day Blow"—a companion story to "The End of Something" in which Nick and Bill drink whisky and Scotch, musing over topics like baseball, books, and Nick's recent breakup with Marjorie while an autumn storm rages outside—also makes use of Hemingway's intimate and immersive constructions of geography. The opening paragraphs are followed by a short passage in which Hemingway positions the two young men as observers of a natural landscape: "they stood together, looking out across the country, down over the orchard, beyond the road, across the lower fields and the woods of the point to the lake. The wind was blowing straight down the lake. They could see the surf along Ten Mile point" (*In Our Time* 39). In traditional narratological terms this passage is written from the third-person point of view, but—again using Genette's distinctions—we can further distinguish the narrative voice as including both one who speaks and one who sees. In this passage Hemingway introduces a second perspective defined by Nick and Bill; their angle of vision gives readers an illusory sense of familiarity with the landscape that a more conventional third-person perspective could not attain. The construction of the clause ("looking out across the country") focalizes the vision momentarily so that we are now seeing the terrain through Nick and Bill's eyes; for a moment we share with them a memory of the landscape that we do not actually possess. For this reason it is unimportant to know what grows in those "lower fields" or what sort of "woods" grow beyond that; they seem clear enough. Likewise, the reference to "the point" is not clarified, and Lake Charlevoix becomes merely "the lake." Both phrases represent language that people would use in describing well-known places; to someone who lived near its shores, to call Lake Charlevoix by its name would be redundant. It would be of much greater interest to note that on this particular day, the wind was strong enough to have raised "surf." The narrative in general seems to come from a mind that belongs, in Carl Fiken's phrasing, to some "Center of Consciousness" other than that of Nick or Bill (qtd. in Brøgger 21); yet at moments like this, it seems fully expressive of their way of looking at the land, a blend of telling and seeing.

Hemingway makes it clear that Nick and Bill have long been part of this geography, especially with the casual yet knowing ways that the young men comment on the storm:

> "She's blowing," Nick said.
> "She'll blow like that for three days," Bill said. . . .
> "It's good when the fall storms come, isn't it?" Nick said.
> "It's swell."
> "It's the best time of year," Nick said. (*In Our Time* 39, 41)

These characters are immersed in the seasonal life of this place, aware that the arrival of the fall storms marks the end of the summer season and the beginning of the cold months to come. Nick and Bill's awareness of their natural environment is not the focus of the story but is instead used to help illuminate their friendship in a number of small details. Bill, for example, brings Nick "a pair of heavy wool socks" and reminds him that "'It's getting too late to go around without socks'" (*In Our Time* 40). Hemingway also shows Nick's youthfulness and his intimate reverence for the natural world in endearing and humorous ways; when the two discuss authors they admire, Bill says:

> "I'd like to meet Chesterton," Bill said.
> "I wish he was here now," Nick said. "We'd take him fishing to the 'Voix tomorrow."
> "I wonder if he'd like to go fishing," Bill said.
> "Sure," said Nick. "He must be about the best guy there is." (*In Our Time* 42–43)

In this coded, private exchange between two longtime friends, readers can see that Nick's desire to take Chesterton fishing is the highest compliment he could pay: Lake Charlevoix becomes, simply, "the 'Voix," and that shorthand moniker bears no further explanation. But the lack of explanation does not detract from the impact of the story or from the clear sense of the natural world's centrality for these characters. When Nick and Bill refer simply to "the lake," "the point," or "the 'Voix," readers are subtly coerced to feel as if they share the same long history with the geography, the same deep attachment to it. At the story's close, the two decide to leave the cottage. "There's no use getting drunk," Nick remarks; Bill replies by saying "No. We ought to get outdoors." And so they emerge into the "gale" blowing outside, moving "down toward the orchard," after which Hemingway's narrator explains that "Outside now the Marge business was no longer so tragic. It was not even very important. The wind blew everything like that away" (*In Our Time* 49).

The relationship between the human and the natural (Hemingway often blends the two categories, calling attention to the artificiality of using these terms as binaries) reminds readers that Nick Adams is, above all else a body bound to and moving within the landscapes of his life. "No nature writer in all American literature save Thoreau," once remarked Alfred Kazin, "has had Hemingway's sensitiveness to color, to climate, to the knowledge of the physical energy under heat or cold, that knowledge of the body thinking and moving through a landscape" (334). In a number of instances throughout the Michigan fiction, we can see Nick Adams as just such a body in place. Alex Shakespeare describes Nick in "Big Two-Hearted River" as "a conscious body that sits down, walks, and wallows, but above all 'watches' and 'looks,'" seeing in that story "the exactitude of a writer who seeks to render in language what it feels like to be in a particular place" (39). In stories like "Big Two-Hearted River," Hemingway indeed renders the natural world down to the most minute detail. But "The Three-Day Blow" and "Summer People" lack that level of geographical rendering. Instead, these stories demonstrate such a hyper-consciousness of the geography around Nick Adams that the details are often strangely inexact and imprecise.

In these very early stories, it is hard to say whether Hemingway was conscious of rendering geography-as-memory *as* a technique, or whether he was simply a writer learning his craft, unable to control the narrative stance sufficiently to distance it enough from his own intimate knowledge of northern Michigan. To a skeptic, narrative slippages such as these might seem like beginner's mistakes. But I think, and I express to my students, that even at this early stage in his career, Hemingway was almost fully in control of his craft. The style can be seen in some light as part of Hemingway's tutelage in the modernist aesthetic.

His sparseness of detail likely originates, in part at least, from the advice on fiction writing that he received from established authors and critics like Ezra Pound. Matthew J. Bolton observes that Hemingway, as part of his correspondence with Pound and his reading of T. S. Eliot's *The Waste Land*, learned how to "[incorporate] the remembered word or image into the fabric of a story.... how to render the text as memory" (37, 38). Bolton also reminds us of Pound's now-famous advice to Hemingway to pare down his writing to the bone, citing the comment from *A Moveable Feast* in which Hemingway notes that Pound was "the man who had taught me to distrust adjectives" (qtd. in Bolton 39).

Upon first reading these stories, though, many students skim over the "outdoor" parts, concentrating instead on dialogue, plot, or subtleties of characterization, and I worry that the reason they find the geography initially uninteresting may be more cultural than literary. For many modern students, a deep attachment to (or even awareness of) place seems to be diminishing, even lost. A student recently commented to me, in a worried tone, that it had been a "long, long time" since she gave any thought at all to where she lived. She went on to explain: "I wake up; I'm scrolling through my phone while I get ready for class. I drive to class. Then I drive to work. Then I get home, and I'm on my phone texting or scrolling through news feeds while reading for next day's classes. I don't even know what the weather was today. I couldn't even tell you if it rained or snowed." This issue has become so noticeable to me that I recently taught a class, Physical and Virtual Environments, in which we explored the extent to which humans are losing the art of paying close attention to physical places. One of the authors I use in class, as a primary model for how to pay close attention to environment, is Hemingway. Hemingway's characters and their connections to their environments remind students, as Matthew Crawford says, that "encountering the world *as* real can be a source of pleasure . . . in light of which manufactured realities are revealed as pale counterfeits, and lose some of their grip on us" (27).

James Howard Kunstler's 1993 book *The Geography of Nowhere* outlines many ways that the suburbanization of the American landscape has altered the way that we live our lives, the way we interpret our spaces. Kunstler writes that "Our obsession with mobility, the urge to move on every few years, stands at odds with the wish to endure in a beloved place.... In every corner of the nation we have built places unworthy of love and move on from them without regret" (173). Richard Louv's 2005 *Last Child in the Woods* studies how contemporary generations of children suffer from "nature deficit disorder" because of lives lived increasingly inside, often in front of various forms of electronic screens (10). Since Louv first published this book, the problem has dramatically increased: there are now camps designed for children and families to "digitally detox" themselves with forced immersion in the natural world. Ideally, then, when many of our students are growing up in such a world, Hemingway's "outdoor" fiction can impart to them a loving familiarity with landscape: Nick moves through the natural world with confidence, tenderness, and a sense of utter belonging. In Nick, Hemingway has created a character who is unquestionably at home in these Michigan geographies, a character who also seems to reflect poet Wallace Stevens's sentiment, expressed in "Esthetique du Mal," that "The greatest poverty is not to live / in a physical world" (286).

Works Cited

Almond, Steve. "Once Upon a Time, There Was a Person Who Said, 'Once Upon a Time.'" *The New York Times Magazine*. 11 Jan. 2013. <https://nyti.ms/2kGXD7T>.

Berman, Ron. "Recurrence in Hemingway and Cézanne." *Hemingway: Eight Decades of Criticism*. Ed. Linda Wagner-Martin. East Lansing: Michigan State UP, 2009.

Bolton, Matthew J. "Memory and Desire: Eliotic Consciousness in Early Hemingway." *Ernest Hemingway and the Geography of Memory*. Ed. Mark Cirino and Mark P. Ott. Kent, OH: Kent State UP, 2010.

Brøgger, Fredrik Chr. "Whose Nature? Differing Narrative Perspectives in Hemingway's 'Big Two-Hearted River.'" *Hemingway and the Natural World*. Ed. Robert Fleming. Moscow: U of Idaho P, 1999.

Crawford, Matthew B. *The World Beyond Your Head: On Becoming an Individual in an Age of Distraction*. New York: Farrar, Straus and Giroux, 2015.

Fleischman, Suzanne. *Tense and Narrativity: From Medieval Performance to Modern Fiction*. Austin: U of Texas P, 1990.

Fludernik, Monika. *Towards a 'Natural' Narratology*. London: Routlege, 1996.

Godfrey, Laura Gruber. "Hemingway and Cultural Geography: The Landscape of Logging in 'The End of Something.'" *Hemingway Review* 26.1 (2006): 49.

Hemingway, Ernest. *A Farewell To Arms*. New York: Scribner, 1929.

———. *In Our Time*. New York: Scribner, 1925.

———. "Summer People." *The Complete Short Stories of Ernest Hemingway: The Finca Vigía Edition*. New York: Scribner's, 1987.

Kazin, Alfred. *On Native Grounds: An Interpretation of Modern American Prose Literature*. New York: Reynal & Hitchcock, 1942.

Knight, Christopher J. *Omissions Are Not Accidents: Modern Apophaticism from Henry James to Jacques Derrida*. Toronto: U of Toronto P, 2010.

Kunstler, James Howard. *The Geography of Nowhere: The Rise and Decline of America's Man-Made Landscape*. New York: Simon & Schuster, 1993.

Louv, Richard. *Last Child in the Woods: Saving Our Children from Nature Deficit Disorder.* Chapel Hill: Algonquin Books, 2005.

Melling, Philip. "'There Were Many Indians in the Story': Hidden History in Hemingway's 'Big Two-Hearted River.'" *Hemingway Review* 28.2 (2009): 46.

Ong, Walter J. "The Writer's Audience Is Always a Fiction." *PMLA* 90.1 (1975): 13.

Reynolds, Michael. *Hemingway: The Paris Years.* New York: W. W. Norton & Company, 1989.

Scarry, Elaine. *Dreaming by the Book.* New York: Farrar, Straus, Giroux, 1999.

Seitz, Susan. "A Final (?) Note on the Textual Errors of Ernest Hemingway's 'Summer People.'" *The Hemingway Review* 11.2 (1992): 3.

Shakespeare, Alex. "'The Names of Rivers and the Names of Birds: Ezra Pound, Louis Agassiz, and the 'Luminous Detail' in Hemingway's Early Fiction." *The Hemingway Review* 30.2 (2011): 39.

Stevens, Wallace. *Collected Poetry and Prose.* New York: Library of America, 1997.

Young, Philip. "'Big World out There': *The Nick Adams Stories.*" *Novel: A Forum on Fiction* 6.1 (1972): 15.

"Summer People, Some Are Not"

Seasonal Visitors, Cottage-ing, and the Exoticism of Hemingway's Michigan

Jeffrey Herlihy-Mera

> "Summer people. Some are not."
> —Graffiti on the drawbridge in Woods Hole, Massachusetts

Each spring I teach several Ernest Hemingway short stories for a humanities course at the University of Puerto Rico. We look into the textual elements of language, weather, flora and fauna, in addition to the portrayals of people and wildlife. Due in part to the climate, demographics, and language (which is generally Spanish, though we read texts in *versión original*), our class discussions do not always map neatly around established critical lines. The uniqueness of a Caribbean classroom invites us as scholars to think critically, ecologically, and historically in a way that is often outside the general perspectives in Hemingway Studies. These conversations have sent my own thinking about Hemingway and nature in new and fascinating directions.

This chapter will discuss my pedagogical approaches (and students' reaction) to one text in particular: "Summer People." The discussion will expound upon how studying the text in a place that receives many seasonal visitors seems to shape the student perceptions of the setting. I will explore how the cottage-ing movement informed Hemingway's impressions of Michigan; how the settler-rituals in the story can be an avenue of critical inquiry; and how the place of composition of the piece—Paris—might have triggered Hemingway to romanticize the role of the natural surroundings. I argue here that when teaching (and reading) about Hemingway's portrayals of nature, we should not limit our inquiries to the sometimes celebrative perspective of the visitor; we should engage this text with the transient status of the characters (and the writer) in mind—this will allow us as scholars to discern how an exotic setting might influence the plot development and the characters' understanding of and interaction with the natural setting.

I feel these topics have particular relevance in Puerto Rico because it is a location with seasonal visitors, and the island itself is often romanticized in texts written by these visitors. And the community has some (post)colonial circumstances that are similar to the Michigan of Hemingway's youth (and the Michigan of today). Generally I endeavor to plan my pedagogy around these topics as discussion axes because they steer us toward the "usable perspectives" of the students—and indeed, since I began teaching this course, the students' reflections on these themes have fascinated me.

Cottage-ing in Michigan

Students are to read "Summer People" and to watch "Hemingway in Michigan, Parts 1–3" on YouTube, before class. I write several key terms of discussion on the board before the lecture. This first part of the ninety-minute session orients our examination of the text toward some relevant historical and cultural contexts. This discussion provides a backdrop for the second part of class, the textual analyses. Using the following terms and concepts as a base for discussion, this introduction on the cottage-ing movement offers a framework to situate the analyses that are carried out later in the class period.

> *Key Topics*
> Cottage-ing and settler-rituals
> Michigan treaties (Saginaw and Chicago)
> Cultural appropriation

Cottage-ing is a form of vacationing that uses recreational farming, fishing, hunting, and other activities to construct a simulated short-term experience in rural life for affluent people from urban or suburban backgrounds. Like dude ranching and safaris, in the early twentieth century cottage-ing packaged an experience in nature in a way that was nonthreatening, complacent, and balanced. Cottagers were "roughing it" in an aesthetic sense, and in this way, notes Frederick Svoboda, compared to their winter lives, the people were "more directly engaged with the natural world" (qtd. in Hendrickson 380). The movement was occurring simultaneously around the American continent, imagining the natural space as a pastoral, controlled area where those with leisure capital may engage their leisure pursuits.

The Hemingways were part of this fashionable trend and purchased a "cottage"—Windemere—up in Michigan, where they would spend summers. The summer narrative in Hemingway's life and writing exists as a countrified, stable environment where displaced urban dwellers and the natural world intermingle—it is important to emphasize here that it is an image constructed on an upper-middle-class, bourgeois experience that was being repeated (and continues to be today) in places like Martha's Vineyard, Cornwall, Aguadilla, and Begur. The Hemingways' simulations of rural life involved Ernest dressing up as Huckleberry Finn and learning to fish and hunt, and the photographs of him engaging in these activities were taken precisely because he is playacting roles that were exotic to him; and they also place him squarely in the narratives of settler-American culture.

Being in nature and repeating the settler, or pioneer, conquest of the space (in the form of a ceremony) had become an important settler-American ritual by 1900. While the Hemingways performed nostalgic cultural rites around Windemere, President Roosevelt was taking trips West, playing dress-up in ridiculous cowboy and Leatherstocking costumes. As innocuous as the costumes and playacting appear, settler-American activities and the eventual literary pieces that treat them are part of a broader narrative that, according to Bill Brown, "aestheticizes the genocidal foundation of the nation, turning conquest into a literary enterprise that screens out other violent episodes in the nation's history" (5).

Nature played a central role in these vacations and in the writing that stemmed from them. The Michigan space itself—sacred to several Native American tribes—was politically appropriated by the United States through the Treaties of Saginaw (1820) and Chicago (1833), which forced Native Americans to relinquish claims to the space. The pioneer activities that reenact the settlement of the area by citizens of the United States are part of the cultural appropriation of the region, which usually, though not always, occurs subsequent to the political annexation. In Hemingway's boyhood, these settler rituals underscored the myth that the presence of U.S. citizens in that space is generally a positive phenomenon (the Native Americans who cohabited the area were not U.S. citizens until 1925, after Hemingway left Michigan for the last time). While for the Hemingways Windemere was "an Eden-like retreat," as Svoboda points out, "nearby were destitute Indians, once lords of the woods, now living in an abandoned lumber camp" (qtd. in Hendrickson 377).

The repeated rites and ceremonies of newcomers to Michigan—like the Hemingways—created a proprietary nostalgia for the place and its nature; these rituals imbued a new sacrosanctity to the region, this time on behalf of the settler-Americans and their perceived community. In the same way that Native American histories, heroic events, and cultural myths were repeated ceremonially in the same space, over time the newcomers' rites became "traditional" to them—and they were (and are) thus, a powerful feature of cultural appropriation process that transitioned the space, in a very short span, from a "foreign" one into the cultural geography of the settler American (that is, U.S.) metropolitan. The young U.S. citizens, like Hemingway, who were from other places existed (and yet exist) in a reality that was controlled and proscribed in such a way that these concepts of cultural proprietorship of northern Michigan were firmly wedded to the newcomers. The emotional value of these traditions is an important dimension in the settler texts that treat them—and Hemingway's short story "Summer People" is no exception.

Despite the frontier aesthetic that the Hemingways attempted to construct during the retreats, theirs was a rather upholstered version of nature. In 1900, as now, the affluent families posing in settler life had all the creature comforts—high-end groceries, for instance, were delivered at an enormous premium to cottages on the lake via boat, and families were often accompanied by their servants. Northern Michigan at that time, as Svoboda has pointed out, "Wasn't really a wilderness. It was actually quite civilized . . . it was more civilized in 1900 than it is today" ("Hemingway in Michigan Pt 1"). Petoskey had trains pass through town every fifteen minutes; there were three opera concerts per day; wealthy, short-term visitors from St. Louis, Kansas City, and all over the Midwest filled out the cottages. "It was a hub," notes Svoboda ("Hemingway in Michigan Pt 1"). For these reasons, the exaggeration of the settler/pioneer rituals, with shotguns, rods and reels, backpacks, and so on, were an expression of a nostalgic and, in some ways, imagined past. Isn't it pretty to think so—that Michigan was once so bucolic, so harmonious, and so pastoral as it is in Nick Adams's life? But such a concept is a construction, one that helps to embed the emotion for the past, a past that never quite existed, as a foundation in the cultural rites of the present.

The cultural appropriation of a space through implementation of nonlocal rituals, languages, symbols, holidays, and ceremonies is also an ongoing reality in Puerto Rico, a nation where many U.S. cultural directives—such as a Thanksgiving Day celebration, the English language, and American flags—intersect with a Latin American society. My students—particularly undergraduates—are often acutely attuned to how such matters function in the Nick Adams stories. "La ceremonias tienen que ver con quién controla el lugar; y como consiguiente, quién controla a quién" (the cultural ceremonies have to do with who controls the space, and as a corollary, who controls whom), was how Ingrid Millán, a student in class, deftly described it. And thus the ostensibly innocuous acts of certain people celebrating the Fourth of July, fishing or hunting or swimming *while* up in nature in Michigan, or writing about those things are dimensions of broader narratives that involve nation states, political rights and citizenships, and the controls on and spreading out of cultures.

Summer People and "Everybody" Else: A Critical View

Following this contextual introduction, the majority of class time is dedicated to textual analysis. I often transition to this second topic by asking students some rhetorical questions that might guide our collective thinking. In this instance, I ask students to imagine what Puerto Rico would be like for someone who comes here for a few weeks each year. After a short discussion on that topic, we examine how the "Summer People" in Hemingway's story perceive their surroundings. It is usually clear that Hemingway and the fictional characters imagine Michigan in a comparable way to how snowbirds and other visitors to the island perceive Puerto Rico. In "Summer People," the place itself and the composition of the different communities within are constructed through several literary devices, one of which is language. I usually focus first on pronouns, as they are often binding signifiers and a clear entry point for criticism. I write these terms on the board:

> *Key Topics*
> "Everybody"
> Summer activities
> Hierarchy of "summer" people
> Contrasting Nick and Odgar
> Place of composition

"Everybody was down there swimming," says Nick (*Complete Short Stories* 496). "Everybody" is a key term here: it sets out the bounds of the community and is inclusive in the same way that it is exclusive. There are year-round residents of Michigan the same age as these characters; some are Native Americans, others are U.S. citizens; but those groups are excluded by the use of this pronoun. The construction of the "summer" people is further layered by their social condition (vacationing for a few weeks) and their shared engagement in leisure pursuits (swimming, fishing, frolicking, sex); and the community dynamic is reinforced by nicknames (Wemedge, the Bird, the Ghee, *Morgen,* and Buttstein). A focus on this in-group etiquette is a useful platform to read the story.

Next, we examine the hierarchy that exists within the summer group, which is constructed on the characters' diverse abilities in summer activities. Nick can realize the acts he desires with relative ease (swimming, diving, and sex with Kate), while Odgar cannot. Kate, the love interest, wishes to "be Wemedge" and Nick's noiseless dive is "absolutely perfect," according to this femme fatale (*Complete Short Stories* 499). They appear to be adolescents, swimming close to shore, while the referent "men" are swimming way out on the lake: this is an ironic phrase as Odgar is thirty-two years old and, conceivably, should be swimming "out there" by now. Like Robert Cohn from *The Sun Also Rises,* he is in a state of arrested development in swimming and sex. These divergences establish Nick as a dominant figure, and part of his strength is based on a contrast to Odgar's apparent poor ability in the same summer rituals.

There are also some organizations of the summer community that are based on economic status. The kids (and the older Odgar) ride home from the lake together in a car that is driven by one of them. Although owning a vehicle and spending summers vacationing (and not working) are certainly markers of privilege, the characters do not perceive themselves in the same ambit as the "*rich* slobs riding behind their chauffeurs" (emphasis mine) who pass them on road from the other direction (*Complete Short Stories* 500). Nevertheless, some of the ostensibly commonplace actions of Hemingway's summer people allude to their affluence—and seem to be present in the text to underscore this status. Just before the amorous interlude with Kate, for instance, Nick procedurally "turned off the light" in the cottage (501). Electricity was in less than 10 percent of rural U.S. residences in 1920, meaning that this Michigan cottage, near a group of RFD (Rural Free Delivery) mailboxes, is extravagantly equipped (Kyvig 55). Once Nick meets Kate in the orchard, her body is described like piano keys from a bourgeois parlor room. They eat chicken together. Chicken, until the late 1920s, "was the most expensive dish you could order in a restaurant; it cost more than lobster or filet mignon" (Morris 1). Nick is also valuated on his dream to become "a great writer" which is contingent upon his literacy, a skill to which many Native American residents of that area had no access (*Complete Short Stories* 503). Each summer person is sharing a lavish existence that is measured through these references: in this reading, nature is a space where one may act out rituals that establish perceived social positions. Being a visitor in Michigan is a symbol of power, and "everybody" in the text shares a dimension of this status.

Summer's Memories: Writing the Romance of Distance and Time

Each year seasonal visitors arrive in Puerto Rico for a few weeks or months, enjoy a brief experience in one dimension of island life, and return north. Once back in their principal residences, some write about Puerto Rico with possessive adjectives. In the literary visions of "winter people," Puerto Rico is often portrayed as a pristine locale—very much analogous to Hemingway's Michigan. An important dimension to bear in mind was Hemingway's distance from northern Michigan when he began to pen stories about it. In this way, Borinkén (the Taíno term for the island) is not unlike northern Michigan, and as a potential extension into term papers or even graduate theses, I encourage my students to look into comparative studies between works from various canons that share a common dimension. (I would be very interested, for instance, to read a comprehensive report comparing "summer" people in Hemingway's Michigan to "winter" people in texts that treats Puerto Rico, and I let my class know this.)

At this point, I like to focus on how and why short-term residents, like Hemingway, tend to idealize the places of their visits when they appear in fictional treatments. After posing this quandary to the class: *Why do people romanticize places from their past, where they spent short periods?* Just as people who spend short periods in Puerto Rico often think of the island in emotional and somewhat unrealistic terms, the same phenomena occurs in other locations. The transience of a retreat experience clouds and, to a certain extent, prohibits a realistic treatment of a region and its natural backdrop. Hemingway began "Summer People" in Paris in 1924, two years after he left Michigan for the last time (Bacon 1). In some ways, his distance from Michigan in space and time when he composed this story is a determining characteristic of how it is constructed. Our cultural situations prohibit any universal "nature" or universal perception of it, and this point of departure can be a fecund one as we think about how, when, and where this story was written: situated perhaps at a Left Bank café, years removed from immersion in American life, Hemingway's writing environment would influence his memory in specific ways. Compared to back home, the paper would be different in size and thickness, and have a different system of lines; the coffee he was taking would be prepared in another method; the cup and saucer and spoon would be of local variety; the table itself would be slightly distinct from a piece of American furniture. Hemingway, when addressing the waiter, barman, or host of the café, would do so in French. The consequence of these details is important: Michigan was a concept that existed in Hemingway's mind; he was writing from experience but also through the filter of cultural, temporal, and geographic distance from the place, events, and communities in the story. This isolation from the events would allow him to control them in his mind in a particular way. The combination of physical and cultural distance from the setting of the piece was a cauldron that crystallized his own perceptions to an important degree, and he famously commented about the link between distance and creativity: "in Paris I could write about Michigan" (*Moveable Feast* 7). And for this, the Michigan he wrote about appears as a romantic, Edenic, and, in many ways, unreal place.

After Michigan: Hemingway's Experiences in Nature in Adulthood

My lecture concludes with a summary of the key concepts we discussed and a short conversation of Hemingway's experiences in the outdoors after he left Michigan for the last time. It is interesting to compare his presence in nature as an adult to his boyhood life in Michigan, as they have significant parallels. Hemingway's later sportfishing, safaris, and recreational hunting were, like cottage-ing, generally brief experiences in an upholstered environment that simulated the natural world—and they were also predicated upon his comfortable socioeconomic status. Hemingway's participation in those activities was similar to his summers in Michigan in that nature was a commodified backdrop that had been exoticized into an element of a leisure pursuit. And in the later texts that involve Africa, fishing, and hunting, the concept of nature is generally bound to these limits, with some important exceptions, like *The Old Man and the Sea*. In *The Old Man and the Sea* we encounter nature not as a bourgeois playground but through the lens of a working-class Spanish immigrant to Cuba—Santiago—whose interaction with the ecosystem is an important part of his livelihood, rather than a space of leisure activity (Herlihy ch. 8).

Small-Group Activities

After the lecture, I divide the class into groups of three or four students and choose from one of the following activities:

1. I write a list of places that receive seasonal visitors on the board—these usually include Cabo Rojo, Aspen, Martha's Vineyard, Orlando, Hawaii, and the French Riviera (which we discussed in a previous class on Fitzgerald). Without knowing the assignment, each group chooses a location. The task is to rewrite the events of the story in the new place. I ask students to pay close attention to the demography of the visitors and to note their use of language and the activities that they would carry out, in each respective location.
2. I write a list of the main characters (excluding Nick) on the board, including Kate, Odgar, "The men," and the absent, year-round resident: a boy and a girl (U.S. citizens) who are the same age as Nick, and a Native American boy and girl, who are the same age as Nick. Each group chooses a character before knowing the assignment. The task is for the students to rewrite the important components of the text from their character's perspective. How would the year-round U.S. citizens perceive the summer people? What about Native Americans? How would the background of each person influence how they perceive the action of the others?
3. I write a list of the main characters of the text on the board—Nick, Kate, Odgar, and "The men"—and I also list those absent, year-round residents: a boy and a girl (U.S. citizens) and a Native American boy and girl, who are the same age as the protagonist. Without knowing the assignment, groups choose a person or group. The task is for the students to write or draw an imaginary Facebook page for their character or group. What is their status? Who would their friends be? What do they "like" and "follow," and what is their hometown? Who are their "people you may know"? I take a moment to ask them to be sure to rehash some concepts that we have touched in the discussion, such as language, background, and markers of cultural orientation.

Writing Assignment

I often involve creative writing exercises in my courses as I feel they can be useful for students to relate texts to their own experiences. As a final component of this period, I ask students to think of a vacation to another place.

(Place is defined however students interpret it in their minds.) We do this in silence. After a few moments, I ask them to write four sentences, each about a particular part of being in that place: food, weather, landscape, and language. In addition to the next session's reading, the homework assignment is a one-page text with four paragraphs. Each sentence they jotted down in class should be the topic sentence of each section. (If that assignment is not interesting to them, I also give students the option of rewriting the task of their small group as an individual.)

Works Cited

Bacon, John U. "Hemingway's Michigan: Summers in Northern Michigan Helped Shape Nobel Laureate." *Ann Arbor Chronicle*. 27 Aug. 2010. <http://annarborchronicle.com/2010/08/27/column-hemingways-michigan/>.

Brown, Bill. *Reading the West: An Anthology of Dime Westerns*. Boston: Bedford Books, 1997.

Hemingway, Ernest. *A Moveable Feast*. New York: Scribner, 1964.

———. "Summer People." *The Complete Short Stories of Ernest Hemingway: The Finca Vigía Edition*. New York: Scribner's, 1987."Hemingway in Michigan Pt. 1–3." *YouTube*, uploaded by Bonnie Bucqueroux. 21 Sept. 2008. <www.youtube.com/watch?v=QNiyDN1thkw>.

Hendrickson, Paul. *Hemingway's Boat: Everything He Loved in Life, and Lost, 1934–1961*. New York: Alfred A. Knopf, 2011.

Herlihy, Jeffrey. *In Paris or Paname: Hemingway's Expatriate Nationalism*. Amsterdam: Rodopi, 2011.

Kyvig, David E. *Daily Life in the United States, 1920–1939: Decades of Promise and Pain*. Westport, CT: Greenwood, 2002.

Morris, Donald R. "Where Do Chickens Come From?" *Baltimore Sun*. 26 Sept. 1996. p. 1.

Organic Space and Time

Using Henri Bergson to Explain Nick Adams's Intuition of the World in "Big Two-Hearted River"

Scott Ortolano

> "There is only a single duration which carries everything along with it, a river without bottom and without banks and flowing without assignable forces in a direction one cannot define."
> —Henri Bergson, *The Creative Mind*

At the turn of the twentieth century, the philosopher Henri Bergson transformed how individuals understood their place in the world by differentiating organic, natural space, and time from a world enthralled to and limited by rational, objective-driven logic. Bergson was immensely popular in America at this time—perhaps even more so than William James, who helped to publicize his ideas in the country. This popularity was put on full display when Bergson briefly visited in 1913 to give a series of lectures at Columbia and the City College of New York and to accept an honorary degree from Columbia University. The scene surrounding his visit was electric and featured record-breaking ticket applications, students crowded out of their seats in classes where he appeared, lecture halls so tightly packed that people fainted, and what many have identified as New York City's first traffic jam (Quirk 53).[1] In *Bergson and American Culture,* Tom Quirk contends that Bergson was held in such high regard because his philosophy "fit into the interstices of the prevailing modes of American thought and life; it encouraged many Americans to believe what they already believed or wanted to believe, and it must have appeared to them, perhaps subconsciously, as perfectly consonant with their national aspirations and historical traditions" (55). Specifically, Quirk is referring to the challenge Bergson's philosophy mounted to mechanistic, naturalist ideologies that were dominant in the nineteenth century and that reduced the world to a series of inhuman, largely uncontrollable forces as well as to Americans' view of their country as an exceptional place of boundless potential and growth. Bergson's ideas seemed to promise that a great new world was emerging and that humanity was breaking free from the shackles of old limitations, a process that Americans saw themselves leading.

Bergson's philosophy would also profoundly shape the ideology and aesthetics of those spearheading the many submovements of modernism—figures including the early Cubists, Paul Cézanne, Gertrude Stein, and Ezra Pound, all of whom helped to shape the aesthetic vision of Ernest Hemingway. While numerous scholars have detailed Bergson's influence on the above individuals and their influence on Hemingway, very little has been written on the presence of Bergsonian ideas in Hemingway's work.[2] Nevertheless, Bergson's philosophy offers a useful lens for understanding the dynamics present in Hemingway's fiction (especially his earliest projects). Most significantly, Bergson can be used to help students grasp the organic reality Hemingway attempts to represent through his aesthetic of omission—a flowing world that is perhaps best embodied in the metaphors, open language, and symbolism of "Big Two-Hearted River."

Bergson maintains that we exist in a dynamic world in which entities (human, animal, and microbial) develop in an unpredictable fashion to meet the physical (and ideological) conditions of their environments—something that simultaneously occurs on multiple, open (rather than singular and fixed) platforms. We fail to see this dynamism because our worlds are saturated by static concepts that have been created by our past exposure to certain stimuli or narratives. This has the effect of flattening our existential field and compartmentalizing our world. Nevertheless, true durational reality continues to evolve beyond such static narratives. The struggle for Bergson (and Hemingway) is discovering how to perceive, exist within, and ultimately represent this fluid reality. Bergson's solution is intuition, a displacing of self within the organic flow of being in a way that discards objective-driven, closed narratives in favor of a sympathetic perceptual process that allows for material, emotional, and spiritual harmony. It is this very process that heals Nick Adams's fragmented psyche in "Big Two-Hearted River," as he enters the stream of life and emerges with a viable understanding of himself and his world.

Introducing students to the above ideas and then comparing them with specific passages in "Big Two-Hearted River" can help clarify the subtle significance of Nick's actions during the story—something with which students often struggle. If the instructor is teaching a high school or general undergraduate course, this is best done by providing a brief overview of Bergson's philosophy (as in the above paragraph) and then pairing quotes that embody his ideas with sections of the short story. The selections presented in this chapter can be used to this end. In advanced courses, students might be asked to read a selection from Bergson before discussing the story, or Bergson's work could be assigned for a class following an initial discussion of the story.[3] If the latter option is chosen, the second class can be used to present an entirely new reading of the story and highlight the deceptive complexity of Hemingway's prose. Teachers may also want to pair Bergson's work and the insights made in this essay with all of *In Our Time*. The book, as a whole, presents the world as an open amalgamation of places and experiences, which makes Bergson's philosophy an immensely useful critical lens.

As the concluding story of *In Our Time*, "Big Two-Hearted River" provides a method of discovering existential fulfillment within the changing environments of "modern" America. The story begins by presenting a world that has fallen into a state of ruin, in which the power of previously dominant—and existentially necessary—unitary structures have collapsed in the face of new social, economic, and technological realities. As Nick steps from the train, he sees a burned over and barren world: "There was no town, nothing but the rails and the burned-over country . . . It [the ruined foundations of the town's main hotel] was all that remained of Seney. Even the surface had been burned off the ground" (163). Numerous scholars have identified this blackened landscape as a symbol for the carnage of World War I and Nick's fragile psychological state. However, this degraded landscape is also a representation of the rapidly fragmenting cultural milieu of the Midwest and the country at large. Cultural historian Jackson Lears explains that the nation's transition to an industrial consumer culture created an obsession with material excess that was itself "streamlined into an exaltation of industrial efficiency," making the "process of productivity" *the* organizing principle of daily existence (18). The existential consequences of this transformation would have been especially visible to Hemingway in the form of the unsustainable lumber industry, which was collapsing in areas of Michigan that had become cutover.

The costs of the lumber industry are explored in other Nick Adams stories, most notably "The End of Something" and "The Last Good Country." Instructors may even point students toward these stories if they want to more fully explore this issue, which provides an informative avenue for discussing what critic Laura Gruber Godfrey identifies as Hemingway's effort to "pass along the histories, memories, and emotional fabrics of the varying communities he observed and of which he was a part" (80). The waste of the lumber industry was so significant and the rate of exploitation so rapid that boomtowns like Seney rose and fell with great frequency. Michigan historian Willis Frederick Dunbar explains that fire was one of the more visible consequences of the industry; they frequently erupted and, fed by plentiful waste material, often raged at uncontrollable rates (481). Thus, the burned over town and countryside are not simply representations of the destruction of the war but also introspective looks at the consequences of industrial efficiency and the rapidly fragmenting regional cultures of America.

Like the practices that produced the ruins of Seney, Nick has spent his life out of sync with his world, moving from one physical-ideological ruin to another, searching for a way to viably exist within his increasingly unstable cognitive landscapes. Those teaching "Big Two-Hearted River" with *In Our Time* can call attention to the presence of these schisms in some of the text's other stories about Nick Adams. For example, instructors might point to Nick's unease with his father's confident narratives of himself and Native Americans in "Indian Camp"; the haunting background of the decaying lumber mill in "The End of Something," a ruin that reflects Nick's cognitively unsettled state, his collapsing relationship with Marjorie as well as the environmental and cultural degradation of Michigan's Upper Peninsula; and Nick's disturbing encounter with the physically and cognitively damaged Ad Francis in "The Battler," whose trauma represents the consequences of existing outside of socially sanctioned modes of being and indicates that the existentially destructive aspects of society cannot be fought on their own terms but require a new logic. All of these stories depict a Nick who is uncomfortable with the cultural fabric of his world as well as the "solutions" offered by those enmeshed in it, whether they are his father's clean yet inaccurate Victorian narratives of life, the self-serving "advice" of his friend Bill, or the tragic madness of Ad Francis. His fishing trip reveals another mode of being—one that is experiential, open, and process-based.

Nick's mental and spiritual recovery is carried out in Bergsonian terms. As previously noted, Bergson advocates rejecting static symbols and concepts and experiencing the world through intuition. The key to such a process is to move outside of scientific-rational modes of perception and encounter and experience reality as it actually exists—before it is imbued with false meaning by our rational intellect. True intuition of the world is "purified, or in other words, released, where necessary, from the molds that our intellect has formed. ... [It] follows the real in all its sinuosities" (Bergson, *Creative Evolution* 363). Entering into this intuitive state offers the possibility of tapping into our *élan vital* (the spiritual force at the center of Bergson's world) and thereby reunifying our fragmented state of being. *Élan vital* can be conceived of as *the* force that drives creation and reaches its apex in human consciousness; it is unquantifiable, omnipresent, and, in the tradition of Bergson, undeniable: "When we put back our being into our will, and our will itself into the impulsion it prolongs, we understand, we feel, that reality is a perpetual growth, a creation pursued without end" (*Creative Evolution* 239). Thus, intuition allows one to experience new, more fulfilling, and unlimited states of existential being.

Hemingway depicts this intuitive process by creating clear images that are not hemmed in by descriptive language but exist in an unconstrained state. In short, "Big Two-Hearted River" depends on an imagist aesthetic, and a basic grasp of imagism is essential to understanding how the story creates and explores an organic environment that is multidimensional. As critics like Natan Zach and Robert Bernard Hass have noted, the tenets of imagism are heavily Bergsonian. Ezra Pound, the movement's progenitor, became familiar with the work of Bergson during his time in Paris and, specifically, through his mentor and friend T. E. Hulme—even lauding Hulme's lectures on Bergson in a letter to his mother (Hass 61). Pound's aesthetics in turn had a significant impact on the young Hemingway, and they are especially evident in "Big Two-Hearted River." Critic Alex Shakespeare goes so far as to call the story a long imagist poem that depends upon Pound's method of collecting and presenting "luminous details," or specific descriptions that present rather than interpret reality (39). This open language has the effect of liberating images from deadening concepts that would imprison their potential meaning. Hass explains that "unlike concepts, which are categorically fixed representations of generic ideas, a series of well-chosen images establishes a surprising matrix of sensations that enables one to apprehend momentarily the flux of immediate experiences" (60). In "Big Two-Hearted River," Hemingway's use of imagist principles allows readers to feel the organic multiplicity of life.

Because imagism is so central to the story, teachers should consider familiarizing students with the overarching objectives of the movement. This can be done by reviewing the imagist tenets Pound outlines in "A Few Don'ts by an Imagiste" and then analyzing "In a Station of the Metro," Pound's noted two-line poem. Both of these texts can be projected onto an overhead or read aloud. As the following lines reveal, the brevity and accessibility of "In a Station of the Metro" makes it especially useful in class discussions: "The apparition of these faces in the crowd; / Petals on a wet, black bough" (111).

These lines embody the ideals of imagism and recreate the experience of the poet by fashioning a hard image that functions as "an intellectual and emotional complex in an instant of time" (Pound, "A Few Don'ts" 95). Explaining how this poem is intended to affect the reader will help students grasp the same dynamics in "Big Two-Hearted River." They can, for example, see that Seney does not just represent the war, Nick's consciousness, the logging industry, or the actual physical environment because the image contains all of these meanings simultaneously. The images in the story, like the moment in the metro, are designed to create firm impressions on readers. The unfurling of these exact images opens a flowing experiential space that is heavily Bergsonian and replicates the organic reality of life itself. Instructors should also use this as a moment to introduce students to Hemingway's "iceberg theory" as a concept and critical strategy for reading his work. Students should be provided with Hemingway's well-known quote about his aesthetic of omission from *Death in the Afternoon* in the same manner that Pound's work was shared.[4] This strategy will be especially useful in lower-level courses because it will help students see how writers work within broader literary movements and use ideas present in these movements to inspire and shape their writing. Furthermore, since the class will have just discussed Pound's aesthetics and imagism, they will be in a position to deconstruct the meaning behind Hemingway's iceberg theory on their own. Instructors should refrain from leading them too much during this portion of the class so that the activity nurtures their confidence.[5]

Failing to see the story as a process-based, experiential narrative can produce severe misreadings, the most notable of which is Philip Young's interpretation in *Ernest Hemingway: A Reconsideration*. Young sees only the fragmented moments that compose the story, describing them as "chronologically ordered, mechanical, deliberate movements which begin to wear on one's nervous system" and are unobjectionable only because they perfectly express that Nick's "terrible panic is just barely under control" (46). Young concludes by comparing Nick's experience to a housewife who has lost her husband and busily does work to avoid reflecting on the loss. He identifies this "clear image" of a man on the edge as "the whole point of an otherwise pointless story" (47). For Young, the story is merely a playing out of "primitivation," or a mind's shutting down of its higher functions to cope with subliminal trauma (168). The absence of descriptive concepts is for him an absence of larger meaning.

In actuality, Nick is not suppressing his cognitive functions but expanding them. The "point" of the story *is* the durational flow of Nick's experiences. The stretching out of time in the story is not meant to wear on the nerves of readers but show them the pulse of life in a world not hurried and constrained by end-driven models of cognition. Bergson explains that ends-based, efficiency-driven life modes—while effective in the production of objects or achieving pragmatic ends—should not be applied as a general life philosophy or artistic technique. He uses an artist painting a picture as an example, contending that time ceases to be something that can be altered by the artist without changing the very fabric of the product: "The duration of his work is part and parcel of his work. To contract or dilate it would be to modify both the psychical evolution that fills it and the invention which is its goal. . . . It is a vital process, something like the ripening of an idea" (*Creative Evolution* 340). It is in this spirit that the repetition of the story occurs. Take, for example, the details that chronicle Nick's making camp and eating dinner:

> Nick sat down beside the fire and lifted the frying pan off. He poured about half of the contents out into the tin plate. It spread slowly on the plate. Nick knew it was too hot. He poured on some tomato catchup. He knew the beans and spaghetti were still hot. He looked at the fire, then at the tent, he was not going to spoil it all by burning his tongue. For years he had never enjoyed fried bananas because he had never been able to wait for them. His tongue was very sensitive. He was very hungry. Across the river in the swamp, in the almost dark, he saw a mist rising. He looked at the tent once more. All right. He took a spoonful from the plate.
> "Chrise," Nick said, "Geezus Chrise," he said happily.
> He ate the whole plateful. . . . He had been that hungry before, but had not been able to satisfy it. He could have made camp hours before if he had wanted to. There were plenty of good places to camp on the river. But this was good. (168)

Far from being an endless monotony solely dedicated to showing Nick Adams's "near breakdown" state, the above passage reflects a Nick Adams entering into the flow of the world and finding his place within it. In a reading of the scene, Joseph Flora explains that the process *is* the iceberg: "Nick's words ['Geezus Chrise'] are not in isolation—he has taken his first mouthful; hence the expression is appropriate to the action of tasting the hot food and to the faith that he feels as regards the future" (162). The experience exhibits his new confidence in a world that he had formerly needed to escape, in which he could neither wait for his food to cool nor settle down to sleep without losing his soul. In the easy, patient way he performs these deceptively simple actions, we see a Nick Adams at peace with the world and his surroundings as they actually exist—a status he has never before achieved.

Hemingway uses "Big Two-Hearted River" to reveal that true meaning is not within the ends of a task (catching fish or eating food) but in the movements of the journey. Nick's recollections of dead trout that have been struck with a fungus after being handled by inexpert fishermen is a reminder than anyone can catch fish. However, the fishing can only be tragic "with other men on the river . . . who were not of your party" and who do not know how to perceive and act within the world (176). The environment in which Nick is enmeshed functions as a site for cognitive-existential healing precisely because it is liberated from the tragic concepts that have been created by others to "regulate" life. Unlike such men, Nick does not exploit his world through an ends-based life philosophy but engages it through process-based progressions that organically evolve from his surroundings.

The concept of existing within the flow of life is most clearly expressed through depictions of trout in the river. As Nick first looks down from the bridge, he sees trout "holding steady in the current," at one with their environment and adjusting with quick angles. The trout are not singular entities but multiplicitous, possessing a not easily perceived yet significant depth: "He watched them holding themselves with their noses into the current, many trout in deep, fast moving water, slightly distorted . . . big trout looking to hold themselves on the gravel bottom in a varying mist of gravel and sand, raised in spurts by the current" (163). These big trout are symbols for an effective existential posture. At one with their surroundings, they endure against and within with the deep currents of their world and the gravelly obstacles erected by its shifting flows. The images of trout merge with that of a kingfisher in flight through the air, yet another symbol of being in a suspended state within an atmospheric current: "As the shadow of the kingfisher moved up the stream, a big trout shot upstream in a long angle, only his shadow marking the angle, then lost his shadow as he came through the surface of the water, caught the sun, and then, as he went back into the stream under the surface, his shadow seemed to float down the stream with the current, unresisting" (163–64). We have here a merging of the various flows of the environment and a model for how to live within a world that does not remain within hard and fast borders but which is always in the process of redefining them. As the trout moves into the air before returning to the current and the kingfisher flies through the atmosphere before its eventual entrance into the water, Nick eats, walks, camps, and enters the stream. In this microcosm of the ever-shifting world, he becomes the Bergsonian ideal, at peace with the flows of life. He does not forcefully enact his will on or passively submit to his environment but moves in tune with its durations and, in the process, comes to a greater understanding of himself and his world. His actions are not performed as individualized fragments (as Young contends) but unified into a flowing duration.

Having healed his splintered consciousness, Nick discovers a suitable means of fishing the stream *and* transposing these lessons to the outside world, which is never really outside of anything. By the conclusion of "Big Two-Hearted River," he has learned not to attempt to ignore or constrain the flow of life but, like a trout, to move and exist with its many currents. Flora explains that the story is "the affirmation that the artist needs a belief that the future matters, a belief he will have a chance to create work that will have a life beyond life" (179). Specifically, Flora cites the final lines of the story as a testament to this fact. At this moment, Nick decides not to go into the depths of the swamp because he sees the river showing through the trees and understands that "there were plenty of days coming when he could fish the swamp" (180). The key to understanding this moment lies in the logic behind not venturing further into the swamp. This is not someone who is avoiding life—as Young contends—but one who has come face to face with himself and, for the first time, is able to see the world clearly. Nick understands that he is an amalgamation of many things, places, ideas, and times and that the world cannot be overpowered but must be lived and explored in a manner in tune with its durations.

Bergson's philosophy offers both a mode of contextualizing Nick Adams's cognitive journey and a model for better understanding and transcending the enduring existential issues Hemingway uses Nick to explore. Bergson explains that "just as the talent of the painter is formed or deformed—in any case, is modified—under the very influence of the works he produces, so each of our states, at the moment of its issue, modifies our personality.... It is right to say that we are, to a certain extent, what we do, and that we are creating ourselves continually" (*Creative Evolution* 7). It is only when we come to peace with this reality that we, like Nick, can find a mode of existence not dependent on the narratives of the past or the narratives of others but on the durational flows of our world, to see the river through the trees and discover methods for exploring our own rivers.

Teachers can scaffold their lessons about Bergson and "Big Two-Hearted River" on to broader projects about Hemingway, modernism, and nature by encouraging students to apply the analytic framework to other works by Hemingway. His writing on fishing in particular provides an accessible and pedagogically useful avenue for students to hone their critical abilities. As scholar Nick Lyons explains, "fishing, which kept him [Hemingway] wedded to the natural world, was an important enough part of his life to affect all of his writing, and understanding its importance helps us understand a lot about the man and a lot about all of his writing" (xix). Lyons's *Hemingway on Fishing*, a collection of Hemingway's reflections on fishing, is ideal for such a project and might be placed on reserve at a school's library or required in courses focused on Hemingway. Alternatively, a teacher could present especially useful selections from the book[6] (ideally one nonfiction essay and an excerpt from Hemingway's creative work) and have students conduct analyses of how Bergsonian concepts can be seen in such works or how they reflect Hemingway's imagist aesthetic, the iceberg principle, or his view of the natural world (see Appendix for sample writing prompts for this and subsequent lessons plans). This would make an especially useful first writing assignment in a literature course as well as a potential take-home exam.

In lower-level courses or the high school classroom, "Big Two-Hearted River" could be used as inspiration for multimodal writing assignments by using free web-based programs like Storify or Medium.[7] These assignments may take a plethora of forms. For example, students might interweave quotes from the story and from Bergson with digital content (websites, GIFs, videos, etc.) about the natural world—all of which could be about the environment of the Midwest, rivers, trout, fishing, or some other linked ecological topic. Putting these texts in conversation with one another should allow students to see how Hemingway's writing allows for a deeper, more spiritual encounter with the environment and world.

A very different multimodal assignment would involve using the discussion of "Big Two-Hearted River" to inspire students to reassess themselves and the various ideas they subscribe to by constructing a crot essay (or a series of interrelated fragments of text and media, which naturally shift tone, style, and subject) that takes the form of an open multiplicity. Here, students would bring together digital media that represents various aspects of themselves (preferably along with quotes from the reading and/or Bergson) into one flowing and open expository essay. While the assignment is very untraditional, such a project answers the call of scholars like Robert Scholes, who advocates shifting the emphasis of

English courses from literary analysis to "textualities" by expanding the range of texts students study and compose (35). The latter assignment would prove especially beneficial with nonmajors who enter literature courses unsure of why the literature they study matters or what it offers to them in both intellectual and existential contexts. Regardless of what specific path instructors take, these types of assignments will help students further appreciate the significance of Hemingway's writing and his engagements with the natural world.

Notes

1. Tom Quirk provides an informative overview of America's reception of Bergson in 1913 in *Bergson and American Culture: The Worlds of Willa Cather and Wallace Stevens* (Chapel Hill: U of North Carolina P, 1990).

2. The most well-known exploration of the relationship between Bergson and Hemingway is Green D. Wyrick's "Hemingway and Bergson: The *Élan Vital*," a three-page article that appeared in a 1955 issue of *Modern Fiction Studies* (then a small journal published by Purdue University's Modern Fiction Club). This article is very abbreviated, oversimplifying Bergson as an antirational primitivist and establishing only superficial, general links between the philosopher and the totality of Hemingway's writing. However, readers should also note that the lack of scholarship on Hemingway and Bergson is beginning to be addressed—a process that has continued as this article has taken shape. One notable example of this correction is Mark Cirino's *Ernest Hemingway: Thought in Action* (Madison: U of Wisconsin P, 2012), a work that recognizes Bergson's important influence on Hemingway along with other philosophers and writers.

3. "Introduction to Metaphysics," an essay from *The Creative Mind*, is an ideal text to use for this purpose as it provides a straightforward overview of Bergson's philosophy.

4. The iceberg theory quote from *Death in the Afternoon* appears at the end of chapter 16: "If a writer of prose knows enough of what he is writing about he may omit things that he knows and the reader, if the writer is writing truly enough, will have a feeling of those things as strongly as though the writer had stated them. The dignity of movement of an ice-berg is due to only one-eighth of it being above water" (192).

5. "The Best Rainbow Trout Fishing" and "The Last Good Country (an excerpt)" are an apt pairing for discussions of "Big Two-Hearted River." They also offer accessible ways for students to identify Bergsonian concepts at work in Hemingway's fiction and non-fiction.

6. This discussion of the iceberg theory can also be used to prepare students for an exam question that assesses their understanding of Hemingway's aesthetic of omission and how it is employed in works about the natural world (see Appendix, Sample Exam Question 1).

7. While Storify (www.storify.com) is currently the more established multimodal composition platform, Medium (www.medium.com) offers students access to a broader array of features and has a useful, free smartphone app. As a result, Medium is probably preferable when not all students have access to traditional computers.

Works Cited

Bergson, Henri. *Creative Evolution.* 1907. Trans. Arthur Mitchell. 1911. Mineola, NY: Dover Publications, 1998.

———. *The Creative Mind: Introduction to Metaphysics.* 1934. Trans. Mabelle L. Andison. New York: Citadel Press, 2002.

Dunbar, Willis Frederick. *Michigan: A History of the Wolverine State.* Grand Rapids, MI: William B. Eerdmans Publishing Company, 1965.

Flora, Joseph M. *Hemingway's Nick Adams.* Baton Rouge: Louisiana State UP, 1982.

Godfrey, Laura Gruber. "Hemingway and Cultural Geography: The Landscape of Logging in 'The End of Something.'" *Ernest Hemingway and the Geography of Memory.* Ed. Mark Cirino and Mark P. Ott. Kent, OH: Kent State UP, 2010.

Hass, Robert Bernard. "(Re)Reading Bergson: Frost, Pound, and the Legacy of Modern Poetry." *Journal of Modern Literature* 29.1 (2005): 55–75.

Hemingway, Ernest. "Big Two-Hearted River." *The Complete Short Stories of Ernest Hemingway: The Finca Vigía Edition.* New York: Scribner's, 1987.

———. *Death in the Afternoon.* New York: Scribner's Sons, 1932.

Lears, Jackson. *Fables of Abundance: A Cultural History of Advertising in America.* New York: Basic Books, 1994.

Lyons, Nick, ed. *Hemingway on Fishing.* New York: Scribner, 2000.

Pound, Ezra. "In a Station of the Metro." 1926. *Personae: The Collected Shorter Poems of Ezra Pound.* New York: New Directions, 1950.

———. "A Few Don'ts by an Imagiste." 1913. *Modernism: An Anthology.* Ed. Lawrence Rainey. Malden, MA: Blackwell, 2005.

Quirk, Tom. *Bergson and American Culture: The Worlds of Willa Cather and Wallace Stevens.* Chapel Hill: U of North Carolina P, 1990.

Scholes, Robert. *English After the Fall: From Literature to Textuality.* Iowa City: U of Iowa P, 2011.

Young, Philip. *Ernest Hemingway, A Reconsideration.* University Park: Pennsylvania State UP, 1966.

Zach, Natan. "Imagism and Vorticism." *Modernism: 1890–1930.* Ed. Malcolm Bradbury and James McFarlene. 1976. New York: Penguin, 1991.

A Darwinian Reading of "Big Two-Hearted River"

The Re-enchantment of Nick Adams?

Michael Kim Roos

A few years ago, I began teaching intermediate composition courses with an evolutionary theme at the University of Cincinnati Blue Ash College, a branch campus with a student body composed of a nearly equal split between those in two-year terminal degrees in a technical field and those intending to transfer to baccalaureate colleges. The course, English 2089, is the second and final required composition course for all students at the university, and it allows faculty to include theme-based readings drawn from a variety of genres. Since I have long recognized strong evolutionary elements in Hemingway's "Big Two-Hearted River," I sometimes included in the syllabus for my evolutionary course an early week devoted to a discussion of the story, which allows students the option of writing one of their required essays on ideas generated by our wide ranging discussion. (See the Appendix for a sample syllabus and writing topics.)

As I prepared for the course and reviewed scholarly commentary on "Big Two-Hearted River," I was surprised to learn that, although a small band of critics have noted isolated evolutionary elements in the story, no one, as far as I could determine, had attempted a full examination of the story through the lens of Darwinian evolution.[1] This puzzled me, given that I see plenty of textual evidence that evolution by natural selection—or, in its more brutal Spencerian phraseology, "survival of the fittest"—seems to have been very much on Hemingway's mind as he composed the story and infused it with evolutionary details that significantly impact the way we should interpret it. What I attempt to do with students in my composition class is to help them recognize that "Big Two-Hearted River" can be read as a profoundly evolutionary tale in which Nick

Adams comes to terms with the natural world, his place in it, and the finitude of all things, especially his own. I want them to recognize that Nick, in symbolic terms, is fishing for meaning in a culture that, according to Max Weber, has become "disenchanted" by science, rationalism, and progress (155). Certainly, within such a reading, a broad range of possible questions for exploration and discussion can open up. I ask students to put themselves in Nick's place and to consider their own places in nature, ponder how they themselves come to terms with natural processes, including evolutionary ones, and ask themselves whether or not they are disenchanted with notions of science, rationalism, and progress.

To begin, I provide students with some biographical background on Hemingway in order to establish that his education, both formal and informal, was indeed steeped in Darwinian theory.[2] In fact, as I have explained in my own previously published essay, perhaps more so than many of today's high school students, Hemingway was thoroughly taught evolutionary theory in his high school zoology class and encountered it full-force in some of the favorite authors of his youth, including Jack London, Theodore Roosevelt, and Havelock Ellis (Roos). In addition, there were frequent childhood trips to Chicago's trailblazing Field Museum of Natural History (even then in the vanguard of presenting evolutionary theory to the public)—all of this before he arrived in Europe in December 1921. This could not have left him unchanged. As Daniel Dennett has written, Darwin's "dangerous idea" is like the "universal acid," one that "eats through just about every traditional concept, and leaves in its wake a revolutionized world-view, with most of the old landmarks still recognizable, but transformed in fundamental ways" (63). Although students may be reticent to speak about it, I feel it is important to have a discussion in class of the ways Darwin's theory can impact a person's religious beliefs. Certainly, this requires a gentle touch. However, by keeping the focus on the young Hemingway, the son of a deeply religious household, I carefully coax students toward an open discussion of how science and religion can conflict. It's a delicate balance for a teacher to walk. While not a scientist, I am honest with students that I trust what the overwhelming majority of scientists tell us and fully accept the scientific evidence in favor of evolution. I share with them the fact that this evidence did indeed have an impact on my own religious beliefs, although not without some deep soul searching. I think it's also important to discuss what it is about faith that provides comfort to people and what the consequences are should that faith be compromised. Eventually, if the classroom atmosphere is managed appropriately, students can become more open to discussing ways to balance science and rationalism with a healthy form of spirituality.

In that light, I offer students the ample evidence that Hemingway himself struggled mightily to find such a balance. Certainly he seriously considered and even adopted a Catholic mode of living in the 1920s and beyond.[3] Apparently, Hemingway needed some reassurance of teleology, an inherent God-given meaning and purpose to life. But as the inexorable march of science was proving in the sixty-five years between the publication of Darwin's *Origin of Species* and Hemingway's writing of "Big Two-Hearted River," the old teleologies, accepted so reassuringly for centuries, were crumbling in the face of mounting scientific data and a rationalism that provided scant comfort to the religiously inclined.

It can help at this point of the discussion to introduce students to Max Weber's 1919 analysis, wherein he declared the world "disenchanted" (155), as well as to Joseph Wood Krutch's 1929 treatise, *The Modern Temper*, in which Krutch identified Hemingway as one of the contemporary writers most emblematic of this disenchanted "modern temper" (9).[4] My goal with students is to show them how "Big Two-Hearted River," a true pinnacle of Hemingway's work in the 1920s, vividly illustrates this temper of disenchantment discussed by Weber and Krutch. In the story, Hemingway's alter ego, Nick Adams, comes face to face with the most elemental of human needs, with nature's realities, with the individual's finitude, and with the dark possibility of meaninglessness—all questions likely to be faced by any evolving young adult. While some critics have identified Nick's problem as a specific war trauma or petty family conflicts or perhaps lurking gender issues, I argue that it is this overarching question of teleology—meaning and purpose—that I believe trumps all else and haunts Nick Adams throughout the story.

Realizing that many students, especially those from more conservatively religious backgrounds, view Darwin and his theory as the great curse of the modern world, I emphasize to them that the question of meaning and purpose haunted Darwin too, according to his biographers.[5] But George Levine, in his engaging book *Darwin Loves You*, has shown how the Victorian scientist was able to maintain an essentially "enchanted" view of the world. In Levine's portrait, Darwin is an "exemplary figure" who can point us "toward a humane and sensitive secularity," without minimizing nature's cruelty but also without losing a sense of its wonder (205). When students closely examine "Big Two-Hearted River," they can learn to see in Nick Adams a fellow human and student of life who encounters the raw elements of natural selection yet achieves a measured sense of enchantment, albeit, as we shall see, a decidedly mitigated enchantment.

After I've laid the groundwork with biographical and cultural background, I ask students to consider the title. We look at the map of the Upper Peninsula of Michigan and identify the actual Two Hearted River, and the location of the actual town of Seney, the setting of the story's opening. Students can clearly see that the river in the story is not the Two Hearted but the Fox, with some alteration on Hemingway's part.[6] For the title, Hemingway borrowed the poetic name of the real river (in the process adding "Big" and the hyphen) and applied it to the Fox, which crosses the rail line at the town of Seney. As I hope that students will see, the details of the narrative suggest that Nick himself is two-hearted—divided essentially between faith and reason, between religion/teleology on the one hand and rationalism/science on the other, as presented in Darwin's account of a world moved by the forces of natural selection. As Weber and Krutch implied, it is never easy to reconcile these opposing worldviews. This is the kind of potentially disenchanting thinking that Nick is trying to leave behind in coming to the wilderness. As a result, he seems unable to let go of either of these worldviews and might be hoping to hyphenate his own two hearts, to link them into some form of coherent unified worldview.

The discussion then turns to the post-apocalyptic scene that greets Nick upon his arrival in Seney. It isn't difficult to get students to recognize how this might represent what has happened to Nick's old values, the faith of his childhood waylaid by science and the rationalism of the modern world—in other words, a stark and vivid representation of disenchantment. Given that there is no indication that this human outpost will ever be reconstructed, we talk about the degree of shock this must represent to Nick and how easy it might be for him to give up hope of a successful fishing trip.

But I ask the students to look at the details that Hemingway provides for reminders that Nick too is a creature of the natural world and may find the means to survive, at least for a time, in a world where death is ever lurking. Not surprisingly, Nick turns first to the river for reassurance—a natural element fire cannot destroy. From the railroad bridge, Nick looks down into a deep pool of "clear, brown water, colored from the pebbly bottom." There he sees the trout "holding themselves with their noses into the current" of "deep, fast moving water" (*In Our Time* 133). Because of their camouflaged coloring, Nick has trouble picking out the largest ones at the bottom. The mottled coloring of the trout, science tells us, is the result of natural selection, protection against the trout's predators. One such predator, a kingfisher, soon appears. There is nothing unusual about this. As a quick check of ornithology websites reveals, belted kingfishers are common birds on the waterways of Michigan, where they feed most commonly on a variety of fish by swooping down from a perch above the water. Once a kingfisher catches its prey, it returns to its perch and kills the fish by beating it against wood or rock. In the story, we note that the kingfisher flies upstream, and one of the big trout shoots quickly upstream ahead of it before reversing itself to take its "post under the bridge where [it] tighten[s] facing up into the current."[7] As Nick watches this drama, his heart "tighten[s]" in response (134).

The verb "tightened" rarely fails to engender some lively discussion as to whether Nick is feeling a positive or negative emotion here. The fact that the word appears twice in quick succession should suggest to the students that Nick identifies with the trout and its response to the presence of the kingfisher. Perhaps from some undefined past experience (taken by many to imply the war), Nick seems to understand and empathize with the trout's defense mechanism. To ensure its survival, the trout finds protection from its predator in the shade of the bridge. As Nick would know, a kingfisher represents death to a trout, and so, as the trout tightens defensively, Nick's heart tightens empathetically, even though he, like the kingfisher, is there to prey on trout. This is the first evidence that death or impermanence is what troubles Nick's heart. However, as a two-hearted observer, Nick relates to the scene as both predator and prey. The sentence that immediately follows, "He felt all the old feeling," is ambiguous enough to contain both roles (134). Students may argue over whether the feeling is positive or negative, but in truth we can't say for certain which is correct. Is it a thrill from past fishing experiences or a post-traumatic reminder of some near-death experience? I ask students to consider that Hemingway may well have intended both meanings.

The next evolutionary detail in the story is perhaps the most important. Nick encounters a black grasshopper, one of many he sees during his hike in the vicinity of the Seney fire—all of them black in color, instead of the more common green-brown. In the space of two finely detailed paragraphs, which I normally read aloud in the classroom, Hemingway makes certain we understand the hoppers are *genetically* black—not just covered with black dust. To remove any doubt, he has Nick take hold of the hopper and turn him over to show us his belly, described as an "iridescent" black, not the dust color of the wings (136). These details require me to bring some more evolutionary science into the discussion, since the color of the grasshopper, in my experience, is one of the most frequently misinterpreted images in the story. It's important for students to understand that Hemingway here is using an example of melanism resulting from natural selection, very much as scientific studies in nineteenth-century Britain showed conclusively that peppered moths changed from speckled gray to black in order to survive in an environment that had become increasingly blackened by soot.[8] It's likely that Hemingway learned about the melanism of moths in his high school science classes. Thus, Nick's blackened grasshopper, far from being an ominous symbol of death, as some have suggested, actually represents, in a Darwinian reading, the vibrancy of life, nature's built-in ability to adapt and regenerate itself in response to catastrophic environmental changes. Nick's mood noticeably lightens as he seems to acknowledge his kinship with the grasshopper by releasing it and speaking to it as a friend. "Go on, hopper," he says, enchantedly. "Fly away somewhere" (136).

Other such evolutionary lessons await Nick as he resumes his hike. For example, the numerous jack pine trees he finds just beyond the charred fire zone are normally the first tree species to appear following a fire. In fact, scientists tell us that jack pines have evolved to be fire dependent. Their cones require the heat of a fire to open and release their seeds (Michigan Department of Natural Resources).[9] Thus without fire, jack pines would not survive. The sweetferns, too, thrive in the immediate aftermath of a fire, and Nick uses them to pad the straps to his heavy pack. Out of death springs life. As Darwin explained, nature regenerates itself through adaptive traits developed through countless generations of natural selection.

On the other hand, the lessons are not all so uplifting: the fact remains that the mortality of the individual organism is inescapable. As a fully conscious human, Nick must acknowledge death and confront it. It is never far away. Consequently, once Nick has quite happily made a home for himself by the river and eaten a very satisfying meal, making coffee reminds him of his long-ago friendship with Hopkins, who, for one reason or another, is no longer in Nick's life, having either died, possibly in the war, or disappeared from Nick's life in some other fashion. Hemingway seems deliberately cryptic here and forces us to speculate. Interpretations by students and critics alike vary. But whatever has happened to Hopkins, Nick seems to be dealing with the essential reality of impermanence. The memory, which may be more painful than the words of the text let on, starts Nick's mind working, although he knows he can "choke" it because he is "tired enough" (142). As if to underscore the idea that death (either literal or figurative) is the real subject lurking beneath the surface, Part I, I point out to students, concludes with Nick's killing of a mosquito and with an ominous reminder of the swamp, silent on the other side of the river, a detail that will become an important focus of Part II.

After briefly discussing with students the appropriateness of dividing a two-hearted story into two distinct parts, we turn our attention to Part II, where, immersed in the stream, flanked by the duality of the swamp on his right and the meadow on his left, Nick actively engages in nature's struggle for existence. I ask the students to consider the possibility that Hemingway intended the swamp to symbolize the faculty of reason and the realities of Darwinian science—in other words, nature at its starkest and potentially most cruel. If we accept that symbolism on the one hand, then it is easy, in the context of a two-hearted story founded on duality, to recognize the meadow as a representation of faith, as nature the nurturing mother, an Edenic comforting paradise, the handiwork of a benevolent creator. Once we've established this essential duality, the two concepts thread their way through the story like counterpoint in a Bach fugue, as Nick and Hemingway attempt to unite them, to hyphenate the two hearts. Beginning with his collection of grasshoppers for bait, Nick is now more forcefully the aggressive predator, albeit a relatively enchanted predator. Although Nick has brought his flybook, I point out to students that he chooses to fish with live bait rather than something artificial. I ask students why he might make that choice. Some are able to recognize the connection to Nick's earlier encounter with the black grasshoppers in the burned over land. In the context of the Seney fire, they were a lesson of adaptation and survival as Nick walked through the fire zone. Now, in the midst of the thriving river, the grasshoppers provide a means for Nick to participate directly in the reality of the Darwinian struggle. Just as Nick had spoken to the black grasshopper as a friend in Part I, here he makes the grasshopper his partner, as he threads his hook through the hopper's body and watches as it spits tobacco juice on the hook, anticipating Nick's own spitting on his bait later in the story for good luck.

I want students to understand that although Nick is a predator, he is a responsible one, respectful of nature, justified in his killing so long as it is necessary to survive. The first trout he catches is too small, and so he releases it, but only after carefully wetting his hand before touching the trout's sensitive skin. If he were to touch it with a dry hand, he knows, a fungus would grow on the spot, and the trout would probably die as a result. He has seen many such fish, "furry with white fungus" from having been touched by careless and irresponsible "fly fishermen." In other words, though he clearly knows how to fly-fish, Nick may be associating fly-fishing with modern civilization and scientific progress. I suggest to students that fishing with live bait on a fly rod may be Nick's way of resisting such progress and thus is another sign of his two-heartedness. Yet Nick also recognizes the trout's camouflaged "clear, water-over-gravel" coloring, the certain result of natural selection. Nick knows that, like all living things in the natural order, the trout's instinct is to survive at least long enough to reproduce. Nick is gentle and caring with the small trout. When it remains unmoving on the bottom of the stream, he touches it to make sure it is okay, and the trout darts away. "He's all right," Nick thinks, reassured that he has done no serious harm to the fish. "He was only tired" (149).

The next fish is the big one that gets away, and I allow students to enjoy the way Hemingway's writing powerfully captures the thrill of the experience. More extended reading aloud is effective here. In the process, I emphasize how each time Nick hooks a fish in the story, his rod comes "alive" (148, 150, 152). Clearly, part of the thrill is the awareness the rod provides of Nick's connection to the life force. In this case, however, Nick loses the struggle. The big trout, which Nick describes significantly as "By God . . . the biggest one [he] ever heard of," breaks the line and escapes (151). Invoking the name of the deity is a reminder to us that the question of faith is ever present in Nick's mind, but catching the fish remains his priority. Nick's disappointment in losing it is so acute that he has to sit down for a while to rest and recover from the intensity of the experience.

The next set of details requires even more careful analysis with the students. Once recovered from his setback, Nick resumes fishing, standing on what is aptly described as the "marly" bed of the stream (152). I ask students to look up the word "marl," and they discover it is "a calcareous deposit found at the bottom of present-day lakes and rivers, composed of the remains of aquatic plants and animals" (qtd. in Shakespeare 50). As such, I point out, it makes excellent fertilizer. Thus, I explain to students that Hemingway's careful choice of terms provides yet another reminder of how death and its by-products are part of the process of regeneration in the natural world. Standing in the marl, Nick effectively lands a nice-sized trout, once again experiencing the aliveness of the rod and the thrill of the struggle to reel in the fish and capture it in his net. He keeps the trout alive in a flour sack immersed in the water of the stream.

To clarify Hemingway's Darwinian thinking, it is helpful at this point in the discussion to share with students the text of the original ending that Hemingway wrote for the story, published in *The Nick Adams Stories* as "On Writing." We have paused at the point in the narrative, with Nick in a distinct state of enchantment, where, after consultation with Gertrude Stein, Hemingway cut the original ending and replaced it with the one published in *In Our Time*. I read for students from Stein's *The Autobiography of Alice B. Toklas*, where she recounts how she stung him with the comment "Hemingway, remarks are not literature" (219). She was, of course, correct. If you are looking for enchantment, it is there in abundance in Hemingway's original ending. To illustrate, I duplicate several pages of the original ending as a handout so that students can more clearly understand the meaning of Stein's comment. As we read together through these selections from the original, I help the students recognize how Nick Adams—the writer who, ironically, came to the wilderness to *escape* thinking and writing—now virtually explodes into an exuberant stream of consciousness, much of which deals with writing but also covers topics such as fishing, painting, bullfighting, marriage, and impermanence. It isn't difficult for students to see that this original ending is badly out of sync with the tenor of the rest of the story. To emphasize the point more fully, I introduce students to Leo Marx's conceptions of sentimental and complex pastorals. Left in place, the original ending would have made the story what Marx terms a simple sentimental pastoral (5–11), a highly enchanted narrative that idealizes nature but doesn't get to the heart of its complexity in the way that the best nature literature does.[10]

In Hemingway's original ending, the troubled urbanite Nick Adams happily escapes the sorrows of civilization to be restored spiritually in a pastoral idyll. The ominous swamp, which all along has provided hints of a darker side to the natural world, is essentially absent in the original ending. Nick doesn't even consider fishing there; he only considers how Cézanne would have painted the swamp (*Nick Adams Stories* 240).[11] In his epiphany, Nick decides he will write "about country" (in other words, the natural world) "so it would be there like Cezanne had done it in painting. . . . He felt almost holy about it" (239). The sacredness of writing, through the sacredness of nature, has revitalized Nick in this original ending, and he can't wait to get back to camp to work on a story. "It [writing] was really more fun than anything," Nick thinks. "That was really why you did it. He had never realized that before. It wasn't conscience. It was simply that it was the greatest pleasure" (238). It isn't difficult for students to see that this is clearly a man enchanted. Unlike the published story, in the original ending Nick fishes no more and even releases his one captured trout alive, claiming to himself that it was too big to eat and he can catch a couple little ones back at camp to make a meal. Furthermore—as if this isn't enchantment enough for the story—along the trail, Nick encounters a dying rabbit, with two engorged ticks attached to its head. Tenderly Nick removes the parasites and squashes them beneath his foot, then lays the rabbit lovingly under a bush, clearly hoping to save its life.

So I ask the students to consider again Stein's criticism and why Hemingway ultimately decided to follow her advice. I show them his letter to Robert McAlmon explaining the revision, wherein he describes the original ending as "the shit" (*Letters of Ernest Hemingway* 170). With these external aids, students can easily identify important differences in the two endings. The swamp in the revision, for example, is brought forward to assume a much more prominent position. Instead of Nick's exuberant ruminations, he resumes fishing, in a way that more clearly emphasizes his *mastery* of nature rather than a sense of harmony with it. Nick does not release the first trout that he caught. Instead, he adds to it with a second, after a somewhat difficult struggle. Thus, with two nice-sized fish in his bag, Nick seems satisfied with the day's catch, and his mind returns to the swamp into which the river ahead narrows—an environment where nature is at its most untamed, a place inhospitable to humans. Here the students and I pause again to consider the following: "It would not be possible to walk through a swamp like that [Nick thinks]. The branches grew so low. You would have to keep almost level with the ground to move at all. You could not crash through the branches. That must be why the animals that lived in swamps were built the way they were, Nick thought" (*In Our Time* 154–55). Students will wonder, as many critics have, why a practical fisherman would even consider fishing such a swamp, when clearly it would only invite frustration. Yet, as I suggest to the students, Hemingway must have recognized in the swamp a powerful symbol to capture what he was now trying for in the story—a meaning that would not sugarcoat the harsher evolutionary aspects of the natural world.

It may help to point out how Hemingway reminds us of the morphology of animals that live in the swamp (the mink mentioned earlier in the story being an excellent example). The animals are the way they are because natural selection has enabled them to adapt to their environments. Humans, as Nick well knows, are *not* well adapted to living in a swamp. I suggest this to students as the reason he uses the odd word "tragic" to describe how it would be if he were to attempt to fish there. Unlike minks, humans have not been selectively adapted to survive in swamps. To attempt to do so would be to invite extinction. The logical conclusion of this thought process is that the swamp can be seen to represent Nick's own inescapable extinction. The result is that the affirmation in the original ending (the movement toward the positive act of writing) is replaced by a negation. Nick flatly rejects the idea of fishing in the swamp, at least for now, because it would be a "tragic adventure. Nick did not want it. He did not want to go down the stream any further today" (*In Our Time* 155).

Students can also hardly fail to notice the difference in Nick's demeanor in the two endings. Here, unlike the original, having brought himself to this face-to-face confrontation with the reality of death, Nick's mood darkens noticeably, and, instead of releasing the two trout he has, he immediately puts them to death, quite unsentimentally, in fact (very unlike the Nick of the original ending), whacking them against a log to break their spines, as a kingfisher does (a very appropriate amplification of the bird's symbolism), thus underscoring Nick's role as predator. Then just as coldly, Nick eviscerates the trout and tosses the offal onto the shore for minks to eat. Thus, I suggest to students that Nick's participation in the bloody natural order, the cycle of life and death and natural selection, by which Nature regenerates itself, is complete.

The final words of the published ending reiterate the importance of the swamp in Nick's state of mind. As he climbs the bank and heads toward "the high ground" of his camp (encountering no stricken rabbit in this version), he looks back one more time at the swamp. The final sentence reminds us "There were plenty of days coming when he could fish the swamp" (156). No thought of writing here. By comparing and contrasting the two variant endings of the story, students can more easily see how fishing the swamp, i.e., resolutely facing death, is now Nick's chief concern, and the published ending more clearly resonates with Part I of the story in a way that the original ending did not. I like to conclude the discussion with the observation that Nick seems determined to fish the swamp—not on this day, but soon, in the "coming" days even—in spite of knowing that it is sure to be a losing proposition. I ask the students why he might be so determined if it is certain to be "a tragic" adventure. Frankly, I don't have a reasonable explanation for this other than to see it as a Sisyphean act of rebellion against the natural order. If that is so, fishing the swamp becomes yet another instance of Nick's two-heartedness. Is he the sentimental romantic, who speaks tenderly to grasshoppers and cares for the well-being of trout and rabbits? Or is he the cold-blooded administrator of death? Both seem to be part of his essence.

Approached in this way, "Big Two-Hearted River" is likely to make more sense than as a simple fishing story in which little happens other than catching a couple nice trout. Seen as an evolutionary tale, the story becomes redolent of meaning—a story by a two-hearted writer exploring the Darwinian realities of the natural world and the attempt of Nick Adams to understand more fully his position in it. Nick does not shy away from the disenchanting implications of Darwinism, but grapples bravely with Nature and with thoughts of his own finitude, so that, successful or not, he might possibly find some sort of teleology, some ultimate meaning in the face of meaninglessness. Students should be able to acknowledge how, in recognition of the harsher aspects of the natural order, Hemingway, through revising the ending, severely darkened any sense of enchantment and may have reached a conclusion that, for him at least, the most satisfactory way to deal with natural law is to rebel against it by becoming an agent of death. Some students may decide they prefer the original ending, for its more sentimental rather than complex pastoralism, but, regardless of which ending they prefer, they should develop an appreciation for "Big Two-Hearted River" as a powerful and compelling work—a two-hearted writer's attempt to come to terms with a two-hearted world.

Notes

1. For discussions of isolated evolutionary elements in Hemingway's works, see, for example, those by Bert Bender, James Green, Glenn Love, and Sarah Mary O'Brien.

2. For a discussion of Hemingway's science education, see Susan F. Beegel, "Eye and Heart: Hemingway's Education as a Naturalist," and my own essay, "Agassiz or Darwin: The Trap of Faith and Science in Hemingway's High School Zoology Class."

3. On the subject of Hemingway's Catholic faith, see, for example, H. R. Stoneback's numerous articles and Matthew Nickel's *Hemingway's Dark Night*. For discussions of religious symbolism in "Big Two-Hearted River," see articles by David N. Cremean, Agori Kroupi, and Jack Stewart.

4. For an in-depth counter discussion of how to overcome this prevailing modern temper and achieve a secular enchantment, see Jane Bennett, *The Enchantment of Modern Life*.

5. See especially David Quammen's *The Reluctant Mr. Darwin* and Darwin's own *Autobiography*.

6. For an excellent explanation of the factual and the fictional details in the story, see Frederick Svoboda's "Landscapes Real and Imagined: 'Big Two-Hearted River.'"

7. The trout's movement is the same kind of evasive action that scientific studies have shown in fish in the presence of overhead predators. See Matthew Litvak's study, "Response of Shoaling Fish to the Threat of Aerial Predation." In the story, it doesn't matter that kingfishers most often prey upon trout measuring only 3–4 inches or that this trout, described as "big" would be in little danger of being attacked by the predator. Natural selection would have ingrained such behavior in the fish from early on, so that even as an adult, the fish would continue to exercise evasive tactics whenever it detects the presence of a predator like the kingfisher. See also Jeff Steinmetz, et al, "Birds Are Overlooked Top Predators in Aquatic Food Webs."

8. The evolutionary process of melanism works something like this: in normal environmental conditions, a small percentage of grasshoppers are born genetically black, but their survival is hindered by relatively ineffective camouflaging, compared to the majority green-brown colored hoppers. However, in the immediate aftermath of a fire, the green-brown grasshoppers are no longer well camouflaged and are thus eaten by predators in much greater numbers than their black brethren. Since grasshoppers reproduce in August and September, the new majority of black grasshoppers will produce the most eggs, which are deposited in the soil for gestation over the winter. The adults all die by October, and the following spring grasshopper nymphs emerge

from the soil, becoming adults approximately two months later, about the time that Nick arrives on the scene to find, as would be expected, that most of the grasshoppers are genetically black in a still blackened landscape one year after the conflagration. For a full scientific explanation, see M. E. N. Majerus, *Melanism: Evolution in Action*. Some species of grasshoppers, according to Majerus, have the ability to change color lighter or darker depending on their background. However, since Nick wonders how long the grasshoppers will remain black, it is all but certain that Hemingway intended for us to understand that the hoppers have become black as a result of natural selection. See also Anders Forsman et al., "Rapid Evolution of Fire Melanism in Replicated Populations of Pygmy Grasshoppers." I am also indebted to my colleague Professor Mark Otten, an evolutionary biologist, who explained the process to me. In addition, Hemingway was probably aware of J. W. Tutt's famous study of industrial melanism in peppered moths, published in 1896. The study showed how, over the course of the nineteenth century, the mottled gray moths had largely been replaced by black ones. Tutt contended the change was the direct result of selective predation as the natural environment of the moths became increasingly blackened from industrial soot. It is furthermore possible that Hemingway was inspired to include melanism in his story by the degree of publicity surrounding J. B. S. Haldane's 1924 article "A Mathematical Theory of Natural and Artificial Selection," published near the time of composition of "Big Two-Hearted River." Haldane included a discussion of Tutt's work with peppered moths and provided statistical analysis and a mathematical formula showing how the results were likely the result of natural selection. His article was widely hailed as some of the strongest evidence yet produced in support of evolution by natural selection.

9. For a discussion of ecological renewal in the story, see Susan Schmidt, "Ecological Renewal Images in 'Big Two-Hearted River': Jack Pines and Fisher King."

10. Marx, in fact, seemingly unaware of the original ending of "Big Two-Hearted River," lists Hemingway among the authors of complex pastorals.

11. In the original ending, Nick also seems to realize that writing may be the best means for him to overcome the realities of death incumbent in the natural world.

Works Cited

Beegel, Susan F. "Eye and Heart: Hemingway's Education as a Naturalist." *A Historical Guide to Ernest Hemingway*. Ed. Linda Wagner-Martin. New York: Oxford UP, 2000. 53–92.

Bender, Bert. *Evolution and "the Sex Problem": American Narratives during the Eclipse of Darwinism*. Kent, OH: Kent State UP, 2004.

———. *The Descent of Love: Darwin and the Theory of Sexual Selection in American Fiction, 1871–1926*. Philadelphia: U of Pennsylvania P, 1996.

Bennett, Jane. *The Enchantment of Modern Life: Attachments, Crossings, and Ethics*. Princeton: Princeton UP, 2001.

Cremean, David N. "Man Cannot Live by Dry Fly Flies Alone: Fly Rods, Grasshoppers, and an Adaptive Catholicity in Hemingway's 'Big Two-Hearted River.'" *Hemingway and the Natural World*. Moscow: U of Idaho P, 1999. 31–44.

Darwin, Charles. *The Autobiography of Charles Darwin*. Rev. ed. New York: W. W. Norton, 1993.

———. *On the Origin of Species: A Facsimile of the First Edition*. Cambridge: Harvard UP, 1964.

Dennett, Daniel C. *Darwin's Dangerous Idea: Evolution and the Meanings of Life*. New York: Simon & Schuster, 1995.

Ellis, Havelock. *The Dance of Life*. Boston: Houghton Mifflin Company, 1923.

Forsman, Anders, et al. "Rapid Evolution of Fire Melanism in Replicated Populations of Pygmy Grasshoppers." *Evolution: International Journal of Organic Evolution* 65.9 (2011): 2530–40.

Green, James L. "Symbolic Sentences in 'Big Two-Hearted River.'" *Modern Fiction Studies* 14.3 (Autumn 1968) 307–12.

Haldane, J. B. S. "A Mathematical Theory of Natural and Artificial Selection." *Transactions of the Cambridge Philosophical Society* 23 (1924): 19–41.

Hemingway, Ernest. *In Our Time*. New York: Simon & Schuster, 1930.

———. *The Letters of Ernest Hemingway: Volume 2 (1923–1925)*. Ed. Sandra Spanier, Albert J. DeFazio III, and Robert Trogdon. Cambridge: Cambridge UP, 2013.

———. *The Nick Adams Stories*. New York: Scribners, 1972.

Kroupi, Agori. "The Religious Implications of Fishing and Bullfighting in Hemingway's Work." *The Hemingway Review* 28.1 (2008): 107–21.

Krutch, Joseph Wood. *The Modern Temper: A Study and a Confession*. New York: Harcourt Brace, 1929.

Levine, George. *Darwin Loves You: Natural Selection and the Re-enchantment of the Modern World*. Princeton: Princeton UP, 2006.

Litvak, Matthew. "Response of Shoaling Fish to the Threat of Aerial Predation." *Environmental Biology of Fishes* 36 (1993): 183–92.

Love, Glen A. *Practical Ecocriticism: Literature, Biology, and the Environment*. Charlottesville: U of Virginia P, 2003.

Majerus, M. E. N. *Melanism: Evolution in Action*. Oxford: Oxford UP, 1998.

Marx, Leo. *The Machine in the Garden*. London: Oxford UP, 1964.

Michigan Department of Natural Resources. *Jack Pine Ecosystem*. 4 June 2012. <www.michigan.gov/dnr/0,4570,7-153-10370_22664-60337-,00.html>.

O'Brien, Sarah Mary. "'I Also Am in Michigan': Pastoralism of Mind in Hemingway's 'Big Two-Hearted River.'" *The Hemingway Review* 28.2 (Spring 2009) 66–86.

Otten, Mark. Email. 4 June 2012.

Quammen, David. *The Reluctant Mr. Darwin: An Intimate Portrait of Charles Darwin and the Making of His Theory of Evolution*. New York: Atlas Books, 2006.

Roos, Michael. "Agassiz or Darwin: The Trap of Faith and Science in Hemingway's High School Zoology Class." *The Hemingway Review* 32.2 (Spring 2013): 7–27.

Schmidt, Susan. "Ecological Renewal Images in 'Big Two-Hearted River': Jack Pines and Fisher King." *The Hemingway Review* 9.2 (1990): 142–45.

Shakespeare, Alex. "The Names of Rivers and the Names of Birds: Ezra Pound, Louis Agassiz, and the 'Luminous Detail' in Hemingway's Early Fiction." *The Hemingway Review* 30.2 (2011): 36–53.

Stein, Gertrude. *The Autobiography of Alice B. Toklas.* New York: Vintage Books, 1990.

Steinmetz, Jeff, Steven L. Kohler, and Daniel A. Soluk. "Birds Are Overlooked Top Predators in Aquatic Food Webs." *Ecology* 84.5 (2003): 1324–28.

Stewart, Jack F. "Christian Allusions in 'Big Two-Hearted River.'" *Studies in Short Fiction* 15.2 (1978): 194–96.

Stoneback, H. R. "Pilgrimage Variations: Hemingway's Sacred Landscapes." *Hemingway: Eight Decades of Criticism.* Ed. Linda Wagner-Martin. East Lansing: Michigan State UP, 2009. 457–76.

Svoboda, Frederic. "Landscapes Real and Imagined: 'Big Two-Hearted River.'" *The Hemingway Review* 16.1 (1996): 33–42.

Weber, Max. *From Max Weber: Essays in Sociology.* Ed. H. H. Gerth and C. Wright Mills. Trans. H. H. Gerth and C. Wright Mills. New York: Oxford UP, 1958.

It's All About a Perfect Drift

Reading the Fishing Metaphor in "Big Two-Hearted River"

Larry Grimes

> "It was not until long afterward that I knew that it was not the duration of a sensation but its intensity that counts. If it is of enough intensity it lasts forever no matter what the actual time was and then it was I that I knew why I loved that fishing too."
>
> —Ernest Hemingway, "On Fly Fishing"

Teaching "Big Two-Hearted River" presents one serious problem: for many readers it is boring. Because the story sometimes reads like a camping and fishing manual, and is boring and off-putting to many readers, a second problem has been created: the story has been abstracted away from the page and into the world of biographical and psychological criticism where things not included in the text are brought to the foreground of interpretation, while hiking, camping, and fishing disappear into the background. So students of the text are torn between boredom and abstract reading, between what they perceive to be either a story about dull stuff or a story about what isn't in the story (the war, the wound, the Native Americans).[1] In this essay I will make suggestions for both enlivening the story and demystifying it.

Before reading "Big Two-Hearted River," it is important to identify the text. Is it the "Big Two-Hearted" of *This Quarter,* published as a stand-alone story in 1924; is it the "Big Two-Hearted" situated among the stories and vignettes of *In Our Time;* is it "Big Two-Hearted" read through its manuscripts; is it "Big Two-Hearted" read through Hemingway biographies; or is it a combination of these texts? In an attempt to address the problems noted above, and because I think many will teach the story from an anthology rather than contextualized in *In Our Time*, I will limit myself to the stand-alone text of *This Quarter*. This means that I will exclude from this reading any knowledge of the protagonist's participation in World War I and any knowledge of war wounds.[2] Instead, I will locate the story in the tradition of the hybrid genre of "nature writing" that springs from Thoreau's *Walden* and runs through Hemingway to writers like Norman Maclean, Terry Tempest Williams, and Rick Bass. As I look at genre, my attention will be focused on echoes from *Walden* in "Big Two-Hearted." I will argue that the story presents Nick Adams as a protagonist who, in the manner of Thoreau at Walden, lives deliberately (simply, intentionally, aware, and awake), rather than as a traumatized young man seeking to control life in a threatening and chaotic world. Moving forward, it should be noted that the word *deliberate* has as its root *libra*, which means balance or scales. On the other hand, the word *control*, so central to biographical and psychological readings of the story, means to dominate, to command, to restrain, and to check. I shall build on this distinction between balance (harmony) and control throughout this essay.

Since I suggest a close relation between Hemingway and Thoreau, students may wish to explore the relationship before beginning a close reading of the story. The approach I suggest is to discuss the nature of "literary influence"—what it is and how one might determine it, especially if an influence seems apparent but not fully and directly established. The tactic I suggest is an inductive one, beginning with reference to the only two nods Hemingway makes to Thoreau.

First, in *Green Hills of Africa*, after making disparaging remarks about the Transcendentalists as a group, Hemingway acknowledges that "they had hard minds, yes. Nice, dry, clean minds" (21). Hemingway goes on to write, "There is one [book, which I presume is *Walden*] that is supposed to be good, Thoreau. I cannot tell you about it because I have not yet been able to read it. But that means nothing because I cannot read other naturalists unless they are extremely accurate and not literary" (21). There is much for students to ponder here. Is Hemingway referring to *Walden*? Has he been told about it but not yet read it, or has he tried to read it and found it unreadable? Did Hemingway violate his own principles about naturalist writing in "Big Two-Hearted" by recounting personal fishing experiences as fiction?

Hemingway makes a second reference to Thoreau in his 1958 interview with George Plimpton. When asked who he considered to be his literary forebearers, Thoreau appears among the thirty writers, painters, and musicians who served in this role. His name is number thirteen on a list that seems in random order. The inventories of Hemingway's reading (Reynolds) and library (Brasch and Sigman) do not include a title by Thoreau, his reference to Thoreau in *Green Hills* is opaque; nevertheless, Hemingway here states that Thoreau was a forebearer in some way.

Is there a way that Hemingway could have come under Thoreau's influence without reading his work? A link can be established between Hemingway and Thoreau—even if he was "never able to read him," whatever that phrase may mean (*Green Hills of Africa* 21). The link begins with the relationship between Thoreau and fellow naturalist Louis Agassiz, a Harvard biology professor, and extends through Clarence Hemingway, Ernest's father.

Thoreau was a friend of Professor Agassiz and collected specimens for him. A very readable account of the relationship can be found in Donovan Hohn's essay, "Everyone Hates Henry." I suggest students read all or part of it.

After students gain some sense of this relationship, share Michael Reynold's account of Ernest's involvement in the Agassiz Club (*Young Hemingway* 31, 101, 112) and Ernest's own reflections in two letters written from Nantucket in September 1910 (10, 11). As students work through this material, they can reflect both on the question of literary influence and on the nature of the work of biographers. The matter of influence explored, students can move to the story.

The reading of the story I advocate here, in the tradition of nature writing, presents Nick as a protagonist of harmony and balance, rather than a character struggling for mastery and control. His trek into the wilderness provides a therapy of sorts, but not a psychological or medical therapy. It does not have to do with a struggle to repress internal horrors or to control terrors that come in the night. Nick sleeps well in the woods. Rather than dealing with "the return of the repressed" or other psychological maladies, Nick undergoes what Thoreau calls a "convalescence" that "lifts the veil of nature" (307).

Appealing to Greek mythology, Thoreau makes a distinction between two kinds of healing quite similar to what I am drawing here. He writes, "I am no worshiper of Hygeia, who was the daughter of that old herb doctor Aesculapius ... but rather of Hebe, cupbearer to Jupiter and daughter of Juno and wild lettuce, and who had the power to restore gods and men to the vigor of youth ... wherever she came it was spring" (432–33). The difference to which Thoreau points is the difference between biological/psychological health (Hygeia) and ontological/spiritual restoration (Hebe). Nature functions in the Transcendental model not as medicine, not as cure, but as the primal state, the fundament of existence. Nick's movement into the primal state is the central drama of this story. His movement is slow, balanced, careful, and deliberate. His successful journey into that state is accomplished step by step, fish by fish.

To encourage student participation in and engagement with the reading of with "Big Two-Hearted River," I suggest that students prepare to read this story by doing any or all of the following:

1. Assemble a tent and pack a backpack to be used for a couple of days on the river and let Nick's inventory serve as a guide; students should, as Nick does, *deliberately* add special items they wish to carry and be mindful that their ultralight, high-tech equipment is unlike Nick's in many ways.
2. Students should ask an experienced angler to give them a hands-on introduction to rods, reels, baits, flies, and casting.
3. Students might actually go camping overnight alone (preferably) or with a group.

Any or all of these activities should help students to engage this very tactile text and do much to end the boredom that comes to those who try to read the story with only urban or suburban experiences of the world.

If time allows, I also suggest that teachers read a short, handwritten diary Hemingway kept on a hiking and fishing trip with his high school buddy, Clarence Clarahan, in the summer of 1916. The diary was published in *The American Fly Fisher*.[3] "Hike Walloon Lake" documents one of two approaches Hemingway took to the natural world in his early years: the objective, scientific approach developed by Louis Agassiz and taught to Hemingway by his father. Teachers should also review Hemingway's letters about fishing, which were written before he entered World War I. The letters[4] illustrate Hemingway's second approach to the natural world, one in which he blends fact with imagination in order to present the affective state created by living deliberately in the natural world.

Here is an example of the "double lens" approach to the natural world that will, I hope, make this way of seeing clear. The diary provides a wonderful contrast to the letters written during the fishing trip. It tends toward a descriptive, Agassiz-like account of the excursion, beginning with a careful catalog of things to be carried and ending with an accounting of the expedition's cost and a tally of the catch day by day, with special attention to rainbow trout. The letters blend an imaginative retelling with objective fact, providing insight into Hemingway's affective and value response to his adventure. Taken together, the diary and the letters provide the reader with a double lens on fishing and the natural world. The contrast between a diary entry on Tuesday, 13 June 1916, and a letter to his sister, Marcelene, describing the same event, illustrates this double-lens effect. In the diary Hemingway writes, "It rained at night and we dried our soaked clothes in front of a roaring fire" (*Letters of Ernest Hemingway* 13). Compare this terse, objective statement in the diary to the wonderfully imagined transformation of the event in a 20 June 1916 letter to his sister Marcelene:

> Ivory dearest you should have seen the old brute doing a war dance in the costume of Adam enveloped by a cloud of mosquitoes on top of a bluff about 300 feet high at night while my clothes were drying on a rack of cedar poles in the driving rain. One hand waved a shoe aloft the other helped me swear. The calm and quiet of the abysmal wilderness of the Broadman river were violated by the old Brute. (31)

As we see in the letter quoted above, in a comic mode, Hemingway offers an Adamic, brute-primitive view of himself in the wilderness and displays himself as an exuberant, playful imp. A great deal of affective information has been grafted to the objective data in the diary, providing a double lens that takes us from Ernest Hemingway, sixteen-year-old angler, to Ernest Hemingway, mythic Adamic brute. Caught in the image of the "Adamic brute" is the fallen innocent, who Thoreau describes this way: "Men nowhere, east or west live yet a natural life. . . . the beauty of the world remains veiled before him. He needs not only to be spiritualized, but naturalized, on the soil of the earth." I argue that Nick deliberately naturalizes himself as he fishes the Big Two-Hearted and that his fishing expedition chronicles what, for Nick, is a convalescence that "lifts the veil of nature" (307).

The older Hemingway who writes "Big Two-Hearted River" finds new ground between the fantastic presentation of the affective in the juvenile letters and the object renderings of the journal where he can write both objectively and affectively in the same sentence or paragraph to create a double-lens viewing of life in the natural world.[5] This double lens, I argue, provides a way of knowing which establishes an ontological unity (harmony) between the thingness of the world and deep, particular affective experience of that thingness. Through this complex lens, forgotten heaven is again visible with the human eye.

Juxtaposing selections from Hemingway's early letters and the fishing diary can make for wonderful writing assignments. The double-lens effect Hemingway achieves is highly experiential. This exercise will give students a chance to actually look through that special lens. Teachers can also ask students to take descriptive naturalistic passages from the story and render them, in the manner of the young Hemingway, as letters to family and friends. This may help them see each part of Hemingway's double lens as well as the binocular effect that occurs when combining the lenses.

Hemingway's double-lens presentation of events calls to mind a comment by R. W. B Lewis in his classic work, *The American Adam*. Speaking of Thoreau, Lewis writes: "The old double, the ideal and the actual, the higher law and the fried rats required a double consciousness and found expression is a double criticism; nature could be satisfied by nothing else."[6] In the movement between object description and imaginative retelling seen in the dialectical contrast between letter material and diary entries, it would seem that even at age sixteen, Hemingway had begun to see the natural world through a double consciousness, in a two-hearted way that controls narrative in "The Big Two-Hearted River."

Thoreau provides a clear path into "Big Two-Hearted" when he writes, "We must learn to reawaken and keep ourselves awake, not by mechanical aids, but by an infinite expectation of the dawn," and in the following paragraph says, "I went to the woods to live deliberately, to front only the essential facts of life, and see if I could not learn what it had to teach, and not, when I came to die, discover I had not lived." (394). To live deliberately, to live intensely, to live awake—these are hallmarks of Nick's fishing life on the Big Two-Hearted. Deliberate living requires that one be intentional with regard to all actions, that those actions be unhurried and savored, and that they be engaged in with the fresh infinite expectation of dawn.

Nick's experience of vibrant, vital life in a seminatural state (comparable to Thoreau's seminatural Walden Pond) is spread across the story. It begins just beyond the fictional ruins of burnt-over Seney at river's edge where Nick watches trout in the pool below the bridge. As the narrator tells us, "it was a long time since Nick had looked into a stream and seen trout" (*In Our Time* 134). While the story does not tell us what Nick has been doing since he last fished for trout, the narrator adds to the carefully observed movement of kingfisher and trout, a doubling lens that allows the eruption of these affective words: "Nick's heart tightened as the trout moved. He felt the old feeling" (134). That "old feeling," the primal state, is attained through a complex apprehension of experience that allows the objective natural world to mingle unmediated with the deep inner state and Thoreau's "higher laws" of human consciousness (490–500). Hemingway/Nick learned to access this state of being as a youth. It is always there to be had when one lives deliberately. It seems to be an Adamic state and is a very "old feeling" indeed. That "old feeling" is well described by Thoreau in words that could serve as the philosophical outline of Part I of "Big Two-Hearted River." Thoreau writes:

> The very simplicity and nakedness of man's life in the primitive ages imply this advantage, at least, that they left him still but a sojourner in nature. When he was refreshed with food and sleep, he contemplated his journey again. He dwelt, as it were, in a tent in this world, and was either threading the valleys, or crossing the plains, or climbing the mountain-tops. But lo! men have become the tools of their tools. The man who independently plucked the fruits when he was hungry is become a farmer; and he who stood under a tree for shelter, a housekeeper. We now no longer camp as for a night, but have settled down on earth and forgotten heaven. (252)

Students could be encouraged to list points of tangency between Thoreau's view of life in harmony with nature and that expressed in Part I of "Big Two-Hearted" as they provide a narrative outline of Part I using the Thoreau quotation as a template.

As a final strategy for teaching "Big Two-Hearted," I will provide a detailed reading of the text, concentrating on the much-neglected Part II. After reading my analysis of Part II, students might be asked to discern and describe my slow, detailed, deliberate method of reading "Big Two-Hearted" and then apply that method to reading sections of Part I.

Part II of "Big Two-Hearted River," I think, gets too little and too narrow attention in Hemingway criticism. What attention it gets seems to be focused on three words: danger, swamp, and tragedy. The bulk of Part II, however, is about fishing—the technical aspects of catching (and sometimes releasing) trout. I shall pay attention here to the catching of fish.

Just before Thoreau's famous line "I went to the woods because I wished to live deliberately, to front only the essential facts of life" (394), he meditates on the need to awaken, taking morning as his metaphor, saying among other things that "Every morning was a cheerful invitation to make my life of equal simplicity, and I may say innocence, with Nature herself" (392) and "Morning is when I am awake and there is a dawn in me" (393). With the heightened consciousness that Thoreau advocates, Nick awakes to a new day, and then he makes an accurate, deliberate, sometimes tactile inventory of the landscape around him. The narrator tells us "Nick was excited by the early morning and the river." We are told that Nick was "really too hurried to eat breakfast but knew he must" (145). Rather than succumb to overstimulation, Nick deliberately slows himself down. He brews coffee, collects and bottles grasshoppers, and makes and eats breakfast. In each instance, he is attentive to detail and works step by step because part of living deliberately is making conscious decisions. At no time does Nick obsess over or struggle with these tasks. His acts are deliberate, relaxed, and balanced nicely, each against the other. The issue is completion of action and not control of events.

Breakfast over, hoppers bottled, Nick turns his attention to fishing. He gets out his fly rod, attaches a leader to the line and then a hook. We see that he has deliberately chosen to fish in an unorthodox way. Although he doesn't directly explain his hybrid choice, we know that he has selected it after studying the trout below the bridge at Seney and observing the feeding pattern of trout near his camp the evening before. It is important when the narrator tells us "Nick felt awkward and *professionally happy* with all his equipment hanging from him" (147; emphasis mine) Even though fly-fishing purists would challenge his decision, it is with confidence in himself and his choices that Nick steps into the river. His step into the river provides his second awakening into the day. He encounters the river as "a rising cold shock" (150). Awake and capable of living deliberately, Nick can begin to fish.

Hemingway's technique for presenting action, including fishing, in "Big Two-Hearted" allows the story to slide along a spectrum of narrative consciousness, moving from objective narrative voice through character-centered consciousness to the sudden intrusion of Nick speaking. It is difficult to detect a move along this spectrum, hard to be sure whether we are observing the surface or reading the deeper story. The river of consciousness, especially when doubled, is two-hearted, and complex, giving to Nick's experience a special verve, a powerful intensity, the thrum of the human heart.

A quotation from Thoreau's *Journal* dated 11 April 1852 seems appropriate here. It speaks to the "river of consciousness" described above and calls to mind Nick's clear and careful look into the river at the beginning of the story. Thoreau writes, "A pure brook is a very beautiful object to study minutely. It will bear the closest inspection, even to the finest bubbles, like minute globules, that lie on its bottom.... Everything is washed clean and bright, and water is the best glass through which to see it" (121). As this passage suggests, Hemingway and Thoreau see the natural world through similar contemplative double lenses, merging careful observation of nature's thingness with transcendent, affective apprehension of that thingness. Indeed, in this special river of consciousness, "water is the best glass though which to see it." What becomes visible is that primal state where all life is in harmony and balance.

Moving forward with my reading, I will describe Nick's experience fish by fish. My purpose is to demonstrate how Nick's deliberate actions, as presented through Hemingway's double lens, establish for Nick an ontological and spiritual balance and harmony in nature that unites him with the fundament of being precisely because he has awakened to the physical world around him and interacts with it deliberately, carefully, slowly, rather than attempting to control, use or dominate it. Nick's actions, I argue, are not aimed at control or undertaken as therapeutic measures in a medical/psychological sense. His engagement with the natural world is ontological and the aim is spiritual balance.

I turn now to Nick at the river, newly awakened, and ready to fish.[7] He will hook Fish One—a fish too little. In this instance Nick, new to the water, deliberately reads the river. First he looks at the swirl of water below each leg.

Next he tips the hopper bottle and one jumps into the water. The objective detail is precise, and, reading the river with care, Nick makes a decision about how to fish this spot.

Although he is using a fly rod, he does not choose to cast for trout nor does he select a fly from the pack in his shirt pocket. Instead, after carefully threading a grasshopper onto a hook, Nick "*dropped* him into the water" (148; emphasis mine). In doing so, he imitates the drop of the first hopper into the water. Nick then strips off line to let the hopper run free in the current, as the first hopper has done. As anticipated in the repetition of the action Nick observed with the first trout, he has a strike.

The objective surface narration here provides excellent instruction for anglers who want to catch fish: read the river carefully, learn what is going on, and fish accordingly—forget the Orvis handbook. The deeper narrative offers instruction in Thoreau's "higher laws."[8] In the phrase "holding the now *living rod* across the current," (148; emphasis mine) there is the doubling effect that metaphor brings to language. There is a compounding and transformation of images as Hemingway's choice of language merges the small trout just caught and released with the big trout that tightened and faced up into the current, at the beginning of the story. As the fish is released, the narrative voice slides toward Nick. Up close to Nick we see that his deliberate action is also restorative action: Nick's touch, if you will, resurrects the trout and we enter into the interior of Nick's being as he thinks, "He's all right.... He was only tired" (149). True for the fish, and by the process of doubling, perhaps, true for Nick as well.

Fish Two—a fish too big. Again Nick reads the river deliberately, carefully. This stretch of river backs up against a pile of logs. It runs smooth and dark, so Nick will be fishing a deep pool. Again, he chooses not to cast. But instead of "dropping" the hopper into the water, this time he chooses to "toss" it "out ahead onto the dark water" (149–50). There is a long tug and again the rod comes "alive." This time the rod is not only alive, the narrator tells us, it is also "dangerous" and underscores the claim by repeating that word (150). On that one explosive word, the turn has been made again from objective surface detail into deeper interior experience.

The nature of the danger is presented first in surface detail—a mechanical shriek testifies that the line went out with a rush. It went out, as the narrator reports it and as Nick experiences it, "too fast." Deliberation and speed, as noted earlier, are incompatible. When things happen too fast to process deliberately, the good place can turn bad very quickly. Under such conditions, nature becomes chaos and not comfort. Under such circumstances, natural stimuli are too strong to process by higher law. The double lens cracks apart and only the brute fact of surface living remains. Nick is at danger here of losing the balanced two-hearted life he has employed in this good place. The narrator tells us that Nick's "heart feeling stopped with excitement." When his "heart feeling" stops, Nick's natural, deliberate playing of the fish ends and the quest for physical control is asserted. He leans back against the current, thumbs the reel hard, and awkwardly inserts his thumb inside the fly reel frame as he momentarily struggles to control the situation. Hemingway's language suggests that the line had become "too hard" (150) in the excitement of the catch and not by the choice of the fisherman. Deliberate fishing dissolved into a struggle for control.

Hemingway reports Nick's process of recovering balance by sliding the narrative consciousness from the surface to deeper into Nick's consciousness. Nick begins to regain balance by moving his catch from objective description toward mythic assertion. He anthropomorphizes the fish, noting its anger. Then he pushes it toward Leviathan status as he thinks, "*By God*, he was a big one. *By God*, he was the biggest one I ever heard of" (151; emphasis mine).

Next the narrator tells us that Nick "did not want to rush his sensations in any way." He wiggles his toes in shoe water, he lights a cigarette and tosses the match into the river. He watches the match float in fast water and sees a tiny trout rise at the match. The absurd act of the tiny trout mirrors the mismatch of Nick and the Leviathan—"Nick laughs." Balance is restored. "It was all right now" (151).

Fish Three—just right. For the first time in the fishing narrative, Nick casts with his fly rod. As described, it is a textbook cast and a trout strikes. The catch proves as perfect as the cast. The "danger" of grass is avoided by deliberate actions taken by Nick: "holding the rod, pumping *alive* against the current, Nick brought the trout in" (152; emphasis mine). Nick is not hurried or overexcited. He deliberately, methodically places the fish in his sack and moves downriver. Only a hint of the doubling text emerges here in the words "danger" and "alive." Otherwise, everything remains calmly on the surface of the story, like the hopper placed so perfectly in the weeds.

Fish Four—the fish that wasn't. Pleased that he now has "one good trout," Nick assesses his options before fishing again. He chooses not to fish upstream in the heavy current, reads the river carefully and chooses not to fish near a downed beech tree, then second-guesses himself and drops a grasshopper "so the current took it under water, back in under the overhanging branch" (153). A trout strikes but the line gets caught in the leaves and branches. The trout gets loose. Bad choice. But Nick is not disturbed. All of this has happened at the level of the surface. He had fished poorly, but he had also fished deliberately and is comfortable with the result.

Fish Five—great catch. Walking down the stream, Nick sees a hollow log and he chooses to fish it head-on. His plan for fishing the log is deliberate and well chosen. He employs a technique that will give him considerable control over the drift of the hopper. His choice is to fish more with his rod than with the line so that he can control of the drift of the hopper. He tosses the hopper out and "held the rod out so far that the hopper on the water moved into the current flowing into the hollow log" (153). While not textbook behavior for a man fishing with a fly rod, this is a wonderfully deliberate act from a man who wishes to catch a fish. He has read the natural world around him and responded well to what he read. He gets a strike. And the narrator tells us that it's as if Nick "had hooked the log itself, except for the *live feeling*" (154; emphasis mine). As when Nick hooked the little first trout, what is true for the fish, by the process of doubling, is perhaps true for Nick as well. There is symmetry here. The echo of "all right" sounds inside the phrase "the live feeling." Nick's morning adventure on the river has gone well. He has read the surface of the natural world around him deliberately and this has given him two fine trout.

Under the surface, we have learned that all is well. It seems easy for Nick to choose not to fish the swamp, just as he has chosen not to fish other places that morning. No big deal, this choice, I suggest. Fishing there now would fit neither the plan nor the man. The tragedy would lie in doing that which does not fit. Nick ends his morning in good shape and he heads back to camp, to the good place, with two fine trout ready for cooking. Upon his return, he may well speak again the words he uttered after setting up a fine camp the night before, the only words he speaks aloud in the story: "Chrise, Nick said. Jesus

Chrise, he said happily" (140). Nick's "cure," I conclude, is neither medical nor psychological, it is natural, transcendental, and spiritual—perhaps in some ways even, as the words spoken aloud suggest, theological.

I have concluded, but probably students are not finished. They may now want to debate the thesis set forth here, one side defending and extending this argument (moving even to the theological), the other arguing in favor of a psychological and therapeutic reading of the story.[9] A third reading might also be explored, arguing that the dichotomy between these two perspectives is a false one and that the two apparently disparate readings in fact collapse into each other. It is good for students to end in vigorous debate rather than with the meaning of the story. If they engage at this moment, you will know that they have not found the story to be boring.

Notes

1. Malcolm Cowley's introduction to the *Viking Portable Hemingway* (1944) focused critical attention on Hemingway's symbolic landscape in "Big Two-Hearted River" and opened the door to psychoanalytic, biographical readings of the story. Philip Young's study of the story, *Hemingway: A Reconsideration,* extended Cowley's reading by explicitly linking the story to Hemingway's war wound and trauma, which Young associated with the wound. Young paved the road most traveled by Hemingway scholars down to the present. It has focused attention on symbol, psyche, and biography and called into the story much that is not literally present on the pages of the text: WWI, war wound(s), even Indians—see Philip Melling for a reading that brings Indians into the text.

2. Robert Lamb provides an excellent discussion of the history of the wound theory from Cowley forward. This provides a good picture of the kind of literary criticism I have moved away from in this essay in order bring readers closer to the text itself.

3. *The American Fly Fisher* journal can be located by your librarian and accessed through interlibrary loan. I heartily recommend that you get a copy of Hemingway's "Hike Walloon Lake," and share it with your class. Scan and project, I think, would be the best way to use it.

4. Spanier and Trogdon have provided a treasure trove of letters from Hemingway's early years. Several letters focus on Hemingway's experience hiking and fishing before being deployed to WWI and just after his return. Among those most useful to readers of "Big Two-Hearted River" are: To Clarence, his father, 10 September 1910; to Clarence, 30 August 1913; to his sister, Marcelene, 20 June 1916; to Clarence, 18 April 1918; to a friend, Howell Jenkins, 9 April 1919; to Jenkins and Lawrence T. Barnett, 26 July 1919; to Clarence, 16 August 1919; to Jenkins, 31 August 1919; to Bill Smith, 28 April 1921.

5. The double-lens technique described here resembles closely Hemingway's description of writing to get "the real thing" (*Death in the Afternoon* 2). In *The American Adam,* quoted below, R. W. B. Lewis locates this technique for writing about the natural world in Thoreau's *Walden.*

6. Lewis's *The American Adam* provides wonderful context for understanding "Big Two-Hearted" in the tradition of Thoreau and Emerson, to which I think it belongs.

7. David Cremean writes in some detail about the mechanics of fishing in "Big-Two Hearted." His focus is on the difference between fishing with bait and with flies. Though useful, I think the distinction too narrow for an analysis of the deliberate fishing done by Nick and the careful reading of the natural world this reflects. Like me, Cremean also places the story into a religious context—in his case, Catholicism. As with the discussion of fishing, I think his focus is too narrow and that the story has more in common with Thoreau's Transcendentalism. Christianity in the story, it seems to me, is hardly orthodox.

8. Don Summerhayes provides a most insightful analysis of the narrative consciousness at work in "Big-Two Hearted." I recommend this to students interested in the narrative process. It could be quite helpful to a bright young writer.

9. If you hold a debate, students who argue contrary to this essay should be directed to the two foundational arguments for a medical/psychological by Cowley and Young referred to above. They should also look at Lamb's summary of this critical perspective.

Works Cited

Brasch, James D., and Joseph Sigman. *Hemingway's Library: A Composite Record*. New York: Garland Publishing, 1981.

Cowley, Malcolm. Introduction. *Hemingway*. Ed. Cowley. New York: Viking Press, 1944. Viking Portable Library series.

Cremean, David N. "Man Cannot Live by Dry Flies Alone: Fly Rods, Dry Flies and Adaptive Catholicity in 'Big Two-Hearted River.'" *Hemingway and the Natural World*. Ed. Robert F. Fleming. Moscow: U of Idaho P, 1999.

Hemingway, Ernest. "Big Two-Hearted River." *In Our Time*. New York: Scribner, 1996.

———. *Green Hills of Africa*. New York: Scribner, 1935.

———. "Hike Walloon Lake: A Diary June 10–21, 1916." *The American Fly Fisher* 15.1 (Summer 1989): 1–9.

———. *The Letters of Ernest Hemingway: Volume 1 (1907–1922)*. Ed. Sandra Spanier and Robert Trogdon. Cambridge: Cambridge UP, 2011.

———. "On Fly Fishing." Item 570. JFK Library. Boston, MA.

Hohn, Donovan. "Everyone Hates Henry." *New Republic* (21 Oct. 2015).

Lamb, Robert. "Fishing for Stories: What 'Big Two-Hearted River' Is Really About." *Modern Fiction Studies* 27.2 (Summer 1991): 161–80.

Lewis, R. W. B. *The American Adam*. Phoenix Books. Chicago: U of Chicago P, 1961.

Melling, Philip. "There Were Many Indians in the Story: Hidden History in Hemingway's 'Big Two-Hearted River.'" *The Hemingway Review* 28.2 (Spring 2009): 45–65.

Reynolds, Michael. *Hemingway's Reading, 1910–1940*. Princeton: Princeton UP, 1981.

———. *Young Hemingway*. Oxford: Basil Blackwell, 1986.

Summerhayes, Don. "Fish Story: Ways of Telling in 'Big Two-Hearted River.'" *The Hemingway Review* 15:2 (Fall 1995): 20–26.

Thoreau, Henry David. *The Journal 1837–1861.* New York: NYRB Classics, 2009.
———. *A Week on the Concord and Merrimack Rivers.* New York: Literary Classics of the United States, 1985.
Young, Philip. *Hemingway: A Reconsideration.* Rev. ed. New York: Harcourt, Brace and World, 1966.

Part Two

Gulf Stream

Not Against Nature

Hemingway, Fishing, and the Cramp of an Environmental Ethic

Rick Van Noy and Dan Woods

The "man against nature" theme is, even for all its generality and gender bias, still cited in literature handbooks as one of the "universal" conflicts in literature. The conflict is to be of an external struggle whereby a hero contends against an animal or a force of nature (Ross 141). Because of the iconic image of Ernest Hemingway as a big game hunter and fisherman, if one were to choose a literary conflict by which to define Hemingway, "man against nature" would seem deserved. According to one writing guide, the "man against nature" conflict is central to Ernest Hemingway's *The Old Man and the Sea*, in which the protagonist "battles" an eighteen-foot marlin, "a conflict between Santiago and the marlin for survival" (Ballon 135). When we teach the novel, we suggest that such a view greatly simplifies the conflict in that story. Rather than win a fight against nature by capturing a fish, Santiago ultimately loses his catch but gains a renewed respect for the fish and nature. In "Big Two-Hearted River" Nick Adams also regains a sensuous contact with nature that had long been dormant. In both *The Old Man and the Sea* and "Big Two-Hearted River," Hemingway presents a view of nature not as person *against* or in conflict with the natural world but as person immersed fully *in* it.

It is more accurate to say that both Nick Adams and Santiago struggle more against themselves than with nature. Nick struggles with his ability to feel restored and whole again, and the old man struggles with that which he has set out to do, catch a fish. The fish is not merely a meal for him, but a statement of his very being. For Santiago, a lifelong fisherman, the marlin is caught to restore wounded pride, to shore up the respect he has lost from the community and "the boy," Manolin, but even before he fastens the marlin to the boat he begins to regret what he has done. He comes to identify with the fish as his "brother," and with the sea as eternal feminine, a kind of mother. Therefore, when we consider Santiago and his "fish," we must consider it together in the literary traditions of characters seeking to recover something of themselves in nature. For Nick and Santiago, and for Hemingway, it is not a matter of man vs. nature, but closer to man *as* nature. Nature is not something to be feared but something to be felt and experienced wholly. Whether in environmental literature courses or in survey classes, we set a goal to help students become actants in the natural world and not merely passive observers, and both texts help to achieve that.

In reading "Big Two-Hearted River," we help students tune in to the symbolic ramifications of the landscape. Early in the story, Nick moves through a "burned-over" scene, one that seems to mirror his state of mind, which he knew "could not all be burned" (135). When we ask what it means, that it "could not all be burned," students seem aware of the layered possibilities, both psychological and war related. In *A Moveable Feast,* we point out, Hemingway wrote that "the story was about coming back from the war but there was no mention of the war in it" (75).

We ask (or they ask) about the style of the story, and most say that it seems tentative, a character seeking to restore something, and in this case something that he hopes to find by returning to the natural world. If the landscape is symbolic for his state of mind, the trout, "keeping themselves steady in the current with wavering fins," seems to point to Nick's own "wavering" situation of trying to steady himself (133). He watches them "holding themselves with their noses into the current," "looking to hold themselves on the gravel bottom in a varying mist of gravel and sand," holding on, like Nick, within the current (133). Nick identifies with the trout, a point Hemingway makes clear: "Nick's heart tightened as the trout moved. He felt all the old feeling" (134). Nick is looking to nature to get that feeling back, looking to nature for a way to live again. He feels like "he had left everything behind," but we ask if that is completely true. Can he completely wipe away the experience of the war?

Busy students relate to how Nick tries to isolate parts of his experience so he can confidently take charge of them—thus the emphasis in the story on the orderly processes of putting up the tent, making food, and baiting the hook. War is indiscriminate, but when he fishes and sets up camp, Nick is deliberate in every way, much like nature. As he does these things, Hemingway mentions that Nick was happy, but we ask students to notice the accompanying pain or displeasure with this happiness, as if it has long been absent or hard won. Examples they come up with are his feeling happy despite the "hard work walking up-hill. His muscles ached and the day was hot" (134). He also "happily" says "Chrise, Geezus Chrise" after nearly burning his mouth on beans and spaghetti (140).

As he makes camp, he is restoring his sensuous, bodily contact—feeling again. The story is rich with satisfying sensory detail and we divide the class into groups or rows and give each a sense to find in the text, listing these on the board in columns. The taste of the hot food and bitter coffee, the sweet apricot dessert. The water he scoops into his canvas bucket is ice cold, the bank white with mist. It is colder by the river than camp where his fire is, and both river and night are quiet, save for a hum of a mosquito and the "satisfactory hiss" when it surrenders to Nick's flame (142). When he walks during the day, we feel the chafing of sweet fern he uses to soften the pack straps and the smell of it, then a nap in the pine-needle floor, its attendant smells, a view of the sky through branches, wind in the upper ones, resting his neck and back until "the earth felt good" (137). Nick walks on that earth all day, the undulating country with "frequent rises and descents," sandy under Nick's feet and he "alive again" (136). What is the effect of that sensory detail? He is reintegrating himself with natural processes, which are healing him[1].

In the morning, Nick repeats some of the evening's food preparation, but there is less emphasis on the sensation as Nick is anxious to get to the stream, excited by the early morning and the river. Nick catches a small trout and is careful to "wet his hand before he touched the trout, so he would not disturb the delicate mucus that covered him" (149). If a trout was touched with a dry hand, we learn, a fungus attacked that spot. Like Nick, trout have a delicate outer covering. Nick tries to touch the trout again when it is released, "steady in the moving stream," but when he touches his "smooth, cool, underwater feeling," the trout disappears into a shadow somewhere downstream (176). "He's all right," Nick says about the trout. "He was only tired," Nick says, which seems to have some implication for Nick's situation: tired but alive (149).

Nick then loses a much bigger fish. And where earlier he had touched the released fish, this one had a "heaviness, a power not to be held" or touched (150). After the excitement, Nick's hand feels shaky from the thrill, and he feels "vaguely, a little sick, as though it would be better to sit down" (150). But then he thinks about "the trout somewhere on the bottom, holding himself steady over the gravel" (150). He knows (or he hopes?) the trout's sharp teeth will cut through the snell. He will be angry, but he, too, will be all right. "By

God," Nick says, "he was a big one," as if to emphasize the mysterious power of the fish. "By God, he was the biggest one I ever heard of" (151).

Students are awakened by the switch. Suddenly, Hemingway suspends his third-person narration to give us a first-person one, as if Nick is the author of his own story. The careful restraint of earlier, of staking tents and setting up camp, gives way to a moment of excitement too thrilling to reign in. As Carl Ficken demonstrates, the point of view moves from the objective report of what happens ("the leader had broken") to Nick's thoughts ("he thought of the trout") to an indirect first person ("By God, he was a big one") to first person. Gradually, what is external becomes internal, what is without now within. The style reinforces that we are reading a "carefully controlled mind," a "man searching for restoration from incoherence" (107). It further represents a moment of contact within nature, yet one almost too strong, too reminiscent of battle. Nick, if only for a moment, is regaining control of his life.

When Nick finally does sit, he regains some of the sensory detail: "smoking, drying in the sun, the sun warm on his back, the river shallow ahead entering the woods . . . light glittering, big-water smooth rocks, cedars along the bank and white birches, the logs warm in the sun, smooth to sit on" (151). It is as if it is not the fish but the experience of fishing and being outdoors that he "catches." And though the feeling of disappointment over losing the fish leaves him, the earlier sensory feeling remains, so that he "was all right now" (151). Nick is both all right, like the trout he earlier released, holding steady, but also alive again in the moment. The disappointment leaves him, like water draining from his shoes. His next sentences are of tying on a new hook and putting a hopper on it.

After sitting for a while, Nick returns to the stream and catches two good trout, one, strangely, from a hollow log.[2] The river has taken him to the place where it narrows and deepens, with a low tangle of branches in the cedars. Earlier, he wanted to avoid a tangle in the braches of a stream. Here, he mentions avoiding the branches on land, making travel difficult. He feels a "reaction against deep wading with the water deepening up under his armpits, to hook big trout in places impossible to land them." In the half-light of the swamp, Nick feels that fishing would be a "tragic adventure" (155).

The word "tragic" is a jarring one, especially in a story otherwise focused on Nick's happiness, and one students are justifiably puzzled by. If fishing was so restorative, we ask, why doesn't he continue? If discussion lags, we offer readings of Nick's characterization of the swamp. Drawing on an original ending where Nick catches another trout and reflects on his writing, Debra

Moddelmog suggests that Nick's evasion of the swamp is an evasion of marriage and fatherhood (605). The two-hearted river is indeed a "good place," but also one of darker depths (139).

In *The Green Breast of the New World,* ecocritic Louise Westling highlights the way Nick's journey takes him away from society and responsibility and into the bosom of Mother Nature, in ways Leslie Fiedler, Annette Kolodny, and Nina Baym have also explained. However, Westling is careful to note that Nick's psychic damage, as manifest by the burned-over landscape, is caused by war and "not by anything feminine" (93). In so much as war represents the ultimate mastery over humans and land, Nick is not looking to command its power. He is, rather, a much different kind of soldier, or pilgrim.

Westling also writes that whatever else Nick's response to losing the big fish may mean, his "reactions demonstrate that he cannot completely control his encounters with the natural world" (93). He does not go into the swamp in part because it requires deep wading where it is impossible to "land" big fish. About fishing in such depths and upstream, Nick earlier tells us "you had to wallow against the current," the water piling on you, like on the Black. And it is "no fun to fish upstream with this much current" (153). Fishing on the Black is one the few memories we are permitted, or Nick permits himself. When he goes back there in his mind, the memory is both pleasant and painful. The swamp is also dark like the "black" river of memory, as if it is consciousness itself.[3] On a symbolic level, Nick's refusal to go into the swamp might be read as his not wanting to go "upstream" against those memories, against consciousness. On a literal level, he simply does not want to go against nature.

If weather and time permit, we gladly take our classes to our nearby river or stream and let them step in (depth permitting) and feel the sensory information of water rushing, noting the difficulty of wading, the details of surrounding trees and birds. We are also not above showing the casting of a fly, presenting it on the water's surface (mimicking creatures on the water), and discussing what it might mean to be a participant in an ecosystem rather than a conqueror of it, which makes for a good writing reflection.

Nick learns to live in the moment, through his senses, with the current rather than against it, and he justifies his choice. As he leaves, Nick looks back: "There were plenty of days coming when he could fish the swamp" (156). Whatever advances Nick has made, he hasn't yet made enough that he can quite manage the murky entanglements of that particular day, though there will be more days to come. We ask someone to keep count, because his hard-won almost painful happiness, his two lost fish—and two gained (one released)—seem a delicate balance. Indeed, Nick seems to have reached a kind of equilibrium he would not upset. As the past has been difficult and the future may be as well, "Big Two-Hearted River" begins in black and also ends dark, but it has much "live feeling" and even some rebirth in-between (154).

As he travels through a landscape of ups and downs, shouldering his belongings, the story would seem to take on allegorical meanings. Fishing, in this sense, can substitute for engagement with nature itself—the line a literal connection to it. If those deeper connections are present in "Big Two-Hearted River," they are also equally present, if not more suggestive, in *The Old Man and the Sea*.

Although the old man fights mightily with the marlin, the story concerns more a fight *within* than one *without*, as manifest by the cramp in the old man's arm. During the long ordeal, Santiago comes to pity the marlin and ultimately respect him. Though he kills the fish, he senses they are bound together in a code of hunting and hunted that he begins to question. Though the cramp is a "treachery of one's own body," it seems to be a treachery of his mind and purpose too. The cramp "humiliates" him, "especially when one is alone" (62). Without the boy present, he has to talk to himself and the fish. As the marlin circles him (rather then he it), the irony builds, and Santiago thinks that "you are killing me fish . . . come and kill me." The doubts continue along with the identification with the fish. He worries his head is becoming unclear: "Know how to suffer like a man," he tells his head. "Or a fish" (92). When the fish comes around again, the old man pulls and feels "the fish's agony" (93). He raises the harpoon high and drives it into the "the fish's side just behind the great chest fin that rose high in the air to the altitude of the man's chest." Chest to chest, man to fish, the contradictions begin to pile up, the fish becoming "alive, with his death in him" (94).

After pointing them out, we ask what is the cumulative effect of those contradictions? The marlin then rises into the air, showing his great "power and beauty" but then falls into the sea. When he does, "the old man felt faint and sick and he could not see well" (94). The blood streams from the heart—earlier on the level with the man's chest—and whereas he talked to his hand earlier, it is now his head he continues to address. "Clear up head," he says to it, and "keep my head clear" (92, 95). And as Santiago brings the fish to the boat, he realizes he wants to feel and see him. Writing about ecological ethics, Aldo Leopold said "We can be ethical only in relation to something we can see, feel, understand, or otherwise have faith in" (251). The old man's cramp of ethics and doubt is most acute now that the fish is next to the boat.[4] "He is my fortune," he thinks, "but that is not why I wish to feel him," and he adds that he thinks he felt, on stabbing him, his beating heart. When he does try to tally the financial value of the fish, he again finds that "his head is not that clear" (97).

When the sharks come, it is as if he knew they would, as punishment for going too far out "beyond all people." We ask students to keep track of the breaking of "weapons—first harpoon, then knife, then tiller—and the purpose of their ineffectiveness. Students suggest it adds to the suspense but also emphasize that the fight is futile. The sharks' stripping the marlin is also inevitable, and he feels remorse and regret. "I am sorry about it fish" (110). He comes to think that it was a sin to kill him: "You did not kill the fish only to keep alive and to sell for food. You killed him for pride" (105). Here Santiago is trying to reconcile his guilt. He knows that he was unprepared to catch such a big fish, yet he pursued one nonetheless. We see early on with the dolphins that Santiago is able to fish well enough to feed himself. Catching the marlin isn't about feeding the physical self, but a matter of ego, and we ask students to write a reflection on when they have pursued something as matter of pride, when pride drove them "too far."

The old man's realization of what he has done is reflected in his apologies to the fish. Its implications are also brought out by the structure of the novel, which leads back to community. Clinton Burhans Jr. claims that *The Old Man and the Sea* shows Hemingway's concern for "the relationship between individualism and interdependence," but Glen Love finds that the novella falls short of "considering that interdependence in the fullest sense" (73, 130). He is "friendly" with porpoises and flying fish, but the Portuguese man-of-war and sharks are enemies. He enjoys the turtles because they eat the man-of-war, but the sharks are adversaries. For Love, "the friends are those who promote Santiago's freedom and happiness, the enemies those who restrict that freedom and happiness" (129). Such anthropocentrism does not acknowledge that the shark is as necessary to the health of the sea ecosystem as the marlin, porpoise, man-of-war, and turtle.

However, Love's sensibility would locate humans outside of both history and the food web. As a fisherman aboard a primitive vessel, sharks were certainly to be feared. And Santiago, a subsistence fisherman, eats what he catches.[5] Though he enjoys watching turtles eat the man-of-war, he in turn eats turtle eggs for strength. Nick eats his catch, and Santiago eats his sacramentally: dolphin, tuna, marlin, and even the tiny shrimp from a floating blanket of sea weed.[6] Killing his "brothers" is ethical so long as it is followed by eating, the act of communion, sharing the blood of life (Beegel 117).

That Santiago would kill these "brothers" is a paradox central to the novella. *The Old Man and the Sea* contains moments of both mesmerizing beauty but also intense destruction and cruelty, and students are often puzzled by the contradiction. Indeed, Santiago describes the sea as "kind and very beautiful. But she can be so cruel," too harsh for some delicate birds (29). The sea is noted for its prisms of light, its phosphorescence, its erotic blankets of seaweed, but also its dangers. Even as the ocean and fish are presented as majestic, the tuna is hit over the head "for kindness" (rather than have it suffocate) and the female marlin is "butchered promptly," though he asks her for forgiveness (39, 50). How is it possible to both "live on the sea and kill our true brothers" (75)? Students who hunt and fish and those who know of the ethics of primitive (and even sophisticated) cultures recognize respect for the kill, asking it for forgiveness, or praying to spirits for its soul.

Though Santiago sins, he is unlike Ahab, who "who would strike the sun if it insulted him" (Melville 140). Ahab fights against nature, a crime for which he pays. Ahab also never repents, while Santiago apologizes to the marlin. As he returns home, Santiago is "inside the current now" and also working with the wind (120). The struggle is over and he is "beaten now finally" by the sharks. But he pays no attention to them, only to "how lightly and how well the skiff sailed now there was not great weight beside her" (119). Santiago, unlike Ahab, does not desire to assert dominion over nature, but only to live within it.

If discussion of "Big Two-Hearted River" might engage Nick's choice not to go into the "tragic" swamp, so too might discussion of *The Old Man and the Sea* turn on the nature of the "tragedy" of the ending. Though Santiago says repeatedly that "he went out too far," did he overreach? Had he not gone "too far," he would not have captured a fish. He has lost a fish and the value it might bring, but he has not really failed. He has too deep a respect for the fish he catches, too deep a love for the sea. After he has killed the marlin, he feels no sense of victory, no pride in accomplishment. If it is a tragedy, the fish skeleton might represent a kind of pyrrhic victory. But the tourists at the end misinterpret that symbol, mistaking it for a shark. What it means is better known among the fishing community, and for Santiago, it is important that the head not be wasted but given to Pedrico to be used in fish traps.

When teaching either the novella or story, we often try a familiar postreading activity, the "what happens next?" writing exercise in which students add another chapter to the book. In our experience, most students envision Santiago's next day as being one that is outwardly peaceful both physically and mentally, yet most also write that as he reflects he will continue to regret taking the big fish. In the character Santiago, students are asked to consider what is enough. When do we go too far in taking what we want or need from nature? Additionally, most believe that the boy goes out again. The thoughtful reflection by Santiago and the continued life of a fisherman for the boy support the idea that *The Old Man and the Sea* is not meant to be story of man in conflict with nature but man as part of it. Neither Santiago nor the boy fishes to fulfill a romantic image of life on the open sea, but simply to survive. Born in a fishing village, they are fishermen.

Though he does not display the classic hubris of a tragedy, Santiago does accept humility. He confronts natural forces but he does not overcome them. We point to the lions that he dreams about, the predators at rest, to suggest a vision of living with nature rather than against it. He dreams not of a single lion but of several who come down to the beach to play together. When he dreams, "he only dreamed of places now and of the lions on the beach" (25). His lion dreams return to an image where he "no longer dreams of conquests" or violence (66). They evoke an innocence but also a peace that the old man returns to after killing and then losing his fish, an atoning for the sinful killing that Santiago has charged against himself. His final dream is of predators at peace, allied as they are with his love for boy and the continuity of life. However, such a dream must be balanced against his comment to the boy that they fashion a killing lance. For now, however, the harpoon is broken, and the boy watches over the broken man, keeping vigil of a man dreaming a dream of nature not in conflict but at play.

One strategy we often employ either at the beginning of class, to gauge reactions to reading, or at the end, to summarize, is the one-word review. Book jackets often have one word taken from a reviewer, "inspiring," "provocative," etc. Students have a hard time with "Big Two-Hearted River." Words like "tragic" come easily, but many more do not, as if reflecting Hemingway's distrust of adjectives. If changed to words about the character, they have an easier time: "re-engaged," "meticulous," "harmonic," "unified," "good for now" (short phrases work too), "simmering," "coping," "at peace." With *The Old Man and The Sea*, students suggest "gripping" (because punning can be fun), "courageous," "magnificent," "enduring," "skillful," "simple," and "natural."

Will students resist a reading of Hemingway's stories that do not pit "man against nature"? In our experience, Hemingway does come with some preconceptions. Many think he is macho, a man's man. Some think of him as the beer commercial's "most interesting man in the world." The stereotypical portrait of him in Woody Allen's *Midnight in Paris* has not helped. Some students do not see him as a person they would "hang with," though in many ways he seemed to live a life students can relate to. Though he indeed fished and hunted for big game, those who profile him in his early years say that he lacked confidence, worked late into the night, feared rejection of the opposite sex, and drank. In other words, he was far more like a college student than his tough-guy image might make him out to be.

Some students, not accustomed to the culture of hunting or the outdoors, may find it difficult to accept that any Hemingway characters express anything but bravado and conquest. The Hemingway "brand" is nearly as prolific as the works it promotes.[7] A quick Google image search will show Hemingway in front of a marlin twice his size. In another, he and his family stand before four marlin. In others, he sits beside a lion, and in yet another, he sits smiling between the twisted horns of a kudu. In her remarks for Fleming's *Hemingway and the Natural World,* nature writer Terry Tempest Williams writes of the men in her family who are driven by "masculine mythologies of hunting." When they hunt, Williams writes, they say they are "somehow more alive, alert, spiritually awake. Life is infused with meaning and import" (13).

Students will recognize the contradiction, killing to feel more alive. And for Williams, Hemingway was a "complicated man with a hunter's heart and a naturalist's eye" (13). The conversation eventually turns to where Hemingway finally stood on the issue of killing and conservation. Did he, like Santiago, express regret? Santiago does not have a radio like other wealthy fisherman, and his "tricks" are mostly basic: follow the birds and know currents and weather (23). Perhaps neither he nor Hemingway could have foreseen the way modern fishing vessels would use fishfinders connected to GPSs—long lines that indiscriminately hook fish and haul them in not by cramped hands but by hydraulic machines. However, there are already shark processing factories present in the novel.

In his essay "Hemingway among the Animals," Glen Love notes that the "Hemingway body count against the earth, in both fiction and in life, is startlingly high" (122). But Love also discusses evidence of a change in sensibility about the time of writing *The Old Man and the Sea,* including son Gregory's account of Hemingway releasing a marlin: "I'd rather release him and give him his life back than immortalize him in a photograph." These changes, for Love, suggest that what we have called Santiago's "cramp of ethics" may be related to his "creator's own questioning of long-held beliefs as he approached the end of his career" and life (131).

Contact with the earth was vital for Hemingway when he was young and his love for nature continued throughout his life. Nick Adams goes on an introspective and restorative journey that is evident in Santiago's voyage. Earl Rovitt and Gerry Brenner write that "Santiago completes the fishing trip that Nick began twenty-seven years earlier" (75). And as important as the natural world was to Hemingway's formative years, his portrait of a regretful Santiago, also in the twilight of his career, might be read as the work of an author who has sinned against his own nature.

Yet, as Love acknowledges, much of the power of Hemingway's work arises from its tensions. In discussions of the natural world, works like Hemingway's that do not overtly polemicize environmental values may in fact have a greater utility in the classroom. Without an overt environmental message, they ask students to reflect on the issues at stake, the contradictions within, and on their own environmentalist and ethical values. The open-ended nature of both fishing stories invites students in, to reflect in the narratives' respective endings and continuation. In this way, they construct students as moral agents, forcing them to ask what *should* happen next. They also ask them to read the evidence closely, beneath the surface of the narrative and the "image" of its author.

In the way that nature heals, "Big Two-Hearted River" should prompt reflection on the importance of contact with nature in students' own lives, and *The Old Man and Sea,* in a sense, completes an environmental journey. The dark swamp is now the depths of the ocean. Early contact with nature has been important to Nick Adams, has restored him when necessary, and a later Nick Adams now questions earlier behavior and even a career. Both stories are about characters who desire contact with nature but who also do not want to go "too far." If that contact is indeed important to students, then both texts allow students to reflect on a right relationship to the natural world without ever quite laying out what exactly it has to be.

It is very difficult to judge writers by today's standards, and Hemingway never made the kind of environmentalist statement that Rachel Carson did in *Silent Spring* in 1962, a year after Hemingway's death. He did, however dramatize how, in the words of Terry Tempest Williams, "the marrow of life is to be found outside" (17). Aldo Leopold was also young and "full of trigger-itch" before he looked into the fiery green eyes of a dying wolf and learned to "think like a mountain" (138). Santiago brings a fish in close enough to feel regret. Before there can be a call to action, there must first be some kind of immersion in the natural world to generate a relationship, a foundation for ethical behavior.

That relationship is something Hemingway held close throughout this life. He wrote of—and was rediscovering late in life—how important it was to be part of nature and not against it.

Notes

1. Drawing on the work of Edith Cobb, environmental psychologist Louise Chawla discusses the importance of early experiences in nature. Michigan seemed to be an "ecstatic place" for Hemingway and Nick, providing a set of "meaningful images; an internalized core of calm; a sense of integration with nature" (23).

2. Sheridan Baker associates this with birth (152).

3. Sheridan Baker suggests that the stream is metaphor for Nick's own consciousness, into his past, an adventure both inviting and to be feared. When he first steps into it, he is of course shocked. Baker suggests the name lends "ominous emphasis to the swift river and the mental process" (152).

4. For a more complete discussion of how this "cramp of ethics" is contingent on time, place, and aesthetics, see Ryan Hediger, "Hunting, Fishing, and the Cramp of Ethics in Ernest Hemingway's *The Old Man and the Sea, Green Hills of Africa,* and *Under Kilimanjaro.*

5. When he was a boy, Hemingway is said to have killed a porcupine and his father made him eat it. See Carlos Baker, 16.

6. Hemingway instructed his own son Jack to never "waste a fish," that it is "criminal to kill anything you aren't going to eat." See Jack Hemingway, 18.

7. Debra Moddelmog discusses a "public relations function for hetereomasculinity" (49) in the representation of Hemingway featured in *Life* and *Look* magazines and other media during the 1950s. See *Reading Desire.*

Works Cited

Baker, Carlos. *Hemingway: A Life Story.* New York: Scribner, 1969.

Baker, Sheridan. "Hemingway's Two-Hearted River." *The Short Stories of Ernest Hemingway: Critical Essays.* Ed. Jackson J. Benson. Durham: Duke UP, 1975.

Ballon, Rachel. *Breathing Life into Your Characters.* Cincinnati: Writer's Digest Books, 2011.

Beegel, Susan F. "Santiago and the Eternal Feminine: Gendering *La Mar* in *The Old Man and the Sea.*" *Bloom's Modern Critical Interpretations: The Old Man and the Sea.* Ed. Harold Bloom. New York: Infobase, 2008.

Burhans, Clinton, Jr. "*The Old Man and the Sea:* Hemingway's Tragic Vision of Man." *American Literature* 31.4 (1960): 446–55.

Chawla, Louise. "Ecstatic Places." *Children's Environments Quarterly* 7.4 (Winter 1986): 22–27.

Fiedler, Leslie. *Love and Death in the American Novel.* 1960. Normal, IL: Dalkey Archive P, 2003.

Ficken, Carl. "Point of View in the Nick Adams Stories." *The Short Stories of Ernest Hemingway: Critical Essays*. Ed. Jackson J. Benson. Durham: Duke UP, 1975.

Hediger, Ryan. "Hunting, Fishing, and the Cramp of Ethics in Ernest Hemingway's *The Old Man and the Sea*, *Green Hills of Africa*, and *Under Kilimanjaro*." *The Hemingway Review* 27.2 (Spring 2008): 35–39.

Hemingway, Ernest. "Big Two-Hearted River." *In Our Time*. New York: Boni and Liveright, 1925. Rev. ed. New York: Scribner's, 1930.

———. *A Moveable Feast*. New York: Scribner's, 1996.

———. *The Old Man and the Sea*. New York: Scribner's, 1952.

Hemingway, Jack. *Misadventures of a Fly Fisherman*. New York: McGraw Hill, 1986.

Kolodny, Annette. *The Lay of the Land: Metaphor as Experience and History in American Life and Letters*. Chapel Hill: U of North Carolina P, 1975.

Leopold, Aldo. *A Sand County Almanac*. 1949. New York: Ballantine Books, 1986.

Love, Glen. *Practical Ecocriticism: Literature, Biology, and the Environment*. Charlottesville: U of Virginia P, 2003.

Melville, Herman. *Moby Dick; or, The Whale*. 1855. New York: Norton, 2003.

Moddelmog, Debra A. *Reading Desire: In Pursuit of Ernest Hemingway*. Ithaca: Cornell UP, 1999.

———. "The Unifying Consciousness of a Divided Conscience: Nick Adams as Author of *In Our Time*." *American Literature* 60.4 (Dec. 1988): 591–610.

Ross, Elizabeth Irvin. *Write Now! Surprising Ways to Increase Your Creativity*. New York: Barnes and Noble, 2003.

Rovitt, Earl, and Gerry Brenner. *Ernest Hemingway*. Boston: Twayne, 1986.

Westling, Louise H. *The Green Breast of the New World: Landscape, Gender and American Fiction*. Athens: U of Georgia P, 1998.

Williams, Terry Tempest. "Keynote Address, Seventh International Hemingway Conference." *Hemingway and the Natural World*. Ed. Robert F. Fleming. Moscow: U of Idaho P, 1999.

Man or Fish?

An Ecocritical Reading of *The Old Man and the Sea*

Allen C. Jones

When I mention that I love Hemingway—on airplanes or in dentist chairs, far from the blindered insight of the university—I always get the same response: "Oh, yes. I read one of his books. The one about the fish!" And while critics have spent a half century discussing Santiago as Christ or embodiment of the tragic Hemingway code, I wonder what might happen if we read this novella as "the one about the fish." Who can forget that first sighting? "He came out unendingly and water poured from his sides. He was bright in the sun and his head and back were dark purple and in the sun the stripes on his sides showed wide and a light lavender" (62). A fish bigger than the fisherman, bigger even than Santiago's boat. But perhaps *this* is not the fish we remember at all. Perhaps, we remember the skeleton left by hungry sharks, and the failure to defend this once beautiful creature. We may even find ourselves standing in the shoes of those tourists who nonchalantly misidentify the remains of the marlin, who "among the empty beer cans and dead barracudas" see nothing more than "the long backbone of the great fish that was now just garbage waiting to go out with the tide" (126). It is difficult to admit, but as the oceans fill with garbage, and the fish fill their bellies with single-use plastics, this final image may come to haunt us.

This argument—that the environment figures centrally in our readings of literature—stands at the heart of ecocriticism. This essay introduces students to the field of ecocriticism, presents the specific ecocritical arguments concerning *The Old Man and the Sea*, and uses this conversation to establish a set of questions for discussing any of Hemingway's texts.[1] These questions can serve as a guide to classroom discussion or as directives for student research. To model this process, I will use this framework to rethink the novella's enigmatic final sentence and argue that the peaceful dream of lions is not peaceful at all. For all its sense of calm, the final image asks us to answer the provocative and disturbing question raised by that lost marlin. In a world literally turning its fish to garbage, this kind of environmentally aware reading of *The Old Man and the Sea* is important because it expands our understanding of the world and our place in it as scholars and as citizens of an increasingly fragile environment.

Ecocriticism is defined as "the study of the relationship between literature and the physical environment" (Glotfelty xviii). This broad definition reflects the values of openness and interconnectedness stressed in the field. The term's root, "eco," is often connected to ecological thinking which, rather than attempting to dissect and codify the world, focuses on the connections between all living things. Within this general definition, however, ecocriticism has taken on four distinct emphases.[2] These emphases can serve to frame our discussion of Hemingway's *The Old Man and the Sea*.

The first emphasis examines how writers represent nature. Common representations include "Eden, arcadia, virgin land, miasmal swamp, savage wilderness" (Glotfelty xxiii). In his seminal work, *The Environmental Imagination*, Lawrence Buell calls these longstanding images "master metaphors" and adds "an economy . . . a chain or scale of being, a balance, a web, an organism, a mind, a flux, a machine" (280–81). Think about how often we reduce the infinite natural processes around us to this simple image: "the circle of life." While some of these metaphors are clearly troubling—virgin land, for example—Buell argues that "we cannot begin to talk or even think about the nature of nature without resorting to them" (281). In other words, these metaphors are so pervasive that even as we critique them, we find ourselves simply replacing one metaphor with another. And it is not just that some of these are more problematic than others. The point is that all of them move our discussion of nature away from nature itself.

Ecocriticism's second emphasis aims to increase awareness of works that treat nature. The first step in this process is to reclaim nature writing as a genre worthy of serious consideration. Norman Maclean once received a one-line rejection letter stating simply, "These stories have trees in them" (Love 13). Three decades of ecocriticism have changed attitudes to some degree; however, the field remains underrepresented. More recent critical work has moved from simply promoting nature writing as a serious genre to examining texts that at first do not seem to be about nature at all. Rather than examine writers we typically associate with nature writing—like Thoreau, Mary Austin, or Annie Dillard—critics now examine everything from the urban to garbage. An ecocritical treatment of Hemingway, a writer we do not traditionally associate with environmentalism, represents part of this project.

The third ecocritical emphasis asks how literature and literary discussions define what it means to be human.[3] A central part of this emphasis is deep ecology, a movement in environmentalism that attempts to value animal and plant life as much as our own: a biocentric rather than an anthropocentric perspective. This biocentric perspective asks if can we read *The Old Man and the Sea* as the story of nature rather than a story about Santiago. While early ecocriticism was sometimes marked by "aggressive anti-anthropocentrism" that seemed to condemn humans for our treatment of the earth, critics now argue that it may be time to ask "what it means to be human in nature" (Love 6). That is, can we conceive of humans as part of nature rather than having dominion over it?

While the theoretical conundrum of being both human and natural sits at the center of ecocritical thought,[4] our final emphasis stems from the environmental movement's focus on the practical and political. As part of this practical approach to literature, many ecocritics avoid the use of jargon, often make not-so-subtle calls to action, and aim at forming readers who will put down the book, walk into nature, and change their attitudes about the world. Glen Love points out that his *Practical Ecocriticism*'s title is an attempt to emphasize this, to connect his work to the "empirical spirit of the sciences ... to the sort of work we do in the real world as teachers, scholar and citizens" (7). While the importance of ecocritics actually becoming fluent in the language of science has come under some criticism, the emphasis on the real-world implications of ecocriticism remains central for many critics (Buell, *The Future* 18). One significant branch of this emphasis is ecofeminism, an approach that examines the connection between the domination of nature and the subjugation of women in society. In a society and university that increasingly asks what is the value of literature, ecocriticism answers that the stories we tell are a powerful force in how we see and treat each other and our environment.

In addition to these four emphases, the following definitions from Lawrence Buell's *The Environmental Imagination* will help us evaluate a text's level of ecocritical engagement:

1. "The nonhuman environment is present not merely as a framing device but as a presence that begins to suggest that human history is implicated in natural history." In other words, human history is presented as part of

a grander scheme of different temperatures, topographies, and wildlife interactions.
2. "The human interest is not understood to be the only legitimate interest." Animals, plants, and natural processes are represented as having their own story above and beyond functioning as a human resource.
3. "Human accountability to the environment is part of the text's ethical orientation." The text teaches us to value nature.
4. "Some sense of the environment as a process rather than as a constant or a given is at least implicit in the text." Nature is active, perhaps even taking on a dynamic role in the movement of the story. (7–8)

We can use these definitions and emphases to evaluate the level of a text's ecocritical engagement and to pursue the specific aspects of that engagement. Here they are simplified for use in discussion:

Evaluating the level of ecocritical engagement (definitions): 1. Does the text foreground nature? 2. Are animals characters? 3. Is the text accountable to the environment? 4. Is nature treated as a process?

Pursuing specific aspects of that engagement (emphases): 4. What natural metaphors are implied by the text? 5. Can we find nature in unexpected places in the text? 6. How does nature in the text reflect upon how we treat each other? 7. How does the text address the practical or political?

Notice that these questions are related. For example, if nature is not foregrounded (number one), we can build tension if we pursue number six. Thus, the definitions are not meant to rule out certain texts; rather they give us a framework to create tension-filled arguments. In fact, a central task in ecocriticism is to find texts that seem to resist an ecocritical reading and then use these emphases to reveal the complex relationship between humans and nature. A complete absence of nature is as much a comment about our relationship with the world as is a story told entirely in the woods.

Now that we have established a research framework, we can examine how these questions play out in the scholarly arguments concerning *The Old Man and the Sea*. This will prepare us to enter the scholarly conversation and will serve as a model of how we might use these questions to analyze a specific scene in the text. We can begin with this essay. My title—"Man or Fish?"—uses a combination of our first and second definitions, encouraging us to read the marlin as more than simply a "framing device" for Santiago's ordeal. I will argue that if we focus on the fish as the central character, we can reinterpret the seemingly passive final scene as a call to action.

Alexander Hollenberg uses the same biocentric perspective as I do; however, he combines it with question number five above (master metaphors) to argue that a metaphor commonly used to dismiss nature—its emptiness—is itself foregrounded in Hemingway's text. Discussing the scene where the tired warbler lands on the stern and Santiago questions him, Hollenberg claims that this bird's sudden appearance from the open sea privileges the vast space of nature. In these moments, "the reader comes to recognize that nature is neither an empty space nor something merely to be worked upon and worked over" (27). Notice how Hollenberg incorporates our fifth question here, arguing that seeing nature as an "empty space" has long been a master metaphor that devalues nature, framing it as nothing but an empty or virgin land that has no inherent value until "worked upon and worked over" by humans.

Simply emphasizing the vast space of nature, however, does not undo this master metaphor's representation of nature as a static resource for humans: an "empty space." The answer to this paradoxical situation, according to Hollenberg, is to foreground not just the landscape but its resistance to interpretation. He points out the warbler's refusal to acknowledge Santiago's questions, using definition two to unpack the particular ways in which the animal-as-character premise resists the interpretive impulse. By resisting interpretation, nature refuses reduction to a metaphor that might result in its dismissal as an inactive entity within the text.

In this example, Hollenberg has used the animal-as-character and nature-as-process questions to address the central problem in ecocriticism; that is, to emphasize and value nature, we divide it from the human, but this very division encourages its devaluation. If the bird resists our interpretation, this does imply that nature has its own character and complex processes beyond our knowledge. This privileging, however, leaves the human/nature divide intact. The danger here is that no matter the complexity we assign to nature, if it remains the other, we automatically assign it a secondary value. While critics like Hollenberg attempt to deal with this central paradox by focusing on the complexities of nature as a process, some critics do exactly the opposite and foreground the author, arguably the most human aspect of a text. If we can reframe Hemingway as a more environmentally aware author, they argue, we can read his texts as also more aware. Notice how this critical move uses question three as its point of entry (the environmental awareness of the text).

We typically see Hemingway's sparse style as a result of Gertrude Stein and Ezra Pound's influence; however, we can also trace this directness back to the Agassiz method of nature writing, a move that allows us to reconsider Hemingway as a naturalist whose style deserves an ecocritical reading. His journals clearly reveal an intense effort to record the natural world as clearly and succinctly as possible. However, even if we accept Hemingway as a "naturalist-scientist-writer-lover" (Beegel, "Hemingway's Education" 57), we must ask ourselves the following questions: Does the author matter? If Hemingway was trained as a nature writer and loved nature, does this change the story? If a writer claims to love nature, yet writes stories without environmental wisdom, can't we argue that his intentions do not matter?

Our seventh question (defining the human) can be of some help here. Ecocriticism asks us to analyze the way we as humans use the natural world to understand ourselves. Therefore, if we can argue that a writer's intentions shape the way we think of nature, then those intentions present an ecocritically valid source of inquiry, even if some critics argue that ultimately those intentions failed. In Hemingway's case, this becomes something of a political question. As he is so central to our understanding of modernism and what it means to be a great writer, our assessment of his intentions as a writer is actually quite important. Notice how this argument makes subtle usage of number eight: interpretation as political action. Reinterpreting Hemingway's intentions turns our interpretation itself into a call to action. It basically suggests that we should read Hemingway as valuing nature because, as environmentalists, we need the power of his personality on our side. If we can read Hemingway, a canonical figure in literature and culture, as an environmentalist, this not only affects our knowledge of his texts, but it demands that as scholars we interact with our real-world accountability to a threatened planet.

Reading Hemingway this way turns out to be a very radical position, one that some critics believe actually undermines its own goals. The difficulty with reimagining Hemingway as environmentally aware is that even as he claimed to love animals, he killed thousands of them for sport. As he aged, Hemingway showed an increasing uneasiness with killing animals for sport; however, as Glen Love points out, "nature exists in Hemingway's work and life primarily as a backdrop for aggressive and destructive individualism" (123). He reminds us that in both fiction and life, "the Hemingway body count against the earth" is substantial (122). And while Hemingway often writes of the degradation of his hunting grounds, of trees cut down and "the earth . . . tired of being exploited" (qtd. in Love 121), Love insists that this impulse always conflicts with

Hemingway's focus on the tragedy of a single man trying to find meaning in an uncaring universe. Love argues that this struggle makes the novella a great book; however, he refutes any attempt to read in its pages the basic concepts of environmental insight: "the interconnectedness of all life, the harmonious sense of oneness with the world, the ability to understand and use complex natural processes without destroying them, the acceptance of death as part of an inevitable and nonthreatening flow of existence" (122).

In the above examples, we see two very different attempts to challenge the problematic binary at the heart of ecocriticism: human/nature. The first privileges nature, presenting it as its own entity resisting our attempt to subjugate it to interpretation; the second emphasizes the ethical position of the author, arguing that if we can see Hemingway as a naturalist, this changes the political effect of valuing his texts. Both of these approaches work to privilege nature, however, neither attacks that central binary directly. Suzanne Del Gizzo does precisely this, proposing a third term to unsettle the binary. While she agrees that Hemingway's thinking grew increasingly biocentric over time, her evidence is, paradoxically, his fascination with people, that is, indigenous people. She argues that his interest in a true intercultural experience, particularly his initiation into the Kamba tribe, was a sign that he embraced the values Love denies him.

There is a great danger in this argument, and it is pervasive throughout all ecocritical reasoning. If we attempt to break down the barrier between humans and nature by placing certain humans closer to nature, we risk simply dehumanizing them. They, like nature, become the other. Del Gizzo recognizes this, admitting that the primitive is often used as an "empty holding place that reflects Western desires and anxieties about its own culture and identity" (498). We look at "primitive" people and use them as an "empty" space to fill with whatever we think will assuage our guilt at allowing our world to be destroyed. This leads to heartfelt but ethically and culturally questionable calls to "live like the Indians." This simplification encourages imperial thinking and the subjugation of non-Western cultures. If we are not careful, humans different from "us" are transformed into that "empty space" metaphor that has so damaged our environment by subordinating it to human need.

In response to the prevalence of this binary, one answer is to simply embrace the division. Rather than trying to undo it, we can work to defeat its valuating function. In other words, the goal of valuing nature is not to displace the human but rather to level the scale itself. We can see this approach when Ryan Hediger points out that Santiago's mistake "is not going too far out to sea . . .

it is trying to bring too much of that othernesss back with him" (53). In other words, the mistake is not to recognize the other (be it nature or the "primitive"), but to think that we can *become* the other. Hediger implies that this process of "going too far out" can be a way of respecting the other without trying to undo its difference. According to him, Santiago realizes his own insignificance and learns to respect the power of the sea. Difference becomes its own value.

But does Santiago truly respect nature when he calls sea creatures prostitutes and the sea itself is reduced to the blatant stereotype of the fickle and vindictive woman: "beautiful" yet "cruel" (29). We can certainly read Santiago's vindictive gendering of the ocean and its creatures as misogyny; however, we can also argue that these disturbing representations are a call to action. Ecofeminism uses this approach, arguing that "the domination of nature is linked to the domination of women and that both dominations must be eradicated" (Adams 114). Gerry Brenner reveals how the text links the feminine to a loss of control, a longstanding gender stereotype: "If she [the sea] did wild or wicked things it was because she could not help them" (*Old Man and the Sea* 30). He argues that this not only reduces the sea to a negative stereotype, it reveals Santiago's view of women as fickle and weak-minded (84).

Thus far I have demonstrated the way scholars use ecocriticism's central questions to analyze the problematic human/nature binary at the heart of this approach. Notice how these approaches focus on the text, the author, or the audience. As ecocritics, we can foreground the presence of nature in the *text*, reassess the values of the *author*, or use the *audience*'s ethical position to critique the text. Now the task is to use this framework to analyze our own scene. In the final section of this essay, I will model this process.

To begin this essay, I argued that poisoning our sea increases the relevance of the novella's final fish image: the great marlin as garbage. David Gallos, the intrepid Titanic explorer, has pointed out that the problem goes far beyond islands of garbage the size of Texas; in fact, plastic bags are disintegrating and being ingested by fish throughout the entire ocean.[5] Fish are now literally made of garbage. This might lead us to reassess the metaphors we use for nature, adding trash to the list. If, however, we read this as a book whose protagonist is a fish (question two), it is hard to ignore the fact that the final image takes us far afield of the sea. We are tempted to echo Santiago's thoughts: "Why are the lions the main thing that is left?" (66). The final line of the novel returns the old fisherman to his dreams of lions on the beaches of Africa. For a book about fishing, this exotic image remains enigmatic, and critics of all sorts have attempted to explain it.

Carlos Baker connects the lions to Manolin, whose age matches Santiago's when he had the amazing African vision of "lions on the beach in the evening" (307). In this context, the beasts become a reminder of Santiago's youth, and the final return fits the longstanding argument that this is a story of resurrection and return. In an ecocritical version of this reading, Beegel argues that, rather than his youth, Santiago has returned to a peace with nature, a place where he is free of the need to dominate nature, to "kill our true brothers" (*Old Man and the Sea* 75). If we push this reading further, we might read the ending as a move not only toward peace with the world but toward biocentrism. If the final metaphor for nature is family, as the word "brothers" indicates, this construction seems to undo the human/nature binary by adding animals to the human world. However, the binary is not completely undone. We still seem to get the human perspective, looking out at nature. Santiago *watches* the lions rather than hunts them, something both Hemingway and his characters became more interested in as the author grew older. His son Gregory recalls his shock the first time he saw his father throw back a fish: "something I'd never seen him do before" (qtd. in Love 131). However, Santiago's actions go further. He is not actually watching the lions at all. He is dreaming. And this is fundamentally important as we assess the text's ability to escape the human/nature binary.

In dreams we have the sense that we are part of the world and yet also above or outside it. This doubling is not unlike the doubling it would take to look at the world from a human perspective and, at the same time, from a natural perspective. In short, we could argue that a dream is a framework that allows the doubling necessary to be both human-centric and biocentric. Note that Santiago no longer dreams of human things, of "women . . . great occurrences . . . fights," but instead dreams only of "places" (25). And in the final dream, Santiago no longer even sees himself in this place, just the lions. Using our ecocentric framing, we can argue that this dream attempts to both remain in a human perspective and also cross the binary, dividing us from nature. In the vision of our unconscious mind, there exists the possibility of giant cats, completely alone, and yet also resting before us on the beach in the African twilight.

This doubling goes further if we use question eight (political call to action) and read the ending not as peace and resolution, but rather as a vacillating, questioning voice, desperately calling us to answer. The book is full of Santiago's incessant vacillation from praising the fish, to saying aloud he must kill him, to noting the injustice of this act.[6] This vacillation represents a battle between desire and reality: the desire to love the fish, yet the reality of having to kill it to survive. Kevin Maier notes this same vacillation in several of Hemingway's texts and calls it an "odd clash of discourses" (733). Hemingway seems to show a growing sensitivity to nature and, at the same time, continues to kill animals for sport. When we as ecocritics ask if this text is accountable to the environment, these competing discourses make it difficult to decide. Most scholars argue that this complex and unanswerable position is what renders Hemingway's seemingly inconsistent position on hunting so powerful. And herein lies the rub. If we accept Beegel's argument that the final image represents Santiago at peace with nature, *and* we accept the argument that a lack of peace—Santiago's incessant self-arguing and his impossible position as lover-killer of nature—makes this text so provocative, then the sweet and peaceful ending of the novel is simply sentimental, a failure to address what makes the book so fascinating to us. But what happens if we read this final line the same way we read the statements Santiago speaks aloud to himself? What if we treat the text itself as a process?

Santiago speaks incessantly, telling himself the fish he catches are his brothers, wishing for Manolin though he knows the boy will not come, telling himself he is not lost when he is, and reminding himself he must kill the great marlin though he knows it is unjust. The final line is not Santiago. It does not seem to vacillate. The narrating voice speaks a line aloud that seems as definitive as the fact that Santiago must kill the great fish. Here we have the text, Santiago and Hemingway's double, speaking aloud what it desires, what it wishes for, and yet it has spent every single page showing us this is impossible. Santiago cannot catch the fish without destroying it; he cannot return to the lions; if we go out "too far," we do not make it back.

The peaceful final image is not peaceful at all. Rather, it is the text speaking aloud one side of an argument that *The Old Man and the Sea has* spent every page training us to doubt. We wish with all our might to cross that dividing line, to lose ourselves in the calm repose of pure nature. But no matter how confidently that final voice speaks, with each passing year, as the environment around us becomes the main character, we will increasingly hear that voice as one of desperation, leaving us in the middle of our own endless vacillating and hope-filled arguments that we can exist as humans in the natural world. Oddly, it is our ability to find doubt in the final definitive statement that renders the book accountable. It is this doubt that defines us as humans, that asks us again and again to turn and look, to dream that nature for us is still possible.

Notes

1. Excellent ecocritical work has been done by Sarah May O'Brien and Robert Paul Lamb on "Big Two-Hearted River," as well as David Savola and H. R. Stoneback on *The Sun Also Rises*. "The Short Happy Life of Francis Macomber" also clearly yearns to respond to many of these questions.

2. The first three emphases come from Glotfelty's introduction; the fourth from Glen Love's *Practical Ecocriticism* where he encourages us to move our examination toward the real world, to think of the environment in a more scientific way, and to consider its relationship with our profession and our lives.

3. According to Lawrence Buell, this emphasis marks one of the key distinctions between "first-wave" and "second-wave" ecocriticism (*The Future* 8). In the early days, critics tended to focus on nature, rejecting anthropocentric critique as a diminishing of the natural. They emphasized texts that were clearly examples of nature writing and advocated direct experience over theory. Second-wave critics, however, have seen the usefulness of considering how humans fit into the picture. This has led to more theoretical explorations and a movement from nature-centered texts to all kinds of writing. This struggle can be seen in Beegel's essay "A Guide to the Marine Life in Ernest Hemingway's *The Old Man and the Sea*," where she argues the importance of focusing on nature in the text. Ryan Hediger also takes up this balance in his essay on hunting and ethics, arguing that this struggle is central to the text.

4. The tension between being human and writing nature can be seen in Beegel's essay "A Guide to the Marine Life in Ernest Hemingway's *The Old Man and the Sea*," where she moves our focus toward the natural. Ryan Hediger also takes up this tension in his essay on hunting and ethics, arguing that it lies at the center of the book.

5. Gallos made this observation at the 2012 iDMAa conference in Miami, Florida.

6. Kevin Hediger explores this at length in his essay.

Works Cited

Adams, Carol J. "Ecofeminism and the Eating of Animals." *Ecological Feminist Philosophies*. Ed. Karen J. Warren. Bloomington: Indiana UP, 1996.

Baker, Carlos. *Hemingway: The Writer as Artist*. Princeton: Princeton UP, 1956.

Beegel, Susan F. "A Guide to the Marine Life in Ernest Hemingway's *The Old Man and the Sea*." *Resources for American Literary Study* 30 (2006): 236–315.

———. "Hemingway's Education as a Naturalist." *A Historical Guide to Ernest Hemingway*. Ed. Linda Wagner-Martin. New York: Oxford UP, 2000.

———. "Santiago and the Eternal Feminine: Gendering La Mar in *The Old Man and the Sea*." *Ernest Hemingway's* The Old Man and the Sea. Ed. Harold Bloom. New York: Chelsea House, 2005.

Brenner, Gerry. *The Old Man and the Sea: Story of a Common Man*. New York: Twayne, 1991.

Buell, Lawrence. *The Environmental Imagination: Thoreau, Nature Writing, and the Formation of American Culture*. Cambridge, MA: Harvard UP, 1995.

———. *The Future of Environmental Criticism: Environmental Crisis and Literary Imagination.* Oxford: Blackwell, 2005.

Del Gizzo, Suzanne. "Going Home; Hemingway, Primitivisn, and Identity." *Modern Fiction Studies* 49.3 (Fall 2003): 496–523.

Glotfelty, Cheryll. Introduction. *The Ecocriticism Reader: Landmarks in Literary Ecology.* Ed. Cheryll Glotfelty and Harold Fromm. Athens: U of Georgia P, 1996.

Hediger, Ryan. "Hunting, Fishing, and the Cramp of Ethics in Ernest Hemingway's *The Old Man and the Sea, Green Hills of Africa,* and *Under Kilimanjaro.*" *The Hemingway Review* 27.2 (Spring 2008): 35–59.

Hemingway, Ernest. *The Old Man and the Sea.* New York: Charles Scribner's Sons, 1952.

Hollenberg, Alexander. "The Spacious Foreground: Interpreting Simplicity and Ecocritical Ethics in *The Old Man and the Sea.*" *The Hemingway Review* 31.2 (Spring 2012): 27–45.

Lamb, Robert Paul. "Fishing for Stories." *Modern Fiction Stories* 37.2 (Summer 1991): 161–81.

Love, Glen A. *Practical Ecocriticism: Literature, Biology, and the Environment.* Charlottesville: U of Virginia P, 2003.

Maier, Kevin. "Hemingway's Ecotourism: *Under Kilimanjaro* and the Ethics of Travel." *Interdisciplinary Studies in Literature and Environment* 18.4 (Autumn 2011): 717–36.

O'Brien, Sarah May. "'I, Also, Am in Michigan': Pastoralism of Mind in Hemingway's 'Big Two-Hearted River.'" *The Hemingway Review* 28.2 (Spring 2009): 66–86.

Ott, Mark P. *A Sea of Change: Ernest Hemingway and the Gulf Stream.* Kent, OH: Kent State UP, 2008.

Savola, David. "'A Very Sinister Book': *The Sun Also Rises* as Critique of Pastoral." *The Hemingway Review* 26.1 (Fall 2006): 25–46.

Shakespeare, Alex. "'The Names of Rivers and the Names of Birds: Ezra Pound, Louis Agassiz, and the 'Luminous Detail' in Hemingway's Early Fiction." *The Hemingway Review.* 30.2 (2011): 36–53.

Stoneback, H. R. "'You Sure This Thing Has Trout in It?': Fishing and Fabrication, Omission and 'Vermification' in *The Sun Also Rises.*" *Hemingway Repossessed.* Ed. Kenneth Rosen. London: Praeger, 1994.

Tyler, Lisa. "'How Beautiful the Virgin Forests Were Before the Loggers Came': An Ecofeminist Reading of Hemingway's 'The End of Something.'" *The Hemingway Review* 27.2 (Spring 2008): 60–73.

Warren, Karen J. "Feminism and Ecology: Making Connections." *Environmental Ethics* 9 (1987): 3–20.

The Sea Has Many Voices

A Maritime Studies Experience of *The Old Man and the Sea*

Susan F. Beegel

For seven years, I taught *The Old Man and the Sea* in a "Literature of the Sea" seminar for the Williams College-Mystic Seaport Maritime Studies program. Each year, twenty to twenty-five students from colleges and universities around the country come to Connecticut for a semester at Mystic Seaport, America's pre-eminent maritime museum. The interdisciplinary program requires everyone to study not only "Literature of the Sea," but also American maritime history, marine environmental policy, and either oceanography or marine ecology, along with the historic maritime skills demonstrated on the Seaport's grounds. Students travel with faculty on an extended field trip to the Pacific Coast and experience a shorter field seminar in at least one other coastal zone. The capstone, however, is ten days of deepwater sailing, sometimes out of Key West.

So when I look at the sunburned faces of Williams-Mystic students settled around a library seminar table and ready to discuss *The Old Man and the Sea*, I am looking at young men and women who have all read *Moby-Dick* and a shelf of other great sea literature. Who have traced the lineaments of America's relationship with its two oceans from the *Mayflower* to post-Panamax super-tankers. Who are passionate about marine conservation and the preservation of traditional fisheries. Who understand the Coriolis effect and the marine food chain. Who are familiar with the marine life of Hemingway's waters from plankton to porpoises. Who can split a codfish, sing a chantey, work a breeches buoy, forge a harpoon, or build a wooden boat. Who know the rudiments of sailing a schooner and navigating by the stars. As a bonus, there's always at least one who's been smacked in the face by a flying fish while taking the helm at night.

Williams-Mystic students are an ideal audience for *The Old Man and the Sea* and almost universally love the book. Intimate with the sea, they appreciate the truthfulness and poetry of Hemingway's descriptions—whether of sea turtles closing their eyes to eat Portuguese man-of-war jellyfish despite their poisonous, stinging filaments (36) or of the "great island of Sargasso weed that heaved and swung in the light sea as though the ocean was making love with something under a yellow blanket" (72). Their sophistication about the ocean world gives them an instant, thorough grasp of the novel's action, freeing them to think widely and deeply about its literary significance.

But with apologies to Herman Melville, these extravaganzas only show that the Williams-Mystic Maritime Studies Program is no ordinary classroom. Most literature students in this country do their learning in serial ranks of plastic chairs, trapped by their tablet arms, their sun a rack of fluorescent lights, their horizon a white board, their captain a teacher with a dry-erase marker. It's a rare department budget that extends to chartering a research vessel. Students from landlocked states may lack even basic literacy about the sea.

So I want to discuss how having taught *The Old Man and the Sea* in a maritime studies program underlies my teaching when I carry this book into traditional high school and college settings. This venture will be two-fold. Some aspects of my Williams-Mystic course work in any classroom. But in classrooms lacking the program's unique resources, and with students lacking a maritime background, I need to supply some interdisciplinary education about the sea.

My "Literature of the Sea" syllabus canvasses a variety of maritime poetry, narrative, fiction, and nonfiction presented chronologically from the eighteenth through the twentieth centuries. I might begin with Samuel Taylor Coleridge's "The Rime of the Ancient Mariner," like *Old Man* a parable about a sin against nature ("With his cruel bow he laid full low / The harmless Albatross) that unleashes an ordeal ("Alone, alone, all, all alone, / Alone on a wide, wide sea!") (50, 32).[1] Herman Melville's *Moby-Dick*—that vast leviathan which seems to have digested all literature of the sea that comes before and influenced all that comes after—is the seminar's unchanging centerpiece. *The Old Man and the Sea* always concludes the course, partly for practical reasons (the novel is blessedly brief, an end-of-term gift for students), but also because it is so obviously a spare, modernist reinvention of Melville's masterpiece, a precursor Hemingway had squarely in his sights as he composed *Old Man* during *Moby-Dick*'s 1951 centennial celebration.[2]

This triad of maritime classics—each belonging to the timeless literary tradition of an anxious voyager hunting for God in an ocean wilderness—forms the skeleton of the course. I flesh out this skeleton with a variety of interdisciplinary readings sufficient for twelve weeks. Titles that work especially well with *The Old Man and the Sea* include Jack London's *The Sea-Wolf* (1904), with its brutal Darwinian vision of man (and woman) in nature; Rachel Carson's *Under the Sea-Wind* (1941), a marine biologist's look at ocean life from the perspective of sea creatures such as Scomber the mackerel; John Steinbeck and Edward F. Ricketts's *The Log from the Sea of Cortez* (1941), combining scientific exploration with spiritual ecology; and Thor Heyerdahl's *Kon-Tiki* (trans. 1950), the Norwegian explorer's best-selling narrative of his 4,300-mile voyage across the Pacific on a balsa raft.

What's the advantage, when teaching literature, of forming a syllabus around the sea—or any habitat or environment? Some scholars may object that an English course focused on an aspect of the natural world, rather than the usual building blocks of author, genre, or period, somehow distracts from literary study, which is, after all, our principal business. I would argue that the opposite is true. Art history has influenced my teaching here—let me give an example. If you were to project four paintings of a reclining nude by four different artists (let's say Titian, Rubens, Watteau, and Picasso) on the same screen, you would be looking not at reclining nudes so much as at the radically different styles, techniques, sensibilities (individual, historic, cultural), aims, colors, and media these artists bring to the same problem.

In precisely the same way, comparing a group of writers all looking at the same external reality acts to foreground their literary differences. Substituting sharks for reclining nudes, below is an example of the type of comparative problem a "Literature of the Sea" syllabus can set for students. The questions they ask and the solutions they discover must be their own.

> HERMAN MELVILLE: "Your woraciousness, fellow-critters, I don't blame ye so much for; dat is natur, and can't be helped; but to gobern dat wicked natur, dat is de pint. You is sharks, sartin; but if you gobern de shark in you, why den you be angel; for all angel is not'ing more dan de shark well goberned." (303)

> JACK LONDON: The shark, a sixteen-footer, was hoisted up against the main-rigging. Its jaws were pried apart to their greatest extension, and a stout stake, sharpened at both ends, was so inserted that when the pries were removed the spread jaws were fixed upon it. This accomplished, the hook was cut out. The shark dropped back into the sea, helpless, yet with its full strength, doomed—to

lingering starvation—a living death less meet for it than for the man who devised the punishment. (163)

THOR HEYERDAHL: We made friends with the shark which followed us today. At dinner we fed it with scraps which we poured right down into its open jaws. It has the effect of a half fierce, half good natured and friendly dog when it swims alongside us. It cannot be denied that sharks can seem quite pleasant so long as we do not get into their jaws ourselves. At least we find it amusing to have them about us, except when we are bathing. (186)

ERNEST HEMINGWAY: The shark was not an accident. He had come up from deep down in the water as the dark cloud of blood had settled and dispersed in the mile deep sea. He had come up so fast and absolutely without caution that he broke the surface of the blue water and was in the sun. Then he fell back into the sea and picked up the scent and started swimming on the course the skiff and the fish had taken. (100)

Naturally, in a "Literature of the Sea" course, whether I'm teaching for a maritime studies program or not, I don't want the actual sea ever to disappear, and I do (passionately) want my students to think and learn about it, for the sake of our survival as a species if no other reason. But, as a professor of literature, and of the humanities, I want to keep the principal focus not on the sea alone, but on writers considering the sea. "The sea," T. S. Eliot reminds us, "is all about us"—and it has "many voices, / Many gods and many voices" (130–31). These "many voices" are the essence of the course.

"Literature of the Sea" assignments reflect the course's comparative method. A midterm paper requires comparison of two works, while a longer final paper asks students to compare three works, one of which must be *Moby-Dick*. Subjects may range from plankton to Providence, from sin to sea turtles, from makos to monomania.

Essay choices on midterm and final exams also require comparisons. One fruitful prompt uses a passage from *The Old Man and the Sea* distinguishing between those who think of the sea "as *la mar* which is what people call her in Spanish when they love her," and those who use the masculine form *el mar* and think of the sea "as a contestant or a place or even an enemy" (30). Students must choose several works from the course, divide them into *la mar* and *el mar* categories, and consider the literary and ethical implications of the ways different authors gender the sea. Another oft-chosen prompt asks students to imagine that they are preparing a *Kon-Tiki* style expedition to cross the Pacific on a raft. They must choose crew members from works on the syllabus and explain their choices. Over the years, no one has ever elected to sail without Melville's Queequeg, a kind of maritime "most valuable player." But Hemingway's Manolin is also a popular choice. In him, students hope to acquire Santiago's knowledge, skills, and sensibility in younger form.

While the students' personal work in the course—their papers and exams—has a comparative thrust, our collective work, when we meet for a weekly, ninety-minute discussion class, focuses on a single reading. To moderate a student-centered discussion of *The Old Man and the Sea*, I remind the class that we have limited time and ask them to consider what single topic they most want to cover. Then, we go around the room and each student offers a topic choice, which I write on the board. With that, we're ready to go. The ice is broken and everyone has intellectual skin in the game. Everyone can see the material we need to cover. My role is to encourage the shy, curb the overenthusiastic, keep discussion moving, summarize results, and watch the clock so we have at least a few minutes to discuss the ending.

This method almost always leads to a lively and important discussion of *The Old Man and the Sea*. The topics covered will differ each time according to the students' choices, but my maritime studies students always choose to focus on the sea. They will argue strenuously about what constitutes a right relationship with nature in the novel and about how they see Santiago or Hemingway performing within that relationship. Baseball, Christian iconography, aging, masculinity, courage, endurance, and the old man's bond with the boy may come up—but discussion will always return to *la mar*.

A comparative syllabus, essays, exams, and student-centered discussion—all focused on literature of the sea—these are the building blocks of my Williams-Mystic course. But when I teach *The Old Man and the Sea* outside of a maritime studies program, I must add something to compensate for the traditional student's lack of experiential and interdisciplinary learning about the ocean world. There are many possible solutions short of requiring students to sail a schooner from Key West to Havana. I can imagine, for instance, taking students on a field trip to an aquarium, or inviting a marine biologist to talk with the class. My personal choice, however, is a slide lecture, the time-honored teaching method of field biologists, who deal every day with the problem of needing to bring living organisms and whole habitats into the classroom.

While I employ Power Point software to create my *Old Man and the Sea* presentation, I use the old-school term "slide lecture" advisedly here to emphasize a particular teaching style. Power Point has unfortunately become synonymous with a business model of presentation, and especially with the bulleted list of words or sentence fragments that the lecturer reads aloud to an audience stupefied by boredom (because presumably, they can read the screen themselves). None of this is a good fit with teaching about the natural world. A "slide lecture," by contrast, fills the screen with dramatic images—photographs, art, scientific illustrations—subordinating text to spare captions or dispensing with it altogether. The lecturer does not read the screen but narrates or explains the images extemporaneously, always alert to student comprehension and potential questions.

The content of my slide lecture follows the Williams-Mystic model, engaging the "many voices" of different disciplines. The strongest emphasis is on science—the oceanography and marine ecology lending drama and beauty to *The Old Man and the Sea*. I touch as well on maritime history and material culture—Santiago's fishery, its boats, equipment, and lifeways. A brief look at marine policy then and now—at ideas of conservation and regulation of fishing practices—prevents students from holding Santiago to anachronistic standards of environmental sensitivity. Around these subjects I weave some relevant Hemingway biography, stressing his authentic prowess as a deep-sea fisherman and marine naturalist. My goals are to enhance respect, understanding, and appreciation for the author, his creation, and the sea.

Because everyone who teaches *The Old Man and the Sea* will have personal ideas about what subjects to emphasize in a slide lecture, as well as access to an ocean of potential illustrations via Google's image search feature, I won't attempt to unload the entire contents of my own lecture here.[3] Instead, let me give a few examples of the topics I narrate and the types of images I use to illustrate them.

To establish the all-important sense of place, I locate Santiago's village (and Hemingway's home port) of Cojímar just east of Havana on Cuba's north coast. National Oceanographic and Atmospheric Administration (NOAA) Chart 11031, "Straits of Florida and Approaches," shows the cities of Havana and Key West facing each other across the ninety-mile width of the Straits—the exit from the Gulf of Mexico into the Atlantic Ocean.[4] Showing water depths and current speeds, as well as aids and hazards to navigation, a nautical chart helps students understand, as the old man does, that the sea is not simply a large body of water but a complex and dynamic environment.

Understanding *The Old Man and the Sea* requires some understanding of the Gulf Stream—one of our planet's great permanent ocean currents. Infrared satellite imagery available online from the National Aeronautic and Space Administration's Visible Earth Collection shows how the Gulf Stream arises in the hot, shallow waters of the Gulf of Mexico and flows through the Straits of Florida into the Atlantic Ocean. At places in the Straits, the current travels at speeds of four to six miles per hour, impossible to row against for long, and is thirty miles wide—a distance that can take three to eight days to cross in a boat without motorized propulsion—long enough to die from dehydration or exposure. Trade winds of eleven to thirteen miles per hour continuously oppose the current, kicking up heavy seas even in good weather. With water temperatures as high as eighty degrees, the Gulf Stream famously breeds its own bad weather, fueling fogs, thunderstorms, squalls—and hurricanes (Mapes).[5]

The Gulf Stream, then, is a supremely dangerous place to be in a small boat, and Santiago's marlin tows the old man deep into its heart (*Old Man and the Sea* 53). Winslow Homer's painting "The Gulf Stream," admired by Hemingway, perfectly illustrates the points I want to make about the current. In it, we see a lone mariner helplessly adrift in a small sailboat that has been dismasted, prob-

Fig. 1. Winslow Homer's "The Gulf Stream." Metropolitan Museum of Art. Catharine Lorillard Wolfe Collection, Wolfe Fund, 1906. www.metmuseum.org.

Fig. 2. Cuban fishermen boating a shark, 1934. Courtesy of the Ernest Hemingway Collection, John F. Kennedy Library, Boston, MA.

ably by the sudden storm raising a waterspout in the distance. He is prostrate in the sun without shelter or fresh water, his only provisions a few stalks of sugar cane. A distant ship might offer hope of rescue, but the small boat is concealed by high waves and the ship is entering a fog bank. Just as they will later threaten Santiago, large sharks menace Homer's mariner, whose boat seems vulnerable to capsizing in heavy seas.

Although *The Old Man and the Sea* offers many poignant descriptions of Santiago's small skiff, students lacking maritime literacy may not be able to visualize the boat accurately. Photographs taken by the author himself help correct that problem. Out sportfishing on *Pilar* in 1934, either Hemingway or a member of his party photographed Cuban fishermen in their traditional watercraft. He kept the pictures for the rest of his life, perhaps to aid his memory when describing these boats in his writing.[6]

Figure 2 shows two fishermen struggling to load a large shark into a small wooden boat similar to the one in Homer's painting, reminding us of the disadvantage Santiago faces in fishing alone. The sail is up and fitted precisely like Santiago's in *The Old Man and the Sea:* "Then he stepped the mast and, with the stick that was his gaff and the boom rigged, the patched sail drew" (97).

Fig. 3. Cuban fisherman with billfish on board. Courtesy of the Ernest Hemingway Collection. John F. Kennedy Library, Boston, MA.

Figure 3 shows another pair of fishermen in a different boat, the mast not stepped, with a large billfish, perhaps a marlin, on board. The boat is so small that the arc of the fish's tail exceeds the width of the stern. Crammed with two grown men, a fish weighing a couple of hundred pounds, the mast, the sail, the oars, the gaff, the boom, the harpoon, and the fishing line, the boat has just inches of freeboard and would easily be swamped by the slightest sea or shifting of weight. The photo speaks to the courage, skill, and sheer desperation of Cuba's subsistence fishermen, who in Santiago's time took boats this size out into the Gulf Stream.

From his small boat, Santiago struggles with a marlin of mythic but possible proportions—"Now alone, and out of sight of land, he was fast to the biggest fish he had ever seen and bigger than any he had ever heard of" (*Old Man and the Sea* 63). Hemingway gives the marlin's weight: "He's over 1500 pounds" (97). An image of legendary deep-sea fisherman Alfred Glassell Jr., posing with a 1,560 black marlin taken off Cabo Blanco, Peru, in 1953, gives students a visual fix on size.[7] The size of Glassell's fish, still the largest marlin ever caught unassisted with rod and reel, contrasts sharply with the frail Cuban fishing boats.

Fig. 4. Alfred C. Glassell Jr. with world record 1,560-pound black marlin. Courtesy of the International Game Fish Association, Dania Beach, FL.

The Old Man and the Sea is dense with marine life, the novel's biodiversity posing a challenge for students who may never have seen a tuna outside of a Starkist can. I show photos of the book's leading animal figures (the marlin, the mako, the *galanos*, and the warbler), taking time to sketch their life histories and consider Hemingway's attitudes toward them. Other creatures—dolphin, flying fish, hawk, man-of-war bird, porpoise, Portuguese man-of-war jellyfish, sea turtle, stingray, sooty tern, and tuna—I handle by rapidly flashing image after image up on the screen without any narrative except to name the subject, pausing just long enough to let students have a good look.

My aim is to enhance students' visual literacy as far as possible in the short time available and to create an aesthetic effect similar to the barrage that concludes a fireworks display. Toward that end, I draw images from internet resources, including the luscious photography of sportfishing magazines, the splendidly relevant art of deep-sea fisherman Guy Harvey, and science sites such as MarineBio, the NOAA Ocean Explorer Gallery, and the Cornell Lab of Ornithology. A slide lecture may be a poor substitute for time spent in nature, but it can leave students bedazzled by the beauty of strange creatures and the vibrant colors of Santiago's world—and better able to appreciate Hemingway's skill at limning them.

Teaching literature with the natural world, an enterprise that ideally involves interdisciplinary and experiential learning, has long been suspect in the academy. As a young teacher, I was once reprimanded for taking my *Moby-Dick* students on a whale watch off Nantucket. "Whales," a senior faculty member intoned, "are extratextual." This is the dubious legacy of deconstruction, of Jacques Derrida's infamous assertion that "*There is nothing outside the text*," that "language is writing as the disappearance of natural presence" (158; original emphasis). "Nature," in his view, is "something that has always already escaped" and that "never existed" (159). Edward Abbey, on the other hand, reminds us that such thinking "is a product of too much time wasted in library stacks between the covers of a book, in smoke-filled coffeehouses (bad for the brains) and conversation-clogged seminars. To refute the solipsist or the metaphysical idealist all that you have to do is take him out and throw a rock at his head: if he ducks, he's a liar" (111–12).

Nature may be a slippery fish, and language a crude and primitive tool for bringing it to gaff, but it exists all right. None of our great maritime writers would ever allow it to "escape" without a fight, let alone Ernest Hemingway, who identified himself as a naturalist and whose own education was interdisciplinary and experiential. *The Old Man and the Sea* is, in many respects, an allegory of his own struggle to "[make] the fish so he is seen and felt by the reader" (qtd. in Brasch 222). Surely one legitimate way to teach this novel is to explore the relationship between the writer and his subject, the natural world. To understand the fisherman we must study the fish.

Notes

With deepest gratitude to my colleague Dr. Richard J. King, research associate at Williams-Mystic, for years of shared ideas and inspiration.

1. Carlos Baker was first to draw a comparison between Coleridge's *The Rime of the Ancient Mariner* and Hemingway's *The Old Man and the Sea*. See Carlos Baker, *Hemingway: The Writer as Artist*, 4th edition (Princeton: Princeton UP, 1972), 303–4.

2. From the beginning, critics noticed the resemblance of *The Old Man and the Sea* to a certain "long novel about a sea captain and a whale." See Gilbert Highet, review of *The Old Man and the Sea*, *Harper's* 205 (October 1952), reprinted in *Hemingway: The Critical Heritage*, edited by Jeffrey Meyers (London: Routledge and Kegan Paul, 1982), 413–14. Hemingway himself was not shy about expressing his ambition "to take Mr. Melville." See *Ernest Hemingway: Selected Letters 1917–1961*, edited by Carlos Baker (New York: Charles Scribner's Sons, 1981), 673.

3. I have published a good deal of my course content elsewhere. See "Santiago and the Eternal Feminine," in *Hemingway and Women: Female Critics and the Female Voice*, edited by Lawrence R. Broer and Gloria Holland (Tuscaloosa: U of Alabama P, 2002), 131–56, 305–7; "A Guide to the Marine Life in *The Old Man and the Sea*," *Resources for American Literary Study* 30 (2006): 236–315; "Thor Heyerdahl's *Kon-Tiki* and Hemingway's Return to Primitivism in *The Old Man and the Sea*," in *Hemingway: Eight Decades of Criticism*, edited by Linda Wagner-Martin (East Lansing: Michigan State UP, 2009), 513–51; and "The Monster of Cojímar: A Meditation on Hemingway, Sharks, and War, " *The Hemingway Review* 34.2 (Spring 2015): 9–35. For teachers developing an interdisciplinary approach to the novel, I also recommend Patricia Dunlavy Valenti's *Understanding* The Old Man and the Sea: *A Student Casebook to Issues, Sources, and Historical Documents* (Westport, CT: Greenwood Press, 2002).

4. The NOAA Office of the Coast Survey maintains a searchable online Chart Viewer for nautical charts of U.S. waters. <www.nauticalcharts.noaa.gov/mcd/NOAAChart Viewer.html>.

5. In this era of concern about global warming and disruption of our oceans' thermohaline circulation, the Gulf Stream—which plays a crucial role in regulating the planet's weather and temperature—is under intense scientific scrutiny. This means a wealth of excellent information about the current available online from a wide variety of research organizations. In addition, sailing experts like offshore training instructor Ed Mapes, quoted here, provide online advice about the challenges of navigating the Gulf Stream without motorized propulsion, as Santiago must do. Teachers wanting to recapture Hemingway's period understanding of oceanography and the Gulf Stream might wish to consult Rachel Carson, *The Sea Around Us*, 1950 (New York: Mentor, 1989) as well as Henry Chapin and F. G. Walton Smith, *The Ocean River: The Story of the Gulf Stream* (New York: Charles Scribner's Sons, 1952).

6. The John F. Kennedy Library in Boston houses a Hemingway Photograph Collection including 11,000 items. Hundreds of copyright-free photographs from the collection are at large on the internet with some high-resolution images available at the library's online Media Gallery. Others, including the photographs of Cuban traditional watercraft used here, are available in digital form for a small fee by request.

7. The Glassell photo is from the now closed archives of the International Game Fish Association, an organization cofounded by Ernest Hemingway and dedicated to sportsmanlike fishing practices, international record-keeping, research, and conservation.

Works Cited

Abbey, Edward. *Desert Solitaire: A Season in the Wilderness*. 1968. New York: Ballantine Books, 1991.

Brasch, James D. "Invention from Knowledge: The Hemingway-Cowley Correspondence." *Ernest Hemingway: The Writer in Context*. Ed. James Nagel. Madison: U of Wisconsin P, 1984. 201–36.

Coleridge, Samuel Taylor. *The Rime of the Ancient Mariner*. 1798. Illustrated by Gustave Doré. New York: Dover Publications, 1970.

Derrida, Jacques. *Of Grammatology.* 1967. Trans. Gayatri Chakravorty Spivak. Baltimore: Johns Hopkins UP, 1976.
Eliot, T. S. "The Dry Salvages." 1943. *The Complete Poems and Plays: 1909–1950.* New York: Harcourt, Brace, and World, 1971. 130–37.
Hemingway, Ernest. *The Old Man and the Sea.* 1952. New York: Scribner, 1995.
Heyerdahl, Thor. *Kon-Tiki: Across the Pacific by Raft.* Chicago: Rand McNally, 1950.
London, Jack. *The Sea Wolf and Selected Stories.* 1904. New York: Signet Classic, 1964.
Mapes, Ed. "Crossing the Gulf Stream." *Sailing Magazine.* 17 Apr. 2009. <www.sailing-magazine.net/how-to/technique/682-crossing-the-gulf-stream.html.>
Melville, Herman. *Moby-Dick; Or, The Whale.* 1851. Berkeley and Los Angeles: U of California P, 1979.

Part Three

Africa

"Shootism" Versus "Sport" in Hemingway's "Macomber"

Gary Harrington

I've found that an effective way to provoke lively and sometimes heated classroom discussion regarding Hemingway's "The Short Happy Life of Francis Macomber" is to begin near the story's end by raising the question of whether Margot deliberately kills her husband. Students are keen to discuss the matter, there is an abundance of evidence both pro and con, and this evidence is so evenly distributed that with a reasonably small class the instructor can simply divide the class down the middle and assign one side to respond "Yes" and the other "No." Depending on the amount of time being devoted to the story, the instructor might even hold a mock trial to inspect the various factors related to Margot's behavior in this crucial episode. When examining this incident, the teacher might also incorporate into the discussion more general features of Hemingway's aesthetic. For instance, the fact that Margot's shot hits Francis in a spot very close to that which Wilson had just a bit earlier specified to Francis as the *coup de grace* area—"take [the buffalo] in the neck just behind the ear" (*Complete Short Stories* 23)—is either an extraordinary coincidence or Margot is a phenomenal shooter. Consequently, readers would very much like to know about Margot's previous experience with rifles and hunting, and the fact that Hemingway largely forgoes providing such information can be used as an illustration of the "iceberg theory" and Hemingway's art of omission.

While discussing this episode, the instructor can point out that in a sense it simply doesn't matter whether or not Margot intentionally shot Francis because her future legal narrative, the way in which the authorities will read her case, will be determined by Robert Wilson, who literally has the last word in the conversation and in the story itself. The guide emphasizes his control over the interpretation of the event when speaking to Margot by alternately referring to the incident as a murder and as an accident. After Francis is killed, Wilson finds himself in a vulnerable position. As Hemingway notes elsewhere, the "white hunter who has a client wounded or killed loses, or seriously impairs, his livelihood" ("Notes" 71), and as if this weren't bad enough, Wilson had recently admitted to Margot that his use of a vehicle in chasing the buffalo was unlawful. While the class can be encouraged to speculate on other reasons for Wilson's implicit blackmail, one indisputable motive is that he wants to ensure Margot's silence regarding his illegal hunting activities. And Wilson's questionable behavior at the end of the story serves as a springboard to discussing his conduct elsewhere, which also proves to be dubious. To mention just a few examples, his sleeping with his clients' wives as a matter of course so that the wives would feel that "they were getting their money's worth" (*Complete Short Stories* 21) and his nonchalant cruelty in whipping the native gun-bearers are both disgraceful. Wilson's unsavory activities and attitudes, when combined with the fact that he serves as Macomber's mentor, raise a serious issue concerning the way in which Macomber's transformation is viewed.

There's no question that Macomber undergoes a dramatic change in outlook and personality during the buffalo hunt, and that this alteration is usually regarded as salutary by students and scholars alike. Among the latter, Philip Young feels that "Macomber, under the tutelage of the guide Robert Wilson, learns courage and honor and to embrace the code" (116); Robert Gajdusek maintains that Francis "makes a redemptive crossover from the territory of boyhood into manhood" (222); and John M. Howell speaks of Francis's "initiation into the code of the hunt, and his discovery of courage and manhood through the confrontation with a dangerous animal" (29). However, the idea of Macomber's changing for the better, of "his discover[ing] courage and manhood," certainly remains open to question; even more unlikely is the contention that he is successfully initiated "into the code of the hunt." Although Macomber learns to slaughter game fairly efficiently, he demonstrates little understanding of hunting ethics. In fact, under the direction of Wilson, Macomber comes to adopt an attitude of "shootism" as opposed to that of "sport," a distinction made in one of the three "Letters" which Hemingway wrote for *Esquire* magazine in 1934, a few years prior to composing "Macomber."

Now most readily available in *By-Line: Ernest Hemingway*, these essays recounting Hemingway's own safari experiences are of much value to students and instructors for they bear directly upon the reader's estimation of the hunting practices which Wilson follows and which he imprints, directly or indirectly, upon his client. Overall the hunting principles and methods articulated in the letters, anticipated and perhaps even influenced by other early twentieth-century safari literature (Martin), suggest a negative assessment of Wilson's conduct. In the episode with the lion, for instance, Wilson does not have the vehicle drive off after Macomber gets out. By contrast, in "Shootism Versus Sport: The Second Tanganyika Letter," while discussing the proper methods of lion hunting Hemingway insists time and again upon the necessity of the vehicle's departing after the hunter exits:

> If you approach the lion in a motor car, the lion will not see you. His eyes can only distinguish the outline or silhouette of objects, and, because it is illegal to shoot from a motor car, this object means nothing to him.... *For a man to shoot at a lion from the protection of a motor car, where the lion cannot even see what it is that is attacking him, is not only illegal but is a cowardly way to assassinate one of the finest of all game animals....* Once you are on the ground *and the car is gone,* lion hunting is the same as it always was.... *if you shoot as you should on the Serengeti, having the car drive off as you get out....* But you will be more of a sportsman to come back from Africa without a lion than to shoot one from the protection of a motor car. (69–71; emphasis mine)

"Protection" here would no doubt include standing in the shadow of the vehicle "where the lion cannot even see what it is that is attacking him," as Wilson essentially dupes the greenhorn Macomber into doing. Wilson, a professional guide, is surely acquainted with this aspect of the safari hunter's code, as was Hemingway's own guide, Philip "Pop" Percival. Concerning the "ethical standards" involved in hunting big game, Hemingway stated that he "had learned them from Pop and Pop, on his last lion hunt and taking out his last safari, wanted things to be as they were in the old days before the hunting of dangerous game had been corrupted and made easy by what he always called 'these bloody cars'" (*True* 47).

Wilson gives his client an enormously unfair advantage by ignoring "ethical standards" and having the vehicle remain in place so that Macomber unwittingly remains in its shadow. Hemingway emphasizes the essential guile involved in Wilson's using this tactic by shifting to the lion's perspective, a shift that sometimes puzzles students:

> Macomber stepped out . . . and down onto the ground. The lion still stood looking . . . toward this object that his eyes only showed in silhouette. . . . Then

watching the object, ... *he saw a man figure detach itself from it* and he turned his heavy head and swung away toward the cover of the trees as he heard a cracking crash and felt the slam of a .30–06 220-grain solid bullet that bit his flank and ripped in sudden hot scalding nausea through his stomach. (*Complete Short Stories* 13; emphasis mine)

Shortly thereafter, Hemingway re-emphasizes that only Macomber's emerging from the shadow of the vehicle allows the lion to see him: "and the lion seeing [Macomber's] silhouette flow clear of the silhouette of the car, turned and started off at a trot" (*Complete Short Stories* 14).

In that same letter in which he discusses the role of the auto in the hunt, Hemingway notes that he and his guide make use of a car only because of the vast distances on the Serengeti, and he outlines the appropriate procedure upon spotting a lion: "You step out of the car from beside the driver *on the side away from the lion,* and *[the guide] gets out on the same side from the seat behind you.* ... You both sit down *and the car drives away.* As the car starts to move off you have a very different feeling about lions than you have ever had when you saw them from the motor car" ("Shootism," 69; emphasis mine).

In "Macomber," however, rather than both hunters exiting on "the side away from the lion," Wilson does not even bother to leave the car, much less have it drive off, and he has Macomber exit from the side facing the lion, with the result that Macomber steps into the vehicle's shadow. Wilson presumably provides Macomber with this unsporting edge to guarantee that his client bags a lion in the open, rather than risking the two of them having to follow a wounded lion into the bush. Consequently, Wilson's disgruntlement with Macomber seems to derive not only from Macomber's having "gut-shot" (*Complete Short Stories* 14) the lion but also from his having allowed the lion to spot him as he moved out of the car's shadow, thus complicating the easy kill, which Wilson had orchestrated.

Macomber, of course, does not realize that Wilson's behaviors violate professional principles. He admits to Wilson, and this is *after* the lion hunt, "There are lots of things I don't know" (8), and it is Wilson's responsibility to acquaint Francis with the honorable as well as the practical features of the hunt, just as Pop Percival had taught Hemingway about those "ethical standards." Wilson not only fails to convey these standards to his client, but he also disregards them himself. Indeed, many other aspects of Wilson's behaviors—in addition to his having the car stay put during the lion hunt—undermine his expertise and integrity as both a hunter and as a hunting mentor.

In "Notes on Dangerous Game: The Third Tanganyika Letter," Hemingway remarks that one of the finest attributes of Pop Percival and Baron von Blixen, the two best guides he has ever encountered, is their close attention to their clients (71). Wilson, however, barely notices crucial aspects of Macomber's condition. Just prior to the lion hunt, for example, Macomber asks a barrage of questions that betray his extreme apprehension: "Is [the lion] very close?" "Where should I hit him . . . ?" "What range will it be?" "At under a hundred yards?" (*Complete Short Stories* 11; and see Bender 13). Wilson fails to note the anxiety such questions and Macomber's demeanor in general reveal. However, as an experienced hunter, Wilson should be *expecting* Macomber's anxiety. Feeling fear on a first lion hunt is so common as to be literally proverbial among the natives. Wilson, however, never informs Macomber about "the Somali proverb that says a *brave* man is *always* frightened three times by a lion" (11; emphasis mine). In my experience, students in recounting the proverb usually forget the word "brave," but it is crucial to refresh their memories in this particular since it posits Macomber's fear as an invariable and universal response (see Hutton 246). Wilson does eventually tell Macomber, "Any one could be upset by his first lion" (10), but this is after the lion incident and so too late to do Macomber much good.

Even after they arrive at the hunt site, Wilson remains oblivious to Macomber's nervousness. When Macomber leaves the car, his hands are shaking, the muscles in his thighs are "fluttering" (14), he finds it "almost impossible . . . to make his legs move" (13), and he tries to fire his rifle with the safety on. However, it is only after Francis presents desperate alternatives to going into the high grass after the wounded lion that Wilson finally notices his client's fear, and even then "as an afterthought," when "he glanced at Macomber and saw suddenly how he was trembling and the pitiful look on his face" (15). Although Wilson rightly dismisses Macomber's objectionable suggestions regarding their next course of action, Wilson himself considers an unethical alternative, as appears in his offhand comment, "We can't bring the car over. Bank's too steep" (15).

When they enter the high grass on foot, Macomber runs away as the lion charges. His doing so brands him, by his own admission, a "coward" (19), a self-assessment with which most students initially agree, but whether this actually reflects Hemingway's opinion is another matter (see Hutton 247). In his introduction to the anthology *Men at War*, published in 1942, Hemingway differentiated between cowardice and panic, the former being blameworthy and the latter being an unconscious, automatic response, and consequently blameless (xxvii). And while *Men at War* postdates the publication of "Macomber," *The Sun Also Rises,* published in 1926, indicates that Hemingway had held this opinion for years prior to writing "Macomber." In that novel, Jake Barnes states that Montoya, the hotel owner and bullfighting expert, can forgive much, including, specifically, "panic" in "a bull fighter who had afición" (137). That Macomber's running from the lion results from panic rather than cowardice is suggested implicitly by Hemingway's emphasizing Francis's flight as a reflexive action and explicitly by the narrator's using the word "panic" in describing it: "Macomber heard the blood-choked coughing grunt, and saw the swishing rush in the grass. *The next thing he knew he was running;* running wildly, in *panic* in the open, running toward the stream" (17; emphasis mine).

Hemingway further underscores that Macomber's response stems from panic, that it is instinctive, by associating Francis with the lion. Their fates are similar: the lion's having half its head blown off anticipates the manner of Macomber's death. Likewise, after being shot, the lion feels that "sudden hot scalding nausea through his stomach" (13), and shortly after shooting him "Macomber stood there feeling sick at his stomach" (14). Wilson suggests that they wait before entering the high grass in order to "'let [the lion] stiffen up'" (15), recalling Macomber's feeling "stiff in the thighs" (14) when he first leaves the vehicle. The hunters encounter the lion as he is preparing to drink at a waterhole; so, too, during the hunt Macomber's "mouth was very dry" (14) and he asks Wilson for a drink of water. Wilson often uses the British idiom "beggar" with reference to Macomber (8, 21, 25); he also calls the lion "'a noisy beggar'" (12); and students can supply many other instances of this convergence.

These correspondences, among other purposes, reinforce Allen Shepherd's contention that "Macomber and his lion are alike in that their cowardice and bravery, in the crisis, are both instinctual" (299)—if indeed the terms "cowardice" and "bravery" even apply. The latter word may well be an inaccurate descriptor of the lion's instinctively determined behaviors. In fact, outside the merry old land of Oz, one might be hard pressed to find a lion either cowardly or courageous. Since Hemingway subtly but firmly links Francis and the lion, and since the lion may not properly be described as courageous, then it follows that Francis should not be deemed cowardly. Even if one were to assume the lion capable of courage and cowardice, it would also be necessary to note that the lion attempts to run into cover as soon as he spies the hunter and before a shot is fired, as Hemingway twice emphasizes (13, 14). Needless to say, no one refers to the lion as a coward for running from Francis, and it is hardly the most useful or accurate phrase to describe Francis after he runs from the lion. Indeed, the instructor might generate discussion by asking students their thoughts on the following proposition: "Macomber should not be labeled a coward for running from the lion; he might, however, be considered a fool for standing his ground against the buffalo."

Francis's "cowardice" is essentially Wilson's faulty formulation: for instance, at one point he mentally refers to Francis as "a bloody coward" (8). Wilson essentially defines courage as having "no bloody fear" (26), but the complete absence of fear in a life-threatening circumstance smacks much more of utter recklessness than of courage. As that Somali proverb which states that even *brave* men feel fear implies, courage consists in taking suitable action despite fear. Hemingway's famous definition of courage as "Grace under pressure," first formulated in 1926 (*Selected Letters* 200), might be seen to signify as much. If there is no fear, then there is no pressure. Consequently, Hemingway's own sense of what constitutes courage seems akin to that of Twain's Pudd'nhead Wilson: "Courage is resistance to fear, mastery of fear—not absence of fear" (101). Notably, nowhere in the story does Wilson himself admit to experiencing fear, whereas both Francis and Margot do so. When Wilson comes nearest to such an admission, he uses the nonspecific second-person pronoun to deflect the feeling away from himself and toward Macomber. He says to Francis during a break in the buffalo hunt: "You're not supposed to mention [the anticipatory elation before action].... Much more fashionable to say you're scared. Mind you, you'll be scared too, plenty of times" (26).

The buffalo hunt in general and the pursuit of the wounded buffalo into the bush especially demonstrates that Francis has embraced Wilson's flawed concept of courage. Wilson's own actions in this incident are even more problematic than those in the lion episode, and I have found it beneficial in class to have students compare and contrast the two episodes. One of the first differences they consistently note is that, unlike with the lion, Wilson chases the buffalo with the vehicle. As even the neophyte Margot notes, such a practice is unsporting; indeed, as Wilson admits (and as Hemingway remarks in "Shootism Versus Sport" 69), it is illegal (*Complete Short Stories* 23). Wilson's attempt to gloss over the use of the vehicle by protesting that the hunters were "taking more chance driving that way across the plain full of holes and one thing and another than hunting on foot" and that they "gave [the buffalo] every chance" (23) rivals in its transparent fraudulence a schoolboy's excuse that the dog ate his homework. Wilson also tries to make it appear as if this tactic were spontaneous: "'Wouldn't ordinarily [chase with a car],' Wilson said. 'Seemed sporting enough to me though while we were doing it'" (23). However, far from being a spur-of-the-moment decision, Wilson had planned in advance to pursue the buffalo with the vehicle. He "had ordered a way shovelled out the day before so they could reach the parklike wooded rolling country on the far side" (21), feeling "if he could come between [the buffalo] and their swamp with the car, Macomber would have a good chance at them in the open. He did not want to hunt buff with Macomber in thick cover" (21). As with the deliberate use of the auto's shadow in the lion hunt, Wilson once again misuses one of "those bloody cars" to minimize his own risk while satisfying his customer—after the lion debacle Macomber had remarked that perhaps he could "fix it up on buffalo" (8) and that he would "like to clear away that lion business" (10).

Even setting aside "sporting" considerations, Wilson's manner of using the car is irresponsible, as students are quick to recognize: certainly barreling rapidly across very rough terrain with each hunter hanging onto a side of the car with one hand and holding his weapon with the other is a less than intelligent or safe procedure. Moreover, Macomber apparently does not have his rifle's safety on during the chase, an eminently dangerous oversight in any case and especially so since Macomber and Wilson jump from the vehicle before it is fully stopped. Macomber even tries to reload his gun while on the "rocketing" vehicle, "dropping shells onto the ground, jamming it, clearing the jam" (22), the participles here, as the instructor might point out, registering the frenetic nature of the action. Surely any conscientious guide would recognize the manifest danger to his client in such behaviors, but Wilson's resolve to ensure his own safety by preventing the buffalo from reaching the bush supersedes all other concerns.

His plan fails, however, as one of the three downed buffalo regains its feet and lumbers into the bush. Wilson's sharpshooting instructions with regard to the upcoming encounter with the buffalo are puzzling, at best: he tells the greenhorn Francis that "The only shot is straight into the nose" (27) and then with a remarkable inconsistency adds a few other potential shots. As Virgil Hutton notes, Wilson's presenting the most difficult shot as the first and "only" choice involves, at best, extremely poor judgment (244). In a similar situation in *Green Hills of Africa*, first published in 1935, Hemingway and Pop discuss going after a wounded buffalo in the bush, and Pop says that if the buffalo charges they'll have to "stop him." Hemingway says, "Right up the nose" to which Pop replies, "Don't try anything fancy" (113–14). Interestingly, Wilson makes precisely this same statement to Macomber (*Complete Short Stories* 27), but only after the guide has recommended as the best option a very "fancy" shot. And, in the event, Macomber does follow Wilson's highly questionable advice and shoots "only" for the charging buffalo's nose, with disastrous results: "Macomber, as he fired, unhearing his shot in the roaring of Wilsons's gun . . . shot again at the wide nostrils and saw the horns jolt again and fragments fly" (27).

Also perplexing is the fact that the rifle Wilson allocates to Macomber when going after the buffalo is not the most powerful available to him and so may not be the best choice of weapon in these circumstances. In *Green Hills of Africa,* when Pop and Hemingway go after that wounded buffalo in the bush, Hemingway initially carries a Springfield rifle, but as they proceed deeper into the bush, he "change[s] to the big gun" (117), a weapon which, as Silvio Calabi observes, would be "a much more effective short-range stopper than the .30–06 [Springfield]" (101). And in a similar circumstance with a wounded rhino, Pop tells Hemingway to "take the big gun" (78). Moreover, Hemingway explicitly addresses the issue of weapon size during a wounded buffalo's charge in "Notes on Dangerous Game: The Third Tanganyika Letter": "I cannot see the buffalo as comparing in dangerous possibilities to either lion or leopard . . . and I see no reason why a man who could wait for [the buffalo] as he came could not be sure of blowing the front of his head in *if he let him get close and shot carefully with a heavy enough rifle*" (72; emphasis mine). Francis lets the buffalo get very close: in death, Francis's body rests "not two yards from where the buffalo lay on his side" (*Complete Short Stories* 28).

Why does Wilson not have Macomber use the most powerful weapon on hand? Wilson rather nonchalantly tells Francis before they go into the bush that he "might as well shoot the Springfield" because he is "used to it" (27), but this explanation seems inconsistent since being "used to it" was not a consideration when Wilson assigned to Francis his "heavy gun" (16) for going after the lion. The guide may not want his client's performance in the buffalo hunt to outshine his own, especially in Margot's eyes (see Bender 15, 18). Additionally, Wilson may fear putting a more powerful firearm in the hands of an unpredictable and possibly antagonistic novice. As they drive out the morning of the buffalo hunt, Wilson thinks, "Hope the silly beggar [Macomber] doesn't take the notion to blow the back of my head off" (*Complete Short Stories* 21), and Macomber is described shortly thereafter as sitting "grim and furious" (21) in the back seat. Wilson's directing Macomber to carry the Springfield seems even odder given Wilson's certainty that Macomber will not run from the buffalo: he asserts to Margot that "It's not going to be a damned bit like the lion" (24). He also tells Macomber that his gun-bearer "can carry your heavy gun" (27), but what good this might do in the mad commotion of a buffalo charge remains unclear.

Wilson's own gun is plenty powerful. He routinely uses a Gibbs rifle, which has "a muzzle velocity of two tons" (17) and which he himself describes as a "damned cannon" (27)—no sharp-shooter he. Pop Percival, on the other hand, felt that the use of a Gibbs was so unsporting "that he himself had never carried one" (Lynn 434), and as Hemingway remarks in "Notes on Dangerous Game," Pop "killed all his own lions with a .256 Mannlicher when he had only his own life to look after" (72). The most likely explanation for Wilson's habitually using such a powerful weapon, even when no one's life is threatened, is that he himself is a coward.

Along these same lines, when the gun-bearer reports that the buffalo revived and entered the bush, the narrator remarks that "they all saw the change in the white hunter's face" (*Complete Short Stories* 24), registering Wilson's dismay over that turn of events. Certainly, the gun-bearer who precedes Macomber and Wilson into the bush reacts with fright when the buffalo charges—he "shouted wildly and they saw him coming out of the bush sideways, fast as a crab" (27). And his fear-fueled response finds its counterpart in Wilson's "duck[ing] to one side" as the buffalo charges. Ostensibly, Wilson does so in order "to get in a shoulder shot" (28), but a much more plausible explanation is that Wilson is saving his own skin by getting out of the way of the advancing animal. It's also possible that Wilson is moving out of Francis's line of fire, but one would think that a competent and careful guide would have made provision for just such an occurrence—would have devised a game plan with his client—before entering the bush. It is in any case noteworthy, as others have mentioned, that Wilson does not try the shot up the nose, which he had recommended as the "only shot" to Francis.

And although the narrator does state that Wilson shifts to the side to try a shoulder shot, the narrator has proven to be less than entirely reliable elsewhere in the story. For instance, the narrator states after the lion hunt that Macomber "had shown himself, very publicly, to be a coward" (6), thereby failing to make that distinction between cowardice and panic which, as we've seen, Hemingway himself endorsed elsewhere. The narrator is also shortsighted in describing the relationship of Francis and Margot (unless one assumes the following quotation to constitute a continuation of the society columnist's remarks): "Margot was too beautiful for Macomber to divorce her and Macomber had too much money for Margot ever to leave him." However, this assertion overlooks the fact that Macomber is wealthy and would be much wealthier in the future while Margot's beauty is fading, and so if Margot's attractiveness is one of the two linchpins in their "sound basis of union" (18), the narrator may well be mistaken in stating that they would always remain together. Thus, the narrative declaration that Wilson dives away "to get in a shoulder shot" is not so definitive as it might initially appear to be. This use of what one might term an "unreliable omniscient narrator," which also calls into question the accuracy of the narrator's assertion that Margot "had shot at the buffalo" (28) during the melee, might be used in conjunction with the long, participle-rich sentences at the climactic moments of the lion and the buffalo hunts to underscore to students ways in which Hemingway was much more experimental in his writing than is often thought.

Whatever Wilson's motivation may be in leaping to the side, he leaves Macomber exposed to the buffalo's charge. And just as Macomber is physically susceptible at this point, so has he been made emotionally vulnerable by his adoption of Wilson's unsound perspective, in terms of which Macomber attempts with such disastrous results to redeem himself, and for that matter feels as if his behaviors with the lion necessitate redemption. As Kenneth Lynn notes, "Macomber" is a "fable about the perils of self-overcoming. It is not wifely malevolence that brings Macomber down, but his own dangerous aspiration to be recognized as intensely masculine" (436). Macomber's stand against the buffalo appears more rash than courageous, and perhaps more foolish than either since no one other than Macomber is in imminent danger; in other words, no one on foot is directly behind him. The same is not true of Wilson, however. When he jumps to the side, there stands Francis—and seconds afterward, there lies Francis, dead. And even though he is not killed by the buffalo but rather by Margot's possibly "friendly fire," Francis would almost certainly have saved himself had he abandoned Wilson's flawed notion of courage and moved out of the buffalo's path.

Consequently, an examination of evidence closely related to "Macomber" leads to an exoneration of Macomber in the lion episode and a censure of his conduct with the buffalo, a reading opposite to that typically advanced—and one guaranteed to generate class discussion. The "Tanganyika Letters" also provide a means by which the class can arrive at a categorical censure of Wilson, a figure who has proven to be one of the more elusive in the Hemingway canon. In other words, in "Macomber" Hemingway condemns Wilson's "shootism"; in the "Tanganyika Letters" and elsewhere he applauds Pop Percival's "sport." In this respect, "Macomber" provides a fictional version of "the central issue of African sporting literature," as identified by Lawrence H. Martin: "It's not the number of heads, the size of the horns, or the rarity of the [prey] that counts, but the approach, the attitude, in effect the style of pursuit and capture that matter most" (93).

Works Cited

Bender, Bert. "Margot Macomber's Gimlet." *College Literature* 8.1 (Winter 1981): 12–20.

Calabi, Silvio. "Ernest Hemingway on Safari: The Game and the Guns." *Hemingway and Africa*. Ed. Miriam B. Mandel. Rochester, NY: Camden House, 2011. 85–121.

Gajdusek, Robert. *Hemingway: In His Own Country*. Notre Dame, IN: U of Notre Dame P, 2002.

Hemingway, Ernest. *By-Line: Ernest Hemingway*. Ed. William White. New York: Scribner, 2002.

———. "The Short Happy Life of Francis Macomber." *The Complete Short Stories of Ernest Hemingway: The Finca Vigía Edition*. New York: Scribner's, 1987. 5–28.

———. *Green Hills of Africa*. New York: Scribner, 1953.

———. Introduction. *Men at War: The Best War Stories of All Time*. Ed. Ernest Hemingway. New York: Crown, 1942.

———. "Notes on Dangerous Game: The Third Tanganyika Letter." *Hemingway's African Stories: The Stories, Their Sources, Their Critics*. Ed. John M. Howell. New York: Scribner, 1969. 71–73.

———. *Selected Letters: 1917–1961*. Ed. Carlos Baker. London: Granada, 1981.

———. "Shootism Versus Sport: The Second Tanganyika Letter." *Hemingway's African Stories: The Stories, Their Sources, Their Critics*. Ed. John M. Howell. New York: Scribner, 1969. 69–71.

———. *The Sun Also Rises*. New York: Scribner, 1926.

———. *True at First Light*. New York: Scribner, 1999.

Howell, John M. "McCaslin and Macomber: From *Green Hills* to *Big Woods*." *The Faulkner Journal* 2.1 (1986): 29–36.

Hutton, Virgil. "The Short Happy Life of Macomber." *The Short Stories of Ernest Hemingway: Critical Essays*. Durham, NC: Duke UP, 1975. 239–50.

Lynn, Kenneth S. *Hemingway*. New York: Simon and Schuster, 1987.

Martin, Lawrence H. "Hemingway's Constructed Africa: *Green Hills of Africa* and the Conventions of Colonial Sporting Books." *Hemingway and the Natural World*. Moscow, ID: U of Idaho P, 1999. 87–97.

Shepherd, Allen. "The Lion in the Grass (Alas?): A Note on 'The Short Happy Life of Francis Macomber.'" *Fitzgerald/Hemingway Annual 1972*. Ed. Matthew J. Bruccoli and C. E. Frazer Clark Jr. Dayton, OH: NCR, 1973. 297–99.

Twain, Mark. *Pudd'nhead Wilson* and *Those Extraordinary Twins*. New York: Gabriel Wells, 1923.

Young, Philip. "The Hero and the Code." *Hemingway's African Stories: The Stories, Their Sources, Their Critics*. Ed. John M. Howell. New York: Scribner, 1969. 116–18.

Pity and the Beasts

Teaching Hemingway's Stories via Sympathy for Animals

Ryan Hediger

At a critical juncture in Hemingway's story "The Short Happy Life of Francis Macomber," the narrative voice assumes the perspective of an injured lion. The lion, "sick" with a gunshot wound, eyes "narrowed with hate," is gathering himself for a final charge on the humans hunting him: "All of him, pain, sickness, hatred and all of his remaining strength, was tightening into an absolute concentration for a rush" (*Complete Short Stories* 16). When the lion does charge, Francis Macomber instinctively, shamefully, turns and runs, embarrassing himself, his wife, and everyone connected to the events in the story. Wilson, the hunting guide, must kill the lion as his client Macomber flees in terror, setting the scene for the Macomber's wife's betrayal and the story's ambiguous ending.

In her essay "Actually, I Felt Sorry for the Lion," Nina Baym writes of observing students scrutinizing this story in the classroom. One student sympathized with the situation of the lion, seeing the events through the lion's eyes as the story asks us to do briefly. Baym argues that a genuine reading of the story is not possible without carefully considering both the lion and, crucially, the final event, when Margot shoots Francis in the back of the head. Baym's primary concern is to show how a gender politics of reading tends to reinforce what she calls a mistaken interpretation of the end of the story; she uses the dynamics of sympathy for the lion to support her case. The present essay extends Baym's argument for a different purpose. I bring sympathy to the fore, arguing that this short story, and much Hemingway writing, powerfully renders sympathy for animals. I use the gender dynamics of the story to help illuminate this sympathy.

This chapter is oriented by two larger questions: How do our readings of Hemingway's writing change when we recognize the pity for hunted animals in them? How does a stance of sympathy affect the way we think about power relationships of many kinds? This approach is effective not only because Hemingway consistently devotes focused attention to the perspectives of nonhuman animals but because thinking about an animal's perspective can dissuade students from pat and easy readings. Once readers sympathize with animals' particularly distinctive perspectives, other perspectives—of various human characters, say—become more visible. Reading for animal sympathy, thus, draws out the complexity of the stories and underscores their quality. It is a practical and effective strategy for student readers, who often readily sympathize and even identify with animals in texts.

"The Short Happy Life of Francis Macomber"

"The Short Happy Life of Francis Macomber" presents a number of different perspectives of its events. Considering these perspectives—the lion's, Margot's, Francis's, and so on—requires careful attention to many of the fundamental elements of teaching close reading: word choice, context, and the like. Studying word choice is especially key at the end of the story, in confronting the interpretive problem the story raises. Francis, having undergone his striking change of courage and now feeling pleasure in the face of serious danger, wounds a buffalo and then begins to pursue it into the brush, thinking the animal dead. Suddenly the gun-bearer, their hunting assistant who had gone ahead to locate the presumably dead buffalo, explodes "out of the bush sidewise, fast as a crab, and the bull coming, nose out, mouth tight closed, blood dripping, massive head straight out, coming in a charge, his little pig eyes bloodshot as he looked at them" (27). The story has already taught us in the episode with the lion not to be surprised by the force of an animal in its death throes charging the hunters. In this case, though, "Macomber had stood solid and shot for the nose, shooting a touch high each time and hitting the heavy horns, splintering and chipping them like hitting a slate roof, and Mrs. Macomber, in the car, had shot at the buffalo with the 6.5 Mannlicher as it seemed about to gore Macomber and had hit her husband about two inches up and a little to one side of the base of his skull" (28).

I like to begin teaching this story by reading this passage closely with students, since it appears to answer elegantly many of the story's most crucial questions. Had Macomber truly learned courage so quickly? Yes, he had "stood solid" despite the great danger, even if his aim was "a touch high." Had Mrs. Macomber intended to kill her husband, nervous now about his newfound courage? No, she "had shot at the buffalo," aiming to save her husband before he was gored. But Wilson—the experienced hunting guide who had witnessed this set of events and recognized Macomber's sudden transformation into a brave and, in the title of the story, "happy" man—offers a radically different interpretation. Just after Francis has been shot and killed, Wilson remarks to Margot, "'That was a pretty thing to do,' he said in a toneless voice. 'He would have left you too.'" Margot responds, "Stop it" (28). Wilson goes on, "Why didn't you poison him? That's what they do in England," suggesting of course that Margot deliberately killed her husband. Readers must negotiate between these interpretations of the ending—do we believe the ostensibly objective narrator's view that Margot shot at the buffalo, or do we accept Wilson's claims?

Baym notes that many critics believe that Margot killed her husband deliberately, but Baym argues compellingly (if not definitively) that this view is wrong. For her, much of the criticism misreads the intricacies of the story. For one thing, the story has confirmed that Wilson is perhaps at least partly right in these final moments: The imperfect Macomber marriage, in light of Francis's new steadfastness, may well have ended had Francis not been shot.[1] But Wilson too is emotionally involved in complex ways that unsettle our sense of his objectivity, since he had "begun to like your husband," as he tells Margot just at the story's end (28); since he was going to be partly professionally responsible for the death under his watch, which would not be good for business; and since he had committed adultery with Margot the night before. The story has set the scene for their adultery not only with Francis's embarrassing failure of nerve, but by showing us Margot's beauty: "She was an extremely handsome and well-kept woman" (5–6). Wilson, who has clearly recognized her attractiveness, also understands Margot's intelligence: "she wasn't stupid, Wilson thought, no, not stupid" (8). These facts must affect how we read the final scene as well, arguably culminating in a negative view not of Margot but of Wilson: Baym reports, drawing from critic Kenneth Lynn, that Wilson's reason for accusing Margot of murder is "to blackmail her into keeping quiet about the illegal car chase that preceded the buffalo kill" (115). Many readers disagree with Baym's view of Margot, though. Mark Spilka, for instance, responds directly to Baym's essay, arguing that her "benevolent" view of Margot is incorrect.[2]

So, what about sympathy for animals at the close of the story? It is debatable whether Hemingway's wording at that moment shows any real sympathy for this second buffalo as it is hunted, but Hemingway at least takes time to describe the animal carefully, as quoted above. Margot, however, makes her perspective of the hunt very clear. When Francis, thrilled with his new bravery, asks her, "Wasn't it marvelous, Margot?" she answers, "I hated it." Indeed, she repeats this same line a moment later, "I hated it," adding, "I loathed it" (25). Margot then further responds to the men's discussion of the hunt, underscoring her sympathy for the hunted animals: "'You're both talking rot,' said Margot. 'Just because you've chased some helpless animals in a motor car you talk like heroes'" (26).

Why does she say this? There is no question that one purpose of the story is to show Margot's fear of her husband's change. Hemingway writes, shortly after the sentence just quoted, "She was very afraid of something" (26). Baym shows that Margot may fear her husband becoming more like Wilson, whom she regards as a brute. But Margot's sympathy for the animals being hunted also seems genuine and is consistent with sympathy expressed not only by other women in other Hemingway texts (Mary in *Under Kilimanjaro,* Catherine in *The Garden of Eden,* the American wife in "Cat in the Rain," and others) but by notably masculine figures in Hemingway's canon like Santiago, the fisherman protagonist of *The Old Man and the Sea,* or the narrator of *Green Hills of Africa*.[3] Sympathy for animals becomes especially pronounced in later Hemingway texts. Indeed, without getting too lost in the compellingly complex dynamics of sympathy and anger established in "The Short Happy Life of Francis Macomber," we must recall that Hemingway himself decided to present Margot's sympathetic statements about the animals. Critics sometimes lose sight of this basic fact as they try to pin simple sexist views on the author of the story. Reminding students of this reality—that authors often dramatize problems rather than simply editorialize about them—enriches classroom activity.

Hemingway underscores Margot's criticism of the men quoted above—that they merely chased helpless animals in a motor car—by noting their lapses in hunting etiquette. First, as they pursue the lion, Francis has difficulty forcing himself even to leave the safety of the car. Wilson says to him, "You don't shoot them from cars. . . . Get out. He's not going to stay there all day" (13). Then later, as they pursued the buffalo illegally by automobile, Francis nearly begins shooting from the car. Wilson exclaims, "Not from the car, you fool!" (22). Francis is not ruffled by the insult and simply stumbles out of the moving vehicle; he shows by his composure and his better shooting that he had in fact changed. But these episodes dramatize the masculine rite of safari hunting with no small amounts of skepticism and irony. We should ask with Margot just how much Francis has proved in this hunt.

Why have these criticisms of hunting sometimes been overlooked by readers? As noted above, a very common interpretive strategy for this story has been to reduce it to an account of the power relationship in a marriage in which a woman, seeing she was losing the upper hand, retakes control by murdering her husband. From that perspective, the interpretive procedure often revolves around a rhetoric of blame. Margot is faulted for behaving horribly first when her husband loses control of himself and then when she loses control of her husband; thus, Hemingway the author is blamed for presenting his heroine in a grossly unflattering light, reinforcing the stereotype of Hemingway as a sexist pig. If we flatten the story in this way, it becomes easy to dismiss Margot's statements about animals too, since she is ostensibly so monstrous a character, driven purely by self-interest.

Certainly that interpretation should be discussed in a full classroom treatment of the text, and indeed it is an interpretation Hemingway himself reinforced when he discussed this story as presenting a mean-spirited woman extracting her revenge. Baym is skeptical of Hemingway's summary, partly because of its timing: he made this claim to an interviewer "seventeen years after the story was published" (Baym 114). For Baym, this reductive reading reveals Hemingway to be caught in the logic of his public gender norms, effectively silencing the complexity of his own story, much as Suzanne Clark shows Hemingway's work (and Hemingway himself) to have been silenced by other political norms (59–96). Further, the fact that Hemingway so famously and so joyously engaged in hunting throughout his life can seem to reinforce the idea that he as author must have sided with the men, against Margot. But there again, a more careful understanding of Hemingway's life and work shows that he always had complex views of hunting and often had significant sympathy for the animals he hunted.[4] In other words, Hemingway's own biographical decisions about hunting and his statements about his work must also be read carefully and contextually, just as diligent readers must register the complexity of what is actually on the pages of the fiction, which lies beyond simplistic interpretations. Underscoring for students this need to interpret both life and text carefully makes for a powerful teaching moment, one that demonstrates the value of the interpretive disciplines in the humanities, and one particularly successful when instructors can mention specific examples such as those cited above.

Bearing these ideas in mind, we can hear additional resonances in "The Short Happy Life of Francis Macomber" when Francis addresses Margot, having been kept awake much of the night by the lion's frightful roaring: "'I've got to kill the damned thing,' Macomber said, miserably" (12). This statement unsettles any easy account of hunting as natural or inevitable. It suggests instead that Francis has to some extent been dragged into this hunting scenario by the norms of his time, norms of masculinity, norms of assumed human dominance over all other animals, and norms of imperialism by which Europeans and Americans believe they have a right to demonstrate their virility and power by traveling to Africa to kill the world's most dangerous animals. Hemingway famously, explicitly argues this last point in *Green Hills of Africa* (285).[5]

The lion has unsettled Francis in his new role as manly lion killer, reminding us that Francis must learn this role. Indeed, this story is largely a tale of pedagogy, of learning lion hunting, with the highest possible stakes—the threats of wrecked marriage and even death. In various ways, it registers ambivalence about this enterprise, but Francis is really never in a position to reverse course without undergoing exactly the kind of loss of dignity he experiences when he instinctively runs away from the charging lion. That scene is almost always read to show simple cowardice, but it can also be understood to reveal Hemingway's complex, inchoate views of sympathy toward animals and of the enterprise of the safari in general. The publication of *The Garden of Eden* and *Under Kilimanjaro*, with their more explicitly sophisticated ideas about hunting, gender, safari, and a great deal more, have helped many critics see more such richness even in earlier Hemingway texts, and I am arguing that we can see more in this famous story, beginning by reading its first key event differently. Francis fleeing the charging lion—viewed objectively, pressed outside the enormously powerful, automatic imputation of shame—reveals significant friction in the pedagogy of hunting norms. His running is embodied, instinctive resistance to the role of lion killer. Pausing with students to consider this situation, perhaps after playing footage of an actual lion charge (easily found on the internet), can lead to a fruitful discussion of both the terror of facing the charge and of the gender norms that govern masculine behavior in such scenarios. The fact that Francis is able to reverse course, to accept those norms quickly by the end of the story, only makes his initial failure more interesting.

The powerful descriptions of the lion's experience are crucial to demonstrating how much more is at stake in this story than who is to blame for the final moment. When Francis has been goaded out of the car by Wilson on the lion hunt, the perspective in the story undergoes its first radical change:

> Macomber stepped out of the curved opening at the side of the front seat, onto the step and down onto the ground. The lion still stood looking majestically and

coolly toward this object that his eyes only showed in silhouette, bulking like some super-rhino. There was no man smell carried toward him and he watched the object, moving his great head a little from side to side. Then watching the object, not afraid, but hesitating before going down the bank to drink with such a thing opposite him, he saw a man figure detach itself from it and he turned his heavy head and swung away toward the cover of the trees as he heard a cracking crash and felt the slam of a .30–06 220-grain solid bullet that bit his flank and ripped in sudden hot scalding nausea through his stomach. (13)

Rarely is an animal's experience of being hunted described so vividly, and pausing with students to recognize this fact is a useful close-reading task. Francis's initial reluctance to leave the car is also palpable; it is presented as parallel to the lion's caution as he tries to interpret the automobile in terms that would be familiar to a lion. When the omniscient narrator's perspective, in the second quoted sentence, migrates out of the province humanity and into that of the lion, we read that the lion sees the car as "some super-rhino." He observes it more worryingly once he recognizes the familiar "man figure," whom the lion understands as an "it," strikingly reversing the long convention of human beings understanding other animals as *its*. The lion's observation of this human thing signals danger and leads him to seek "the cover of the trees." Revealing their similarity, the lion does what Francis will soon do in facing mortal danger: seek cover. But it is too late. The lion is shot. The narrative continues to detail the lion's suffering, devoting two more long sentences to his painful experience, with "blood sudden hot and frothy in his mouth" (13).

This shift to the lion's perspective effectively builds the story's intensity and suspense, certainly, but it also presents a radically different view of Francis, of hunting, of humanity more generally. The passage quoted above moves from careful attention to the details of Francis's experiences and fears, to humanity becoming simply a smell on the wind and a shape that detaches from another mere shape vaguely resembling a rhinoceros. Humanity is radically estranged, a technique that reaches its dramatic height at the moment when Francis becomes the animal being shot, his body finally lying in death parallel to the buffalo's. Similarly, I noted that Francis and the lion are presented in parallel fashion at first, although the lion is said to lack fear. Here then, compounding the reversal showing a human being as an *it*, the lion offers an image of what Francis will become by the end of the story, once he has understood what it means to confront danger. The lion is the model of bravery.[6] Hemingway underscores how much Francis must change by noting that "Macomber had not thought how the lion felt as he got out of the car. He only knew his hands were shaking and as he walked away from the car it was almost impossible for him to make his legs move" (13). Francis is too immersed in his own personal dramas and dreads to really appreciate the full situation, and we require the narrator's interjection to see it. Emphasizing these dynamics for students illuminates how sentence-level craft can couple with a text's larger plot architecture to create robust significance.

These questions of knowledge are central to the story's dramatic tension. Wilson upbraids himself when he suddenly recognizes just how frightened Francis is: Wilson's "entire occupation had been with the lion and the problem he presented." He "had not been thinking about Macomber," but when Macomber asks why they do not simply "leave him there?"—that is, leave the injured lion behind—Wilson "suddenly felt as though he had opened the wrong door in a hotel and seen something shameful" (15). Here again is a sentence to pause upon and read carefully with students, so they better understand what is at stake. But Wilson then changes his mind about Francis when the latter apologizes. Francis admits, "There are a lot of things I don't know" about hunting and safari norms (8). Francis is learning; Wilson knows much more. About the lion's experience in particular, having watched his fight in the face of death, Hemingway writes, "Wilson knew something about it and only expressed it saying, 'Damned fine lion'" (18).

This issue—what we can know about the lion and about other animals—is a major crux in Hemingway's thinking on hunting (and in most debates about animals). When I teach Hemingway or other texts centered on animals, I make a point of mentioning this fact. Hemingway explains in *Green Hills of Africa* that he felt justified in pursing hunting activities partly because he knew what the animals on the other end of his gun experienced, having suffered a very painful wound himself (148). That statement, admirable for its honesty in facing the reality of animal suffering, also perhaps presumes more knowledge than Hemingway possesses. Further, it might seem willfully sadistic, even masochistic. Should someone embrace this kind of suffering and even impose it on others at moments when it is not necessary? One's answer to that question—yes or no—will point toward one's ethics regarding hunting and animal issues more generally.

In any event, the lion is presented in a careful and sympathetic fashion. If readers approach this story by looking for its animal sympathy, the ending grows more complex, a compelling view of its critical history emerges, as noted by Baym, and a host of other possible questions about gender norms, hunting rituals, and knowledge itself arise. The story also opens a route into discussing what scholars today call *posthumanism*, which recognizes human beings as one more animal, however powerful, in a complex biosphere.

Close Reading as Sympathetic Understanding

A larger pedagogical point underlies this chapter, one that is worth emphasizing to students in a literature or cultural studies classroom: the enterprise of closely reading fiction, since it requires exploring the perspectives of various characters, depends partly on sympathy. Indeed, writing a number of perspectives convincingly into a story itself requires sympathy from an author.[7] When we recognize sympathy as a crucial element of fiction in general and these stories in particular, beginning with its most stark and surprising example—the sympathetic treatment of the very animals being hunted and killed in the narratives—the stories become richer. Their craft comes more clearly into view, and they seem less bound by their time. More generally, this reading strategy rehabilitates the role of sympathy and the emotions in human life, which are often treated nervously in cultural criticism and are routinely dismissed under the often-vague insult of "sentimental." The emotions are a fundamental biological talent of the human animal, giving us necessary guidance, helping us determine many of our key decisions and beliefs.[8] They are essential as we find our place in the human and natural worlds, something Hemingway knew intellectually and instinctively.

Notes

1. One piece of evidence for this idea appears when Margot asks Francis about his new bravery, "Isn't it sort of late?" Francis responds, "Not for me" (26), implying that they may go separate ways. But there are other ways to read this moment.

2. See Kenneth K. Brandt and Alicia Mischa Renfroe for a recent treatment of this story; they include a brief summary of the critical debates about whether Margot killed her husband deliberately or accidentally (24, note 1).

3. The narrator of *Green Hills of Africa*, who is closely modeled on Hemingway himself, shows thoughtful sympathy for an animal he hunts on 271–72.

4. For instance, see Carey Voeller, "He Only Looked Sad the Same Way I Felt." Also, in my articles "Hunting, Fishing, and the Cramp of Ethics" and in "The Elephant in the Writing Room," I focus on sympathy in a number of Hemingway texts.

5. As I argue in "Hunting, Fishing, and the Cramp of Ethics," even this claim is more complex than it looks; Hemingway's uneasiness about the norms and impact of hunting are visible in the text.

6. Baym sees the lion in this way, as the standard of bravery, but Spilka argues that the lion is "disqualified" from that status because lions "are not natural cowards" while "men are" (197; Spilka is reporting what he understands Hemingway's view to be). More can be said on this issue than I have room for here, but a brief reply: The lion does show fear physically in the story, as noted in my discussion, and further, Wilson's compliment that this was a "damned fine lion" reveals that different lions respond differently to such events. The story itself and critics' responses to it are entangled in unresolved, competing views of animals, animals' fear, and humans—that animals are naturally all the same and more machine-like than emotional humans, for instance, an idea roundly criticized by biologists like Bekoff and De Waal.

7. Psychologists David Comer Kidd and Emanuele Castano demonstrated that spending time reading literary fiction—as distinct from popular fiction and other forms of writing—improves readers' social abilities, helping them to become more empathetic and socially perceptive.

8. For insights about the biology of emotions, see De Waal, Bekoff, and many of the other texts they cite. For the importance of the emotions in human decision making, see Dan Ariely.

Works Cited

Ariely, Dan. *Predictably Irrational: The Hidden Forces that Shape our Decisions.* New York: Harper Collins, 2008.

Baym, Nina. "Actually, I Felt Sorry for the Lion." *New Critical Approaches to the Stories of Ernest Hemingway.* Ed. Jackson J. Benson. Durham: Duke UP, 1990. 112–20.

Bekoff, Marc. *The Emotional Lives of Animals.* Novato, CA: New World Library, 2007.

Brandt, Kenneth K., and Alicia Mischa Renfroe. "Intent and Culpability: A Legal Review of the Shooting in 'The Short Happy Life of Francis Macomber.'" *The Hemingway Review* 33.2 (2014): 8–29.

Clark, Suzanne. *Cold Warriors: Manliness on Trial in the Rhetoric of the West.* Carbondale: Southern Illinois UP, 2000.

De Waal, Frans. *Primates and Philosophers: How Morality Evolved.* Princeton: Princeton UP, 2006.

Hediger, Ryan. "The Elephant in the Writing Room: Sympathy and Weakness in Hemingway's 'Masculine Text,' The Garden of Eden." *The Hemingway Review* 31.1 (Fall 2011): 79–95.

———. "Hunting, Fishing, and the Cramp of Ethics in *The Old Man and the Sea, Green Hills of Africa,* and *Under Kilimanjaro.*" *The Hemingway Review* 27.2 (2008): 35–59.

Hemingway, Ernest. "An African Story." *The Complete Short Stories of Ernest Hemingway: The Finca Vigía Edition.* New York: Scribner's, 1987. 545–54.

———. "Cat in the Rain." *The Complete Short Stories of Ernest Hemingway: The Finca Vigía Edition.* New York: Scribner's, 1987. 129–31.

———. *The Garden of Eden.* New York: Scribner, 1986.

———. *Green Hills of Africa.* New York: Scribner, 1935.

———. *The Old Man and the Sea.* New York: Scribner, 1952.

———. "The Short Happy Life of Francis Macomber." *The Complete Short Stories of Ernest Hemingway: The Finca Vigía Edition.* New York: Scribner's, 1987. 5–28.

———. *Under Kilimanjaro.* Ed. Robert W. Lewis and Robert E. Fleming. Kent, OH: Kent State UP, 2005.

Kidd, David Comer, and Emanuele Castano. "Reading Literary Fiction Improves Theory of Mind." *Science.* 18 Oct. 2013. <http://science.sciencemag.org/content/342/6156/377>.

Spilka, Mark. "Nina Baym's Benevolent Reading of the Macomber Story: An Epistolary Response." *Hemingway: Up in Michigan Perspectives.* East Lansing: Michigan State UP, 1995. 189–201.

Voeller, Carey. "'He Only Looked Sad the Same Way I Felt': The Textual Confessions of Hemingway's Hunters." *The Hemingway Review* 25.1 (Fall 2005): 63–76.

Teaching the Conflicts in "The Snows of Kilimanjaro"

Sean Milligan

Although "The Snows of Kilimanjaro" remains one of Hemingway's most popular works, it is also one of his most controversial. Even a cursory survey of the criticism of the story turns up a variety of contradictory opinions about the themes and aesthetic quality. For instance, in recent years, the story's racial politics have become a point of contention among critics. While many have identified race as one of the story's central issues, not all critics agree about what the story does with the issue of race. Amy L. Strong, for instance, sees the story as undermining racism and colonialism. Marc K. Dudley, however, sees the story as reinforcing racist stereotypes. Another point of disagreement for critics, especially critics in the early to mid-twentieth century, is the story's natural symbolism. As Oliver Evans points out in his 1961 essay, "'The Snows of Kilimanjaro': A Revaluation," "Even critics who have praised the story without reservation have differed widely in their interpretation of it.... The fact is that no other story of Hemingway's has caused quite so much critical controversy, and the main reason for this is disagreement on the meaning of the symbols" (601). At first, these various controversies may seem problematic to anyone teaching "Snows." Novice instructors, in particular, may find it intimidating to address some of these issues (especially sensitive issues, like race) in the classroom. However, there is a way in which the critical controversies surrounding the story can be an asset when presenting the story to students.

In a day and age when what gets said and what gets read on college campuses is under extreme scrutiny, it is important that teachers are aware of how to present texts like "Snows" to their students. The question of whether or not a problematic text like "Snows" should be anthologized and taught is beyond the scope of this essay. Instead, the question I would like to pursue here is: how should we teach a text that is as problematic as "Snows" in a contemporary context? The answer, I believe, is found in Gerald Graff's theory of teaching the conflicts. Much like *The Adventures of Huckleberry Finn,* another problematic literary text that Graff has devoted significant attention to, "Snows" is ideal for "teaching the conflicts" because of the controversies and disagreements within the criticism surrounding it.

Despite the fact that teaching the conflicts is an excellent way of presenting problematic texts to students, it can be a difficult method to implement in the classroom. Even Graff has acknowledged that his work leaves many teachers curious about concrete techniques for teaching the conflicts. In the foreword to David Richter's anthology *Falling Into Theory,* Graff himself poses the question, "Just what does 'teaching the conflicts' mean, especially when it comes down to what an instructor actually does on an actual Monday morning in a roomful of actual undergraduates?" (v). This method can be especially problematic because, as Elaine Showalter notes in *Teaching Literature,* teaching the conflicts is an inherently combative pedagogical approach and, "without a clear purpose, teaching the conflicts may leave students feeling battered" (32). It is my goal with this essay to offer "a clear purpose" for teaching the conflicts in Hemingway's "The Snows of Kilimanjaro." I will begin by presenting an overview of Graff's theory, explore the different critical controversies surrounding the story, and provide some concrete techniques for presenting these controversies in the classroom.

Graff first articulates his model for teaching the conflicts in his 1992 book *Beyond the Culture Wars.* To illustrate the type of conflict that Graff believes students should be exposed to, he frames a hypothetical debate between a young female professor and an older male professor over their different interpretations of Matthew Arnold's "Dover Beach." The older male professor makes claims such as "'Dover Beach' is one of the great masterpieces of the Western tradition," while the younger female professor makes assertions like "we should teach ["Dover Beach"] as the example of phallocentric discourse that it is" (38). Graff believes that this dialogue illustrates conversations that are played out behind the scenes on college campuses on a daily basis. Graff argues that it would benefit students to have these disagreements played out in the classroom, not behind the scenes. Graff recommends a number of ways of doing this, including staging debates between students, inviting guest speakers into classrooms, and introducing students to literary criticism.

While exposing students to literary criticism would seem to be the most straightforward way of teaching the conflicts in English classes, many college instructors are reluctant to do so. Graff, however, believes that these instructors are doing their students a disservice. In *Beyond the Culture Wars*, Graff discusses the effect that reading criticism had on his own education. Graff tells the story of his experience as a young English major at the University of Chicago. Unlike many English majors, Graff claims that he did not grow up loving books and that he only became interested in literature after a course introduced him to the critical debate surrounding the ending of *Huckleberry Finn*. Graff writes,

> It was through exposure to such critical reading and discussion over a period of time that I came to catch the literary bug, eventually choosing the vocation of teaching. This was not the way it is supposed to happen. In the standard story of academic vocation that we like to tell ourselves, the germ is first planted by an early experience of literature itself.... The standard story ascribes innocence to the primary experience of literature and sees the secondary experience of professional criticism as corrupting. In my case, however, things had evidently worked the other way around: I had to be corrupted first in order to experience innocence. (69–70)

Throughout his work, Graff is critical of the romanticized notion that students, early in their educational careers, should only be exposed to "literature itself" without engaging criticism and theory. For instance, in his essay "Organizing the Conflicts in the Curriculum," Graff gets at the tendency among many college teachers to shield younger undergraduate students from literary criticism in order to keep the experience of "literature itself" pure and not overwhelm students with complex theories and interpretations. Graff writes, "Some teachers actually discourage undergraduates from reading criticism and they certainly discourage them from reading literary theory, on the ground that criticism and theory can only distract students from literature itself" (65). But what if students find themselves overwhelmed or confused by the literary text? Wouldn't exposing them to literary criticism be a way to help students understand a work and articulate their own responses to it? After all, as Graff points out, when we ask students to write essays or even contribute to class discussions, literary criticism is exactly what we are asking them to do (65). So why not expose students to criticism as early as possible?

Reading criticism not only helps students to better understand and appreciate the literary works that they read; it helps them to master the type of academic discourse that they are required to utilize throughout their college careers. Graff writes, "Students need to master academic discourse not only in order to make their way through the university, and not only in order to get ahead in an information-oriented culture which increasingly rewards those who can use analytic and argumentative forms of speaking; they also need to master academic discourse to become more critical as thinkers and more reflective as citizens" ("Organizing the Conflicts" 65). Of course, teaching the conflicts is not the only way to introduce students to the rhetorical skills they will need in college. But, throughout his work, Graff makes a compelling case for why this methodology should be adopted by teachers. The question becomes how does one utilize this approach in the classroom?

In what follows, I will focus on the critical controversies surrounding "Snows" and discuss some of the works of literary criticism that teachers could utilize in the classroom. In particular, I will focus on two critical controversies: the disagreements over the story's natural symbolism and the issue of race. I am not going to provide my own analysis of the story, and I will avoid making any kind of commentary on the arguments made by these critics. Instead, I want to attempt to put the critics into dialogue with one another and then show how they can be presented in the classroom.

In the 1961 essay "'The Snows of Kilimanjaro': A Revaluation," Oliver Evans summarizes many of the critical opinions of the symbolism in "Snows," and this essay is a good place to begin for any instructor interested in teaching the conflicts surrounding the natural symbolism in the story. As I discuss in more detail below, it is also a good piece to bring into the classroom, as it is fairly short and relatively free of jargon. In the article, Evans presents a rather comprehensive discussion of the critical reactions to the story from over a quarter century of criticism.

Evans first considers the opinions of New Critics who see the natural symbolism in "Snows" as one of the story's shortcomings. In particular, Evans cites Ray B. West, and Caroline Gordon and Allen Tate. West considers "Snows" to be one of Hemingway's best stories. Nevertheless, he writes that the story is "spoiled for me by the conventionality of its leading symbol: the White-capped mountain as the 'House of God'" (131–32). In their short story anthology *The House of Fiction*, Gordon and Tate are even more critical of "Snows" and argue, "The symbolism seems something the writer has tacked on, rather than an integral part of the story" and that, "the story itself lacks tonal and symbolic unity" (421–22).

In contrast to these critics, Evans also cites critics who see the natural symbolism as one of the story's strengths. E. W. Tedlock, for instance, argues that the symbols are "perfectly . . . integrated with the story" (item 7). Carlos

Baker, who is in agreement with Tedlock, writes that the natural symbols in the story "have been very carefully selected so as to be in complete psychological conformity with the locale and the dramatic situation" (193). As with any arguable issue, there are more than just two sides. The middle ground in this conflict is articulated by Marion Montgomery in her essay "The Leopard and the Hyena: Symbol and Meaning in 'The Snows of Kilimanjaro.'" Montgomery argues that while Hemingway's use of the hyena as a symbol is "extremely skillful," he does not make "efficient use of the leopard and the mountain" (149).

One way to foreground this controversy in the classroom, as it is presented in Evans' article, would be to have students map the critical disagreements using a synthesis tree. Essentially, a synthesis tree is a diagram (resembling a family tree) that represents the various schools of thought on a given controversy. Students would start by reading Evans' article. (The article could be presented to students before they come to class. However, it is short enough that students should not have a problem reading it during class.) In class, the instructor would discuss the article with students and help them to identify the points of agreement and disagreement among the authors. Student would then, individually or in groups, create a synthesis tree that groups the critics Evans cites based on their similarities and differences. At the top of the diagram, students should put the question, "Is Hemingway's use of symbolism in 'The Snows of Kilimanjaro' effective?" From there, each branch of the synthesis tree would group authors based on their answer to this question (West would be grouped with Gordon and Tate, Baker with Tedlock, etc.). On each branch, students would identify the authors and summarize the authors' critical evaluation of the story. If teaching in a computer lab (or if students bring laptops to class), this assignment could be done using the free Family Tree template on Prezi. If access to technology is an issue, students could simply draw out a family tree using pencil and paper. After completing the synthesis tree, students would write a short essay in which they articulate their own response to this question, citing both Hemingway's story and Evans' article. (A more formal write-up of this assignment is available in the appendix.)

One advantage of this assignment is that students may find it more interesting than a typical article summary or writing prompt. More importantly, it should help students to begin to articulate their own opinion on this controversy. When I teach research and argumentative writing, I often have students complete synthesis trees in order to understand the intricacies of the topic they are writing about. Grouping critics in this way will help students to understand the way that critics relate to one another within an academic conversation. A more advanced version of this assignment could have students complete the synthesis tree by conducting their own research to find the sources that Evans cites.

Another good way to use this conflict to teach the story would be to bring in the sources that Evans cites and have students respond to these essays. For instance, instructors could present Gordon and Tate's commentary to the students along with Tedlock's article and then simply pose a question such as, "Does the symbolism weaken the story, as Gordon and Tate assert, or is the symbolism one of the story's strengths, as Tedlock claims?" This is, admittedly, reductive, but as Graff points out in *Beyond the Culture Wars,* "In teaching, one often has to start out with a reduction in order to go anywhere beyond" (58). Students would then be given time to articulate their own opinions in response to the critics. When asked to respond to the critics, students should demonstrate that they understand the different critical perspectives and argue for their own responses. This could take a number of forms. Students could be required to write a rebuttal essay in response to one or the other of the articles after reading them. Students could also be divided into small groups to discuss the merits of the critics' arguments. Students should then share their responses with the whole class. After this, students could read Montgomery's essay (in part or in whole) in order to understand that a critical response can also fall somewhere in the middle. Some of these sources are quite dated and are not as accessible as Evans' essay, so using this method would require more research on the instructor's part ahead of time.

In recent years, criticism of "Snows" has shifted from an emphasis on the story's aesthetic qualities to an emphasis on the story's cultural politics. Yet, despite this shift, critics still remain divided in their interpretations of the work. Obviously, it can be more difficult to address political issues, such as race, than aesthetic questions in the classroom. However, because of the difficulties inherent in these sensitive topics, I would argue that it is even more important to introduce students to criticism that deals with these issues.

One critic who could be particularly helpful in the classroom is Amy L. Strong, who, in her book *Race and Identity in Hemingway's Fiction,* presents an interesting and nuanced analysis of the racial themes in "Snows." Strong writes, "The opening epigraph, the story's title, the 'boys' who tend to Harry and Helen, and the final dream flight to the top of the mountain all raise issues of capitalism, colonialism, and the destructive power of white privilege" (72). In a chapter dedicated to Hemingway's African stories, Strong argues that "Snows," "functions as a critique of the capitalist, colonialist mindset" (74). Strong admits that the story initially seems to offer us white characters that have no real "connection to the country where they have been set" (72). But, for Strong, it is the way that Harry approaches Africa that leads to his demise. She writes, "Harry has traded his old life for an embrace of white privilege and power at the expense of nonwhites" (78). Ultimately, Strong sees "Snows" critiquing the white privilege that Harry enjoys.

An interesting piece to put into dialogue with Strong is Marc K. Dudley's discussion of Hemingway's African stories in his book *Hemingway, Race, and Art: Bloodlines and the Color Line*. Dudley sees Hemingway's treatment of race in his early stories as a "progressive aesthetic exercise." However, he sees the African stories, including "Snows," as "a regression of sorts" (112). For Dudley, "The Indian stories and the African American-centered works all demonstrate an intention to forge racial difference and establish Anglo primacy where, the author eventually shows us, there is actually none.... However, the early African writings show us something slightly different" (114). What we find in the African stories, including "Snows," is a reinforcement, rather than subversion, of racial stereotypes.

There are, of course, a number of ways that these works can be presented to students. For instance, students could be asked to consider their own reactions to the representation of the African characters in "Snows." Then, students can read the portions of Strong and Dudley's books that deal with the story. (Both Strong and Dudley deal with other stories in their chapters addressing "Snows." So, unless engaged in a survey of Hemingway's work, it would probably be best to pull excerpts from these chapters.) Students can then reassess their opinions of the story to see if either of these arguments has changed their opinion of the treatment of race in this story.

Another, more recent, work of criticism that deals with cultural politics is Samuli Helama's short piece titled "Ernest Hemingway's Description of the Mountaintop in 'The Snows of Kilimanjaro' and Climate Change Research." In the essay, Helama shows how climate change activists have used Hemingway's description of Kilimanjaro in the story. Although Helama is more concerned with the rhetorical uses to which Hemingway's central symbol has been put, this piece could be very interesting to use in a teaching the conflicts lesson as it foregrounds a controversial issue that, unlike the debate about the story's symbolism, has a direct impact on students' lives.

While it would be best to bring in some of these articles to read with the students, not all of the essays and commentaries mentioned above would be useful in a classroom discussion. Baker and West, for instance, both discuss Hemingway's work beyond just "Snows," so these texts would not be very useful, unless you are engaged in a survey of Hemingway's work as a whole. Dudley also discusses "Snows" alongside *Green Hills of Africa* and "The Short Happy Life of Francis Macomber." Students who have not read these other stories may find themselves confused by the chapter (especially considering the fact that most of the chapter deals with *Green Hills*). However, it may also be a good way to show students how "Snows" demonstrates concerns that recur throughout Hemingway's work.

One of the things that students should take away from these types of activities and discussions is the fact that meaning is indeterminate. When we interpret literature, there will never be a right or wrong answer. However, in reading the criticism, students will discover that while literary texts are open to interpretation, one must be able to argue convincingly for any given interpretation. For some students, especially those who did not particularly enjoy the experience of reading the story (and there will be those students), it may be exhilarating to discover that not all literary professionals agree about the merits of a work, even one that has achieved canonical status. Even if students do not respond to criticism the same way that Graff did, they may nevertheless find themselves more engaged by the class material than they were before. When students see that even professionals do not always agree, it may give them the courage to articulate their own responses. It also benefits students to see academics engaged in a dialogue that requires both interpretation and argumentation. If they do, students will have a better chance of developing these skills themselves.

Works Cited

Baker, Carlos. *Hemingway: The Writer as Artist*. Princeton: Princeton UP, 1963.
Dudley, Marc K. *Hemingway, Race, and Art: Bloodlines and the Color Line*. Kent, OH: Kent State UP, 2012.
Evans, Oliver. "'The Snows of Kilimanjaro': A Revaluation." *PMLA* 76.5 (1961): 601–7.
Gordon, Caroline, and Allen Tate. *The House of Fiction: An Anthology of the Short Story with Commentary*. New York: Charles Scribner's Sons, 1950.
Graff, Gerald. *Beyond the Culture Wars: How Teaching the Conflicts Can Revitalize American Education*. New York: Norton, 1992.
———. Foreword. *Falling into Theory: Conflicting Views on Reading Literature*. Ed. David Richter. Boston: Bedford Books, 1994. v–vi.
———. "Organizing the Conflicts in the Curriculum." *The Journal of the Midwest Modern Language Association* 25.1 (1992): 63–76.
Helama, Samuli. "Ernest Hemingway's Description of the Mountaintop in 'The Snows of Kilimanjaro' and Climate Change Research." *The Hemingway Review* 34.2 (2015): 118–23.

Hemingway, Ernest. "The Snows of Kilimanjaro." *The Complete Short Stories of Ernest Hemingway: The Finca Vigía Edition*. New York: Scribner's, 1998.

Montgomery, Marion. "The Leopard and the Hyena: Symbol and Meaning in 'The Snows of Kilimanjaro.'" *Hemingway's African Stories: The Stories, Their Sources, Their Critics*. New York: Charles Scribner's Sons, 1969. 145–49.

Showalter, Elaine. *Teaching Literature*. Malden, MA: Blackwell Publishing, 2003.

Strong, Amy L. *Race and Identity in Hemingway's Fiction*. New York: Palgrave MacMillan, 2008.

Tedlock, E. W. "Hemingway's 'The Snows of Kilimanjaro.'" *The Explicator* 8 (1949): item 7.

West, Ray B. "Ernest Hemingway: The Failure of Sensibility." *The Sewanee Review* 53.1 (1945): 120–35.

Part Four

Europe

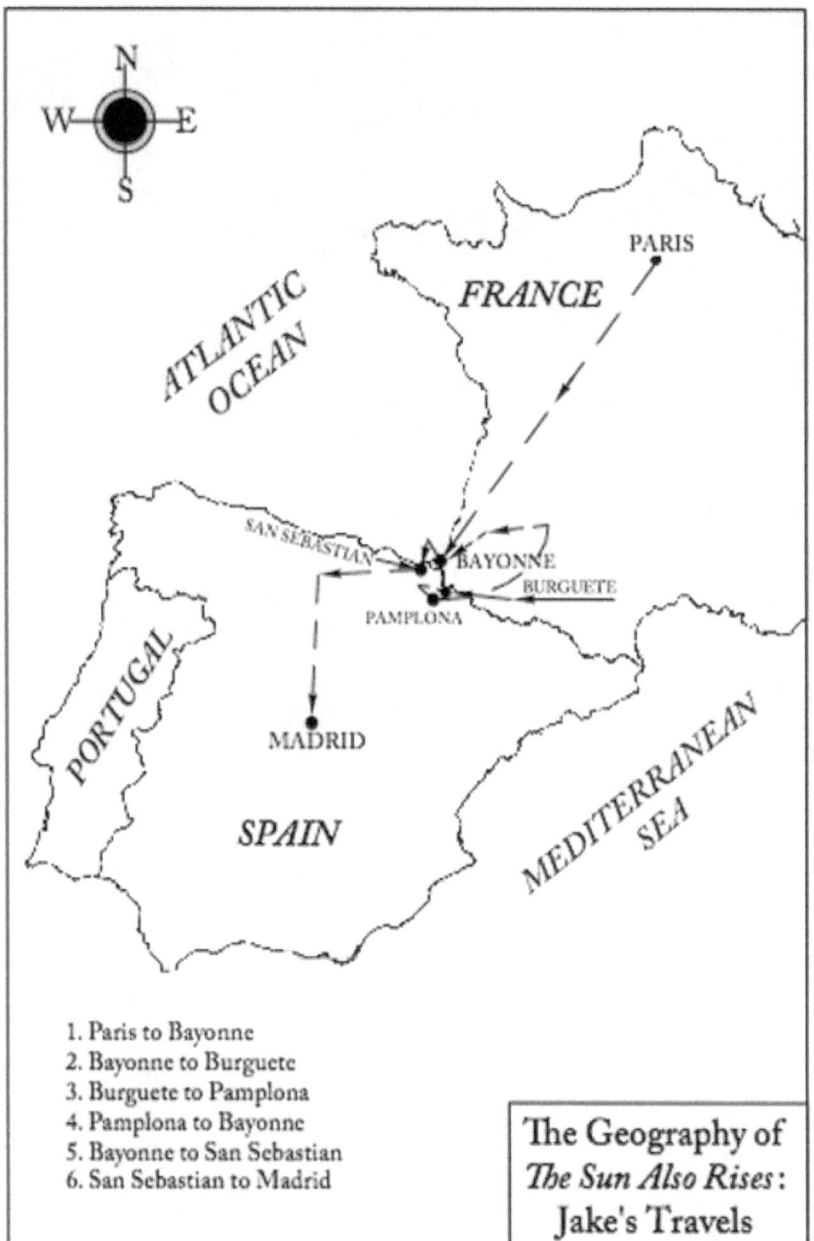

"I Hated to Leave France"

The Geography and Terrain of Hemingway's *The Sun Also Rises*

Donald A. Daiker

> "His prose was wonderfully rooted in geography and linear movement."
> —Paul Hendrickson, *Hemingway's Boat: Everything He Loved in Life, and Lost, 1934–1961*

The physical geography of *The Sun Also Rises* is clear and straightforward. Readers can easily follow the travels of the novel's narrator and protagonist Jake Barnes through two countries—France and Spain—and six major locations: Paris and Bayonne in France; and Burguete, Pamplona, San Sebastian, and Madrid in Spain.

Jake and his good friend Bill Gorton travel by train from Paris to Bayonne, where they spend a night before traveling by car with Robert Cohn across the Spanish frontier to Pamplona. After a night there, Jake and Bill travel by bus to the remote Spanish village of Burguete for several relaxing days of fishing. They return to Pamplona for a fiesta week with Robert, Lady Brett Ashley, and Brett's fiancé Mike Campbell. When the fiesta ends, Jake goes by car to Burguete and then by train to San Sebastian, spending a night alone in each location before traveling by himself to Madrid, where Brett has gone off with the bullfighter Pedro Romero. As the novel ends, Jake has arranged to travel back to San Sebastian by train with Brett. Jake's physical travels seem straightforward and clear.

But the emotional geography of Jake's travels—and of the novel as a whole—is more complex and, at least at first, more problematic. What may initially seem especially problematic is Jake's decision to travel from Bayonne to San

Sebastian in the novel's concluding chapter. On the day after the fiesta in Pamplona ends, one day after Brett had left for Madrid with Romero, Jake bids good-bye to Mike Campbell, who will be staying at the coastal French village of Saint Jean de Luz, and then to Bill Gorton, who is headed back to Paris by train. Jake himself decides to spend the night in Bayonne, the "nice town" (90) where he had earlier stayed with Bill and Robert.

But the next morning Jake leaves Bayonne, France, for San Sebastian, Spain—and it is this decision that initially seems hard to explain. In fact, Jake has a difficult time justifying it to himself. When he arrives at Irun, the Spanish border town where he has to change trains and show passports, he seems on the verge of changing his mind: "I hated to leave France," Jake says. "I felt I was a fool to be going back into Spain." He even repeats that reluctance a sentence later: "I felt like a fool to be going back into it" (233). So the question becomes, what is the motivation and significance of Jake's hesitant return to Spain?

The explanation of Jake's ambivalence lies in the clearly established contrasts between France and Spain in the novel's concluding chapter. Because Jake stays not only in the same Bayonne hotel but even in the same room he had earlier occupied, he feels at home there. For Jake, Bayonne emanates "a safe, suburban feeling" (232)—a sense of familiarity reinforced when he buys and reads a copy of the *New York Herald*, the American newspaper with a Paris bureau on the Avenue de l'Opéra with a "window full of clocks" (15). The clocks point to the predictability and rationality of life in France, "a country where it is so simple to make people happy" (233). In France, you can make a waiter "happy" by simply overtipping him. By contrast, "you can never tell whether a Spanish waiter will thank you." Because "everything is on such a clear financial basis," France is "the simplest country to live in." In France "no one makes things complicated by becoming your friend for any obscure reason" (233), but in Spain Jake's friendship with the innkeeper Montoya is based not on the simplicity of finances but on something both more complicated and more obscure: their shared *afición* for bullfighting.

At first it seems that San Sebastian may be little different from Bayonne, a French town that is nevertheless "like a very clean Spanish town" and whose cathedral is "like Spanish churches" (90). In Bayonne "they were sprinkling the streets of the town" (90) just as the streets of San Sebastian "feel as though they had just been sprinkled" (234). Each locale evokes from Jake a sense of morning freshness: Bayonne "had a cool, fresh, early-morning smell" (91) and "San Sebastian has a certain early-morning quality" (234). As H. R. Stoneback observes, San Sebastian is "the least Spanish of Spain's resorts" (276). And when in Bayonne Jake anticipates enjoying himself in San Sebastian, it seems that it, too, is safe and suburban:

> It would be quiet in San Sebastian. The season does not open there until August. I could get a good hotel room and read and swim. There was a fine beach there. There were wonderful trees along the promenade above the beach, and there were many children sent down with their nurses before the season opened. In the evening there would be band concerts under the trees across from the Café Marinas. I could sit in the Marinas and listen. (232)

But Stoneback misses the point when he insists that San Sebastian is "exactly the same" (276) as Bayonne. If it were, there is no reason why Jake would hate to leave France and feel such a fool in doing so.

San Sebastian may be physically similar to Burguete but, for Jake, the two venues carry vastly different associations. Bayonne for Jake means a "nice hotel" with a "cheerful" staff and a cathedral that is "nice and dim" (89–90). But San Sebastian means much more: San Sebastian is the place where Lady Brett, the woman Jake desperately loves, has slept with Robert Cohn. Jake knows that the reason Brett had left Paris for San Sebastian was the recurring frustration of their relationship. "I'm going away from you," Brett had frankly told Jake after their most recent attempt at physical intimacy in the bedroom of Jake's Paris apartment had failed. "Better for you. Better for me" (55), she had explained. Brett had sent Jake a casual postcard from San Sebastian, but only after she returns does she reveal that she had lived there with Robert Cohn. That revelation so pains Jake that, for the only time in the novel, he responds to her with angry sarcasm. "Congratulations," he says to Brett. When Brett tries to rationalize her behavior by saying, "I rather thought it would be good for him," Jake's sarcasm—which Brett rightly considers "nasty"—continues: "You might take up social service" (83–84), he suggests.

But San Sebastian contrasts with Bayonne not simply because it has been the setting of Brett's tryst with Jake's rival. San Sebastian is different for Jake precisely because it *is* located in Spain, a country that Jake now understandably associates with pain and defeat. It was in Pamplona, Spain, that, against his best judgment and in violation of his highest moral standards, Jake reluctantly but willingly brought Lady Brett Ashley to Pedro Romero so that the two could go to bed together. His pandering—Robert Cohn is absolutely right in labeling Jake a "pimp" (190)—causes Jake to feel dirty. It is immediately after reproving Cohn—"You called me a pimp," Jake later complains—that Jake first voices his need for cleansing: "I wanted a hot bath. I wanted a hot bath in deep water" (194). Neither Cohn's retraction of his accusation nor his sincere apology to Jake—"Please don't remember it. I was crazy" (194)—is enough to take away Jake's sense of dirtiness. But when Jake finally locates the hotel bathroom and its deep stone tub, he turns the taps only to find that "the water would not run" (195). It is this dirty feeling[1] that Jake now consciously connects with Spain. When he arrived at his Bayonne hotel the day after the fiesta, he noticed that his "car was powdered with dust. I rubbed the rod-case through the dust. It seemed the last thing that connected me with Spain and the fiesta" (232).

In Spain, the woman that Jake has loved "off and on for a hell of a long time" (123) has lived with Robert Cohn and, thanks to Jake himself, begun a sexual liaison with Pedro Romero, which Jake knows to be wrong. Little wonder that Jake feels foolish to be returning to a country so clearly identified with his defeat, humiliation, and guilt. So why does he do it? Why does Jake return to Spain? "I felt like a fool to be going back into it, but I stood in line with my passport, opened my bags for the customs, bought a ticket, went through a gate, climbed onto the train, and after forty minutes and eight tunnels I was at San Sebastian" (233–34). The major reason Jakes goes "back into it" is that he expects to hear from Brett again—and sooner rather than later. Indeed, in twice calling himself a "fool" for returning to Spain, Jake is echoing Brett's earlier explanation—"I was a fool" (75)—for leaving Paris. Brett, who has "had affairs with men before" and even "gone off with men" (143), had hinted that her dalliance with Romero might be short-lived when she originally pleaded for Jake's help: "Oh, darling, please stay by me. Please stay by me and see me through this" (184). In asking Jake to "see me *through* this," Brett suggests that her affair with Romero may not last long, that she expects to be through or over it soon.

And sure enough, within two days of his forty-minute, eight-tunnel trip to San Sebastian, Jake receives two identically worded telegrams[2] from Lady Ashley: "COULD YOU COME HOTEL MONTANA MADRID AM RATHER IN TROUBLE BRETT" (238–39). Jake is not surprised. "I suppose, vaguely, I had expected something of the sort" (239), he says. Because he has anticipated Brett's call for help,[3] he knows exactly what to do. He immediately asks the concierge to get him a berth on the Sud Express that will leave from San Sebastian for Madrid that very evening.[4]

It is precisely because Jake has anticipated Brett's call for help that he had left safe, suburban France for the country where "you could not tell about anything" (233). In moving from the simplicity and safety of France to the complexity and danger of Spain, Jake is emulating the behavior of Pedro Romero and moving closer to "the terrain of the bull": "In bull-fighting they speak of the terrain of the bull and the terrain of the bull-fighter. As long as a bull-fighter stays in his own terrain he is comparatively safe. Each time he enters into the terrain of the bull he is in great danger" (213). Pedro Romero has "the greatness" (216) because, unlike his rivals Belmonte and Marcial, he works always in the terrain of the bull. Whereas other bullfighters use "tricks . . . to make it look as though they were working closely," Romero "always quietly and calmly let the horns pass him close each time. He did not have to emphasize their closeness" (167–68). On the last day of the fiesta, although in sharp pain from Cohn's beating, Romero worked so close to the bull that the bull's horns ripped his shirt out from under his sleeve and the two "were one" (218).

Of course San Sebastian with its children and nurses is certainly not the terrain of the bull. But it is closer to that dangerous terrain than either Bayonne or Burguete—and that is precisely the point. Hemingway has carefully structured his novel about its alternating geographies:

Alternating Geographies in The Sun Also Rises

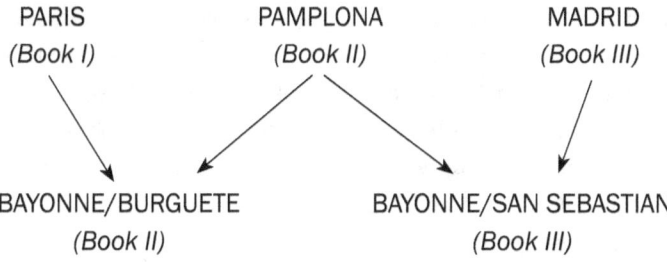

What the upper-level locations—Paris, Pamplona, and Madrid—have in common is that they are areas of tension and conflict for Jake Barnes because of the presence of Lady Brett Ashley, the woman he loves but cannot have. In the lower-level locations—Bayonne, Burguete, and San Sebastian—life is relatively tranquil and serene for Jake because Lady Ashley is not there. In Burguete, for example, Jake sleeps well, waking "only once in the night" (111), a sharp contrast to his customary night in Paris "when you could not sleep" (30).

Like Mark Twain's *Adventures of Huckleberry Finn*, the novel that according to Hemingway "All modern American literature comes from" (*Green Hills of Africa* 22), *The Sun Also Rises* lends itself to classroom teaching that focuses on contrast. For example, the novel's opening chapter contrasts the physical prowess of Robert Cohn, once middleweight boxing champion at Princeton, with his emotional subservience in allowing others, especially women, to dominate him. Frances "evidently . . . led him quite a life" (7), Jake observes. If asked to point other early contrasts, students might recognize differences in the novel's two epigraphs, one from Gertrude Stein focused on a single generation, the other from *Ecclesiastes* on all generations; in Jake's casual treatment of the prostitute Georgette and his deference to Lady Brett; in the happiness of Count Mippipopolous versus the despair of Georgette, Harvey Stone, and Frances Clyne; and, above all, in Jake's self-knowledge, sense of humor, and wisdom versus Cohn's naïveté and immaturity. These contrasts prepare students for the even more important contrasts to be introduced in Book II through the fiesta and the bull fighting of Pedro Romero and in Book III, notably through echo scenes in bedrooms, bars, and taxicabs.

Because of Brett's presence, Paris, Pamplona, and Madrid represent the terrain of the bull for Jake. They are places of risk and danger where he can be emotionally hurt—and perhaps destroyed—by Brett, the bull in his life.[5] Just as Robert Cohn is identified as the steer when Michael says, "I would have thought you'd loved being a steer, Robert," (141), so Brett becomes the bull in the novel's taurine typology when, following a scene in the bull ring where a steer trots along with a bull, Michael asks, "*Is* Robert Cohn going to follow Brett around like a steer all the time?" (141; original emphasis). Brett represents the powerful, menacing, and potentially destructive force of the bull for men like Robert, Michael, and Jake who allow themselves to be controlled by their desire for her.

In the novel's opening two chapters, before Brett arrives on the scene, Jake's life in Paris seems tranquil enough. It at first appears that his most serious problem lies in humoring his friend Robert Cohn, who—convinced that life is passing him by—urges Jake to travel to South America with him. Jake genuinely enjoys his work as a journalist—he is the Paris bureau chief for a North American newspaper—and his evenings seem dull rather than tense. On a characteristic evening he sits at an outdoor café as dusk falls, watching the crowds pass and the traffic signals change. He picks up a prostitute and treats her to dinner not because he is "getting damned romantic," as Brett suggests, but rather because he is "bored" (23). But once Brett reenters Jake's life, boredom ends and his troubles emerge: he has long loved Brett, who says she loves him in return, but a serious sexual wounding in the war—apparently his penis has been shot off—prevents Brett from marrying or even living with Jake. Although Jake tries to "play it [his injury] along and just not make trouble for people" (31), his meetings with Brett invariably lead to tears, sleepless nights, feeling "like hell again" (34), and "a bad time." Brett successfully parries even the most modest of Jake's attempts to be with her: "Couldn't we go off in the country for a while?" he pleads. No, "Not with my own true love," she answers (55). Brett's last words to Jake before she leaves Paris for San Sebastian with Robert Cohn are, significantly, "Oh, don't!" (65).

Once Brett is gone, Paris is no longer the terrain of the bull for Jake, and he is no longer in emotional danger. He passes time safely and pleasantly by working—he spends extra time at the office readying it for his departure—going to the races, dining with friends, and welcoming his best friend, Bill Gorton. But when Jake and Bill arrive in Pamplona after a lovely week of hiking, fishing, and camaraderie in Burguete, they are reunited with Robert, Michael, and of course Brett—and Jake has once again approached the terrain of the bull. It is a dangerous time for Jake, as the pervasive military imagery suggests. Their first meal together, Jake says, is "like certain dinners I remember from the war" (146). When the fiesta "exploded" (152), war images multiply: the café becomes a "battleship stripped for action," and the air is filled with bursting rockets, bright flashes, and a "ball of smoke [that] hung in the sky like a shrapnel burst" (153). Just as bulls become dangerous only when they are separated from the herd—"They only want to kill when they're alone," Jake explains (141)—so Brett becomes especially dangerous for Jake when she detaches herself from their friends. It is at this point—when Brett explodes at Robert, "For God's sake, go off somewhere. Can't you see Jake and I want to talk?" (181)—that Jake is most vulnerable, that he most clearly resides within the terrain of the bull. When Brett first asks, "Do you still love me, Jake" (183), and then, after Jake repeatedly resists her entreaties to bring her to Romero, pleads, "Oh, darling, please stay by me. Please stay by me and see me through this" (184), Jake consents to do what he knows is dreadfully wrong. Although he has told Brett, "You oughtn't to do it" six different times in six different ways and although he later agrees with Mike that Brett's going off with Romero was a "Bad thing to do. . . . She shouldn't have done it" (223), he finally cannot withstand her forceful and repeated charges. But his bringing Brett to Romero makes him feel immediately dirty—as the objective correlative "a waiter came with a cloth and picked up the glasses and mopped off the table" (187) suggests. Later, feeling "like hell," Jake tries to get over his "damn depression" by drinking glass after glass of potent absinthe and becoming "drunker than I ever remembered having been." That Jake tries to drink himself into oblivion even though he knows "it won't do any good" (223) is a sign both that he has become disgusted with himself and confirmation that, according to his own standards, he has acted immorally. "Immorality," he had earlier reflected, is defined by acts "that made you disgusted afterward" (149).[6] The scene—and the fiesta—ends with a casualty report reflecting his profound sense of loss: Jake, Bill, and Mike "sat at the table, and it seemed as though about six people were missing" (224).

In stark contrast to Jake's defeats and drunkenness in Paris and Pamplona stands his idyllic week with Bill Gorton in the more natural world of Burguete—far from the terrain of the bull. Jake and Bill enjoy their bus ride with friendly Basque peasants, their fishing trip to the Irati River, their friendship and moderate drinking with the vacationing Englishman Harris, and—best of all—each other's nonthreatening, noncompetitive company. When Jake tells Bill that the fish he has caught are "all about the size of your smallest," Bill—accustomed to Jake's reticence in competitive matters—replies with friendly skepticism, "You're not holding out on me?" (120). Not only is Brett not present in Burguete but for several days there is "no word from Robert Cohn nor from Brett and Mike" (125). There are no bulls to be seen anywhere in Burguete, neither the metaphorical nor the literal kind, only tame, harmless animals: "two donkeys that were sleeping in the road," "white cattle grazing in the forest," and playful goats that watch Jake dig for worms (93). Burguete is not only safe and suburban like Bayonne but simple and domestic as well. There are "no side-streets" here, and "families sitting in their doorways" (109) watch Jake and Bill walk from their bus to the only inn in town.

Only one tense moment briefly disturbs the tranquility of Jake's Burguete interlude. It occurs when Bill asks whether Jake has ever been in love with Brett. Jake answers with a tight-lipped "sure" (123), hoping to end the conversation there, but Bill persists with questions about Brett until Jake says, "I'd a hell of a lot rather not talk about it." That Jake swears in four consecutive responses—swearing is unusual for Jake[7]—is one reason why Bill thinks that asking about Brett may have made Jake "sore." So, good friend that he is, Bill first changes the subject to Jake's Catholicism and then closes the conversation with light, self-directed irony: "Don't keep me awake by talking so much" (124). But Jake's barely checked anger over Brett even in pastoral Burguete, far from the terrain of the bull, anticipates his more serious loss of control in Pamplona—initially in his becoming "very drunk" (147) on his first night there with Brett and later, with far more painful consequences for himself, Cohn, Mike, Romero, and Brett, when he asks her, "What do you want me to do?" (184), knowing that whenever she calls him "Darling" and pleads for help he will do whatever she commands, even if that means betraying his friends, profaning his *aficion*, and committing an immoral act. "'Come on,' Brett said. 'Let's go and find [Romero]'" (184). And that's exactly what Jake does for her.

But once the fiesta is over and Brett has left for Madrid with Romero, Pamplona is no longer the terrain of the bull for Jake. Danger has passed as children appear on the square to pick up spent rocket-sticks, and cast-iron tables and severe folding chairs are replaced by marble-topped tables and "comfortable" white wicker chairs at the cafés (227). Jake's next stop in Bayonne, France, is no more dangerous with its "safe, suburban feeling" and waiters made happy by overtipping (232). "It felt comfortable to be in a country where it is so simple to make people happy," Jake says (233). But when Jake crosses the Spanish border into San Sebastian the next morning, he no longer feels comfortable: he feels like a fool traveling to a country where "you could not tell about anything" (233).

Nevertheless it at first seems as if Jake's stay in San Sebastian might merely duplicate the Burguete interlude a week earlier. After all, both San Sebastian and Burguete are Spanish places far removed from the hot and crowded streets and cafés of Paris and Pamplona. Like Bayonne, which is "on a big river" (90), each is associated with water and the natural world—the Irati River at Burguete and the beach and harbor at San Sebastian. Each is a cool resort that provides Jake with peaceful surroundings. In each venue Jake drinks moderately, spends wisely, sleeps easily, and enjoys himself thoroughly. And in each, Jake's actions mirror his efforts to reorder his life: in Burguete he carefully packs layers of freshly caught trout between layers of fern; and in San Sebastian he "unpacked [his] bags and stacked [his] books on the table beside the head of the bed, put out [his] shaving things, hung up some clothes in the big armoire, and made up a bundle for the laundry" (234). Lady Brett is not to be found in either Burguete or San Sebastian.

But San Sebastian is finally not Burguete. Not at all. The similarities between the two locales are designed primarily to point out more compelling contrasts. The key difference, of course, is that Jake goes to San Sebastian by himself. Jake misses the hearty companionship of Bill Gorton he so enjoyed at Burguete[8]—the "empty" train tracks that signal Bill's departure (231) also register Jake's sense of aloneness—but he knows he must be alone in order to prepare himself for Brett's eventual call. Burguete and San Sebastian contrast in other ways as well. Remote Burguete is a move backwards in time—Jake sees an "old diligence... left from the days before the motor-buses" (112)—or even outside of time—"Wonderful how one loses track of the days up here in the mountains" (127), Harris says. By contrast, in modern San Sebastian Jake is fully aware of time: "I set my watch again. I had recovered an hour by coming to San Sebastian." Unlike Burguete,

San Sebastian means a return to schedule for Jake. As soon as he arrived in San Sebastian, he "calculated how many days" (234) he would be there.

Brett does not literally appear in San Sebastian any more than in Burguete, but her presence is felt much more strongly—and not just because Jake knows that Brett had earlier traveled there and cohabited with Robert Cohn. Brett is present in San Sebastian through association. First, she is there figuratively when Jake swims out to a raft in the bay. "A boy and girl were at the other end. The girl had undone the top strap of her bathing-suit and was browning her back. The boy lay face downward on the raft and talked to her. She laughed at things he said, and turned her brown back to the sun. I lay on the raft in the sun until I was dry" (235). The boy and the girl suggest Jake and Brett through the sensuous details—the undone bathing strap and the brown back—and through the boy's lying face down on the raft, an echo of Jake's saying, "I lay face down on the bed" (55) when Brett was last in his Paris apartment. But if Bill's asking about Brett in Burguete caused Jake to react in pain and anger, this is a changed Jake, one who is relaxed enough to remain on the raft near the couple until he dries off. Second, Brett is even more powerfully present the next morning when Jake goes to the beach and sees "nurses in uniform" and a "soldier" with "only one arm" (237). Jake, too, had been a soldier—he was wounded flying on the Italian front in World War I—and he, too, is missing a portion of his anatomy. It was precisely Jake's wounding that led to his meeting Brett in an English hospital, where she worked as a nurse's assistant in the Voluntary Aid Detachment during the war. Brett "loves looking after people" (203), Mike says. By reminding him of his first meeting with Brett, the sight of the uniformed nurses and the wounded soldier quietly reinforces Jake's determination to continue planning for Brett's eventual call, his reentry into the terrain of the bull.

He does so by swimming in San Sebastian bay—a return to the natural world as well as a final contrast to his experiences in Burguete. Jake had been physically active in Burguete as well, but although hiking with Bill to the Irati River was tiring, the fishing there was anything but a challenge. Unlike the dangerous fishing in "Big Two-Hearted River," *The Old Man and the Sea*, and the "Bimini" section of *Islands in the Stream* and unlike the abortive fishing trip in "Out of Season," fishing the Irati River is a breeze. While Jake is baiting his line, he sees two trout jump out of the water. No sooner is his line in the water than a trout strikes—and in "a little while" (119) Jake has effortlessly caught six. Apparently it makes no difference whether you fish with live bait like Jake or a fly like Bill or whether you fish the dam or above or below it. "They're plenty" (118) no matter where or how you fish. It seems as if the trout can't wait to be hooked.

But the swimming in San Sebastian is different, more challenging—signaled by Jake's walking "up the street to the Concha" (234), San Sebastian's semicircular bay and beach that had been pictured on the postcard Brett had earlier sent Jake when she was living with Robert Cohn in San Sebastian (69). On the first of Jake's two days at the Concha, with the tide going out, the swimming through "slow rollers" (235) was not difficult. But on the second day, with the tide in and the surf up, swimming out into the bay through the faster and larger rollers is not easy for Jake, forcing him "to dive sometimes." He then swims back in, "trying to keep in the trough and not have a wave break over me. It made me tired, swimming in the trough" (237). But if swimming in San Sebastian bay takes more effort and energy than the effortless fishing in Burguete, it is Jake's two days of diving that show him carefully preparing, both physically and emotionally, for Brett's eventual summons. On the first day, Jake tries several dives from the raft, once diving deep and "swimming down to the bottom" of the bay. Then, Jake "dove once more, holding it for length, and then swam ashore" (235). The diving details suggest that something more than water sports is going on here. On some level, conscious or otherwise, Jake is recreating a self that will be capable of resisting Brett when she again tries to reassert her control and rekindle his affection for her, as she had earlier in Paris by inviting him to leave the dance floor with her and, even more obviously, in Pamplona, by asking, "Do you still love me, Jake?" (183). Jake's diving on the second day, which occurs just minutes before he receives Brett's two imploring telegrams, reveals a new sense of power, purpose, direction, and determination: "I sat in the sun and watched the bathers on the beach. They looked very small. After a while I stood up, gripped with my toes on the edge of the raft as it tipped with my weight, and dove cleanly and deeply, to come up through the lightening water, blew the salt water out of my head, and swam slowly and steadily in to shore" (238). But just as the real test for Nick Adams of "Big Two-Hearted River" lies within "the plenty of days coming when he could fish the swamp" (180), so the real test for Jake, the confrontation in Brett's bedroom in Madrid, the unequivocal terrain of the bull, also lies ahead, metaphorically suggested when Jake says, "I thought I would like to swim across the bay but I was afraid of cramp" (238).

Just as San Sebastian is not Burguete but a nearer approach to the terrain of the bull—the "smooth and firm" and "yellow" (234) sand of the beach recalls the "firm and smooth" and "yellow" (211) sand of the bull ring—so Madrid fits the pattern of the novel's alternating geographies without repeating Jake's emotional defeats in Paris and Pamplona. When Jake answers Brett's call for help and travels to Madrid, he has prepared himself to reenter the terrain of the bull not only through his swimming, diving, and other acts of recovery at San Sebastian[9] but through his watching and learning from the bullfighting of Pedro Romero. From Romero, Jake has learned both how to wipe out the effects of past defeats, as Romero does in recovering from Cohn's beating—"Each thing that he did with this bull wiped that out a little cleaner" (219)—and how to directly confront powerful forces that threaten to destroy you unless you first control and subdue them.[10]

Madrid is like Paris and Pamplona in its heat—it is "very hot in the summer"—its traffic, and its complexity. It is a "hot, modern town." But Madrid is at the same time "like a country town" (240), suggesting that Jake's experiences there may compare in important ways to his pleasant times in suburban Bayonne or pastoral Burguete or off-season San Sebastian. And so they do. In contrast to Paris and Pamplona, where Brett has fully controlled their relationship—asking Jake to leave the *bal musette* with her, barging into his apartment unannounced in the middle of the night, refusing to live with him, pushing him away when he is kissing her, leaving town with Robert Cohn, and finally using his love to persuade him to set her up with Pedro Romero—Jake takes complete charge of events in Madrid. His dominance, a principle he has internalized from the bullfighting of Pedro Romero, is made clear when he kisses Brett and he says, "While she kissed me I could feel she was thinking of something else. She was trembling in my arms. She felt very small" (241). It is Jake who decides they will have drinks at the Palace Hotel and then lunch at Botin's restaurant. Brett herself has never been to Madrid before. It is Jake who decides they will return to San Sebastian that evening and so arranges and pays for their "berths on the Sud Express" (243); Brett, who "can't go anywhere alone" (102), doesn't "have a sou" (242). It is Jake who suggests that they take a "ride through the town" that Brett has never seen before and who tells the taxi driver where to drive (246). And it is Jake whose last words in the novel—"'Yes.' I said. 'Isn't it pretty to think so'" (247)—effectively and permanently end forever his subservience to Lady Ashley. In gently but firmly telling Brett that it is foolish to believe that the two of them could ever, ever have had a good life together, Jake is emulating his teacher Pedro Romero, who "dominated the bull by making him realize he was unattainable" (168).

Guided by the pattern of alternating geographies that Hemingway establishes in *The Sun Also Rises*, we can now more readily follow Jake's physical and emotional journeys from dangerous to safe terrains, from Paris through Bayonne and Burguete to Pamplona and then back to Bayonne. We can also now better understand Jake's risky but necessary move from Bayonne to San Sebastian, risky because it takes him away from safe, suburban, predictable France to more complicated and more dangerous Spain, necessary because it enables him to anticipate and prepare for the expected call from Lady Brett Ashley. When it arrives, Jake follows the lead of Pedro Romero—first in moving from San Sebastian to Madrid, from the terrain of the bullfighter to the terrain of the bull, and then in controlling and dominating the woman who used to control him but has never been able to control herself: "I can't help it" (183), she acknowledges in Pamplona, and "How can I help it?" (245) she pleads in Madrid.

The novel's final image is appropriately one of control: the khaki-clad mounted policeman who directs traffic. Brett, who is apparently looking at Jake to gauge his response to her latest come-on—"'Oh, Jake,' Brett said, 'we could have had such a damned good time together'" (247)—does not see the policeman, but Jake, who is looking "ahead," does. Jake sees that the policeman "raised his baton" (247)[11], an act that both recalls the "fixed batons" (211) and drawn sword of Romero's bullfighting and reminds us that, alone with Brett again, Jake has located himself wholly within the terrain of the bull. The raised baton also functions as an objective correlative to signal Jake's newly won position of authority and control, his power to stop for good the mutually destructive relationship with Brett. And in the last words of the novel—significantly they are his—Jake does precisely that.

Notes

I am grateful to Miami University Theatre Professor Emeritus Mike Griffith for creating the map of Jake's travels.

    1. I ask my students if they remember earlier references to bathing. One or more usually recalls Brett's words as she returns from San Sebastian after living there with Robert Cohn: "must clean myself" and "must bathe" (74).

    2. A student will sometimes ask, "Why print the text of both telegrams? Isn't one enough?" Another student may respond that the duplication drives home to Jake the point that the patterns of his relationship to Brett repeat themselves over and over again.

    3. In outlining his novel, at a time when he was still calling Brett "Duff" and still referring to Jake as "I," Hemingway wrote, "I go on down into Spain and bring Duff back" (*Sun Also Rises, Facsimile*, I, 316).

    4. During class discussion, I ask my students whether they would think more or less of Jake if he had telegrammed this to Brett: LADY ASHLEY HOTEL MONTANA MADRID YOU GOT YOURSELF INTO THIS MESS NOW GET YOURSELF OUT OF IT? Discussion often leads back to Jake's definition of morality and his philosophy that "The bill always came. That was one of the swell things you could count on" (148).

5. In "The Affirmative Conclusion of *The Sun Also Rises*," I argue that Brett represents the potentially destructive force of the bull in Jake's life and that in the course of the novel Jake transforms himself from a steer to a bullfighter in relation to Brett the bull.

6. That Jake's definition of morality is also Hemingway's is made clear in *Death in the Afternoon*, Hemingway's first-person paean to bullfighting: "So far, about morals, I know only that what is moral is what you feel good after and what is immoral is what you feel bad after" (4).

7. Hemingway considered swearing central to the novel's experience. When his Scribner editor Maxwell Perkins asked him to cut down on profanity, Hemingway resisted: "I never use a word without first considering if it is replaceable," he wrote to Perkins. "I've tried to reduce profanity but I reduced so much profanity when writing the book that I'm afraid not much could come out" (*Selected Letters* 211, 213).

8. I ask my students if the way that Jake says good-bye first to Mike and then to Bill (231) shows how much closer he is to Bill.

9. For especially insightful analyses of Jake's recovery in San Sebastian, see Knodt, Steinke, and Vopat.

10. In "Jake Barnes as Teacher and Learner," I contend that in trying to teach Lady Brett about bullfighting, and especially the significance of Romero's bullfighting, Jake in fact teaches himself.

11. The manuscript version of *The Sun Also Rises* does not include the sentence "He raised his baton" (*Facsimile* II, 616). That Hemingway chose to add this sentence when he revised his novel is one sign of its importance.

Works Cited

Daiker, Donald A. "The Affirmative Conclusion of *The Sun Also Rises*." *McNeese Review* 21 (1974): 3–19. Rpt. in *Critical Essays on Ernest Hemingway's* The Sun Also Rises. Ed. James Nagel. New York: G. K. Hall, 1995. 74–88.

———. "Jake Barnes as Teacher and Learner: The Pedagogy of *The Sun Also Rises*." *The Hemingway Review* 27.1 (Fall 2007): 74–88.

Hemingway, Ernest. *The Complete Short Stories of Ernest Hemingway: The Finca Vigía Edition*. New York: Scribner's, 1987.

———. *Death in the Afternoon*. New York: Scribner's, 1932.

———. *Ernest Hemingway: Selected Letters, 1917–1961*. Ed. Carlos Baker. New York: Scribner's, 1981.

———. *Green Hills of Africa*. New York: Scribner's, 1935.

———. *Islands in the Stream*. New York: Scribner's, 1970.

———. *The Old Man and the Sea*. New York: Scribner's, 1954.

———. *The Sun Also Rises*. 1926. New York: Scribner's, 1954.

———. *The Sun Also Rises: A Facsimile Edition*. 2 vols. Ed. Matthew J. Bruccoli. Detroit, MI: Omnigraphics, Inc., 1990.

Hendrickson, Paul. *Hemingway's Boat: Everything He Loved in Life, and Lost, 1934–1961*. New York: Knopf, 2011.

Knodt, Ellen Andrews. "Diving Deep: Jake's Moment of Truth at San Sebastian." *The Hemingway Review* 17:1 (Fall 1997): 28–37.

Steinke, Jim. "Brett and Jake in Spain: Hemingway's Ending for *The Sun Also Rises*." *Spectrum* 27.1–2 (1985): 131–41.

Stoneback, H. R. *Reading Hemingway's* The Sun Also Rises: *Glossary and Commentary*. Kent, OH: Kent State UP, 2007.

Vopat, Carole Gottlieb. "The End of *The Sun Also Rises:* A New Beginning." *Fitzgerald-Hemingway Annual* (1972): 245–55. Rpt. in *Brett Ashley*. Ed. Harold Bloom. New York: Chelsea House, 1991. 96–104.

A Few Practical Things

Death in the Afternoon and Hemingway's Natural Pedagogy

Ross K. Tangedal

> "No. It is not enough of a book, but still there were a few things to be said. There were a few practical things to be said."
> —Ernest Hemingway, *Death in the Afternoon*

> "*Death in the Afternoon* is not merely a stepping stone to help us interpret Hemingway's life or his work. It is not background, but foreground: a complex book that richly rewards critical and textual analysis."
> —Miriam B. Mandel, "Subject and Author," *A Companion to Hemingway's Death in the Afternoon*

How do teachers effectively approach Ernest Hemingway's nonfiction texts? Widely considered the least accessible of the author's major works, the nonfiction (specifically *Death in the Afternoon* [1932] and *Green Hills of Africa* [1935]) proves difficult for the classroom. Both texts have complex structures, dense descriptions of foreign lands and traditions, and decidedly self-indulgent writing from Hemingway. Few contemporary readers (between the ages of eighteen and twenty) find bullfighting or big-game hunting as fascinating as Hemingway did; however, I find that students react well to challenging material, especially when they have been primed to receive the challenge. *Death in the Afternoon* provides a fascinating blueprint for writing confidently, since composition students tend to think very little of their own writing skills. I begin with *In Our Time,* where students discover their reading abilities through an intensive experience with some of Hemingway's finest short fiction. Once they recognize the style and essence of Hemingway's writing, they are prepared to tackle his difficult bullfighting book. The book then takes on a pedagogical and artistic function, since Hemingway not only displays his writing prowess through a carefully controlled narrative, but he also crafts an essential writing handbook. Students both puzzle over and willfully address the author's approach, and once they see just what Hemingway is trying to accomplish, they find themselves better for having taken the journey.

In no uncertain terms, Hemingway's *Death in the Afternoon* lives on as the ultimate text on Spanish bullfighting, though my students notice his simultaneous delivery of an eloquent, passionate, and direct examination of writing, authority, and textual endeavor. This confidence of purpose plays well in the classroom, especially when a teacher's goal is to foster the same kind of confidence in student writing. However, bullfighting and writing remain a tough sell. On the surface the two fields do not mix, and Hemingway relies on this circumstance in order to fully attract and sustain reader attention. His approach depends on two major factors: discourse and its natural forms. In order to flesh out the intensities of bullfighting, Hemingway must also consider the merits of writing (both fiction and nonfiction) while driving a new model of experimental narrative.

John Raeburn argues that the book "signalled the shift in his relationship with his audience, and, more comprehensively than anything else he wrote, it formulated his public personality" (38). With this text Hemingway attempted to characterize and position his writing style as true, clean, and simple. He claimed that "the truly great killer must have a sense of honor and a sense of glory far beyond that of the ordinary bullfighter. In other words, he must be a simpler man" (*Death in the Afternoon* 232). In defining his work this way, Hemingway engages in a rhetorical experiment, with bullfighting the conduit for living life well. He decidedly separates himself from readers by repeating the word "truth" (and its derivations: "true" and "truly"), for he must become the generator of that "truth" and they the beneficiaries of his experience. Hemingway provides these impressions through careful textual/visual arrangement, consistent authorial power/authority, and a defiant confidence. Robert O. Stephens contends that Hemingway records "his struggle to learn to see the vision in the experience" (213), and it is here that a natural pedagogical moment emerges, a specific combination of skills Hemingway gleaned from experiencing, traveling, and reading the ritual landscape of Spain's bullfighting traditions. While utilizing this natural landscape as a key to unlocking writing skills, Hemingway reads his own artistic landscape and develops the essential teacher-student relationship with his readers. As we read, we also watch, learn, and consume; in doing so, we attribute our perspective to the one showing us where to look—Hemingway himself.

Consequently, Hemingway directs emphasis onto writing (and reading) by fusing the aesthetic endeavors found in the written word and in the bullfighting arena. Hemingway grants full access into the complicated and fascinating tradition of bullfighting, with chapters dedicated to specific matadors, arenas, bulls, and business. Hemingway adroitly focuses the readers' attention on an entity (bullfighting) few American readers had experienced, and even fewer understood. On 6 December 1926, Hemingway informed editor Maxwell Perkins that "[the bullfighting book] might be interesting to people because nobody knows anything about it—and it is terribly interesting—being a matter of life and death" (Bruccoli 53). Six years prior to publication, Hemingway already saw the aesthetic and pubic value possible if given the right treatment. More importantly, he knew how best to approach the topic ("the gradual finding out about it"), which displays Hemingway's regard for a "solid and true" book that grants knowledge and spectacle, art and instruction, life and death (53).

Intentionally, Hemingway expects his readers to trust him regarding bullfighting, and in turn readers trust his writing instruction. However, this trust is gained through carefully written and edited prose. In order to achieve aesthetic and instructional cohesion, Hemingway reworked his manuscript extensively. Robert Trogdon notes that Hemingway's "marked galleys showed that he made 405 substantive emendations and 461 emendations to punctuation and spelling in the text. His revisions were so extensive that the firm charged him $145.25 for the alterations that had to be made to the type, the only time Hemingway was ever charged for proof corrections" (112). These emendations prove that the author spent more time changing and shaping this text than any other. He also obviously sought to create something altogether challenging and expansive, which required extensive revision, a hallmark of good writing. Even with the extensive editing, the text defies characterization. Biographer Michael Reynolds suggests that *Death in the Afternoon* is "a book without models or comparisons, a book in several voices, many tenses, and doubling points of view. . . . It is a discursive book of huge risks which no publisher would have encouraged had the author not been Ernest Hemingway" (41). Indeed, Reynolds's use of "discursive" in defining the text places Hemingway in a prime pedagogical moment. He carefully constructs an environment of aesthetic experimentation and relies on reader aptitude and analysis. As I noted earlier, to properly teach the text, I assign various short stories (or *In Our Time* in its entirety) in order to establish Hemingway's style and aesthetic model. From there students recognize a variety of tendencies at play in *Death in the Afternoon*, and our conversations usually begin with definition. What is this text? It is difficult to characterize because Hemingway does not want it characterized. Miriam B. Mandel insists that "more aggressively and insistently than any of his earlier work, it mixes, blurs, and finally breaks through the limits implicit in concepts like subject, style, genre, experience, research, and invention" ("Introduction" 8). Even Hemingway's preliminary intentions for the book resulted in an abandoned form, as the author wrote Perkins, "It [a bullfighting book] is a long one to write because it is not to be just a history and text book or apologia for bull fighting—but instead, if possible, bull fighting its-self" (Bruccoli 53). Such means bear out the remarkable dexterity the author possessed and ensure his readers of two things: he can write, and he can show us how to understand it.

This essay focuses on key pedagogical factors within Hemingway's text, how he uses the natural landscape of Spain, the cultural epoch of bullfighting, and the technical confidence of *aficion* to both cast a critical eye on writing and teach his readers how to write like him. Students react well to Hemingway's instruction, especially after gaining confidence with his short fiction. Better than most writing manuals, Hemingway's book shows *and* tells students how to write effectively about a given topic. He develops a distinct pedagogy, expects his readers to endure both technical explanation and aesthetic critique on a level playing field, and delivers his instruction through a unique medium (bullfighting). The fusion of writing technique and *aficion* represents an intense shift in endeavor for Hemingway, for he intended always for his book to *be* bullfighting. The text had to encompass not only an entire country's national tradition, but also express a new type of readership, a new adherence to style, mode, reception, and transference. Hemingway's text operates on the level of newness, not only because of its alien content but also its pedagogy, its author's intention to teach at various levels. This "natural" pedagogy allows for *Death in the Afternoon* to function as a bullfighting manual, Spanish history travelogue, and reading/writing handbook. Hemingway is a teacher, and his text provides several teaching moments derived specifically from the natural landscape of Spain and its cultural heritage. His tight aesthetic model urges reader response, as well as participation, and through the competing modes of truth and fiction Hemingway dually creates and enacts intense pedagogical moments for readers and students. When properly recognized and used by instructors, these methods lead to increased student confidence, creativity, and respect for the writing process. This text encourages interpretation, discussion, argumentation, and refutation, but, above all, it encourages an adherence to creative, practical instruction, something students thrive on. It is the recognition and application of Hemingway's pedagogy that I teach, and students find that they have two writing instructors for the two weeks we spend with *Death in the Afternoon*.

However, Hemingway's methods are only effective when paired with specific themes. Of the many themes present in *Death in the Afternoon*, death drives Hemingway's entire narrative. Peter Messent argues that "Hemingway sees the condition of modern man locked in an existential battle, looking to live with dignity and courage in a naturalistic universe where, in the face of the constant presence and pressure of death, pain and violence, 'winner take nothing'" (132–33). Messent's point clearly establishes Hemingway within a continuum of natural factors, including fate, determinism, and order. For Hemingway, knowledge results in power, and accessing that knowledge requires immersion in the cultural and natural confines of Spain. Knowledge of death and its determinants allows him to structure a confident argument for the relevance of simplicity and fundamentality in all things, especially writing. He bridges the gap between novice readers and writers and his learned authorial persona, as Hemingway begins, "The only place where you could see life and death, *i.e.*, violent death now that the wars were over, was in the bull ring. . . . I was trying to learn to write, commencing with the simplest things, and one of the simplest things of all and the most fundamental is violent death" (*Death in the Afternoon* 2). The death frame allows for Hemingway to begin a difficult text (structurally and aesthetically) with a universal where students immediately grant judgment.

Death allows for an initial moment of clarity, and Hemingway explains the metaphor in terms of bullfighting and writing, thus beginning his ultimate pedagogical fusion. He follows the simplicity of violent death with the added complexity of death's spectators: "I had read many books in which, when the author tried to convey it [death], he only produced a blur, and I decided that this was because either the author had never seen it clearly or at the moment of it, he had physically shut his eyes, as one might do if he saw a child that he could not possibly reach or aid, about to be struck by a train" (2–3). Not only does Hemingway require students' attention, but he forces it with a complete idea: death is inevitable, and the explanation of death should be given clarity in order to appreciate its significance. Continuing, Hemingway clarifies the position of looking away as possible—not because of carnage, but due to death itself being an "anti-climax." However, "in the case of an execution by a firing squad, or a hanging, this is not true, and if these very simple things were to be made permanent, as, say, Goya tried to make them in *Los Desastros de la Guerra*, it could not be done with any shutting of the eyes" (3). Death needs qualification in certain instances, but the ability to react to and interpret the aura of death and death itself forms the complete metaphoric device espoused throughout the text.

Interpretative knowledge of death leads Hemingway into a state of pedagogical directness, for understanding death also means understanding the rituals by which death interacts with life. Hemingway indirectly explains as both bullfighting guide and writing guide, driven by reactions to a natural order. If students "sense the meaning and end of the whole thing even when they know nothing about; feel that this thing they do not understand is going on, the business of the horses is nothing more than an incident. If they get no feeling of the whole tragedy naturally they will react emotionally to the most picturesque incident" (8–9). Bullfighting is a carefully controlled tragedy, designed (as Hemingway explains) to increase the intensity and honor of the ordered event. My students make connections between this definition and writing, since writing is also equal parts inspiration *and* order, creativity *and* tradition. In synecdochic fashion, Hemingway continues to explain the relative insignificance of small deaths (i.e., horses) in relation to the grand death being exacted. Specifically, Hilary K. Justice argues that "in the economy of art, such partial judgments can lead to changes on the whole that will detract from the experience of those who understand and appreciate the work of art in its entirety" (100). I stress to students the importance of process resulting in product, though the product is the ultimate goal. Failure to recognize the greater operation renders the operation moot, and art in any form (bullfighting, writing, or otherwise) must adhere to this precept.

Relating to another universal, Hemingway provides readers with a discussion of symphonic music in order to bridge the gap between understanding synecdochic relevance. A "sense" of the whole drives Hemingway's explanation, for "without an ear for music the principle impression of an auditor at a symphony concert might be of the motions of the players of the double bass.... The movements of a player of the double bass are grotesque and the sounds produced are many times, if heard by themselves, meaningless" (*Death in the Afternoon* 9). Intuitive emotional reactions must instead be controlled in order to fully appreciate a profound sensory experience, for "a man of culture and knowing that symphony orchestras are wholly good and to be accepted in their entirety he probably has no reactions at all except pleasure and approval. He does not think of the double bass as separated from the whole of the orchestra or a being played by a human being" (20). Listeners (and viewers) release their senses to the operation in order to fulfill certain personal criteria. Failure to recognize the fine line between personal criteria and aesthetic wholeness troubles Hemingway, and here he offers his initial directive separating essence from preconception. Indeed, Justice argues for the separation between "author" and "writer" in *Death in the Afternoon*, contending that "within Hemingway's logic, writer and author are necessarily connected but not synonymous: the writer is the individual artist—someone who *does*—whereas authorship is but a professional role, distinguishable from the writer by being no less a product of writing than the characters a writer creates" (93). No less important are the roles played by author and writer throughout the text, which leads to a more pedagogical approach from Hemingway. For Justice, this approach relies on separating specific structural entities (author/writer), much like Hemingway separates essence from preconception. Both exist, and both perform specific functions. In turn, this separation pays great dividends when students begin to recognize confidence as the key to good writing.

As he describes essential bullfighting weather conditions and cities, Hemingway centers on yet another specific: Madrid. In his reasoning, Hemingway fully explains the controlled simplicity of the city (similar to the bullfight itself) as well as the city's position in relation to tourist preconception. As the essential bullfighting city, Hemingway writes, Madrid "is modern rather than picturesque, no costumes, practically no Cordoban hats, except on the heads of phonies, no castanets, and no disgusting fakes like the gypsy caves at Granada. There is not one local-colored place for tourists in the town. Yet when you get to know it, it is the most Spanish of all cities, the best to live in, the finest people. . . . It is in Madrid only that you get the essence (*Death in the Afternoon* 51). This introduction serves two pedagogical purposes. One, Hemingway realizes the preconceived tourist knowledge of Spain, citing Cordoban hats, castanets, and gypsy caves as evidence. In order to reinterpret bullfighting for the American reading public, he must signify the simplistic grace of a singular Spanish city, indicative of both central aesthetic possibility and bucking generalized tourist unfamiliarity. Two, Hemingway must introduce "essence." Similar to his work on the senses earlier, "the essence, when it is the essence, can be in a plain glass bottle and you need no fancy labels, nor in Madrid do you need any national costumes; no matter what sort of building they put up, though the building itself may look like Buenos Aires, when you see it against that sky you know it is Madrid" (51).

The insistence on categorizing Madrid well above any other Spanish city provides Hemingway with the platform to lay out his natural pedagogy. Not only does Madrid possess "the essence," but Hemingway teaches readers to see that essence without ornamentation. He goes so far as to say, "it makes you feel very badly, all question of immortality aside, to know that you will have to die and never see it again" (53). The simplest natural beauty turns Hemingway loose, for he not only shows students how to read Madrid, but how to read (and use) the very book in their hands. The combination of reading landscapes and reading texts elevates Hemingway's text beyond treatise or guidebook and into the realm of artistic fusion. Without Spain there is no experience, and without experience there is no writing. Students then write their own experiences with a personal place, such as a hometown or a favorite vacation spot. They are charged to distill the essence of that space (much like Hemingway does), and frequently students unearth sensual attributes first, geographic specifics second. Hemingway's experiment provides a firm grounding in structured description essential to good writing, and students appreciate being able to recollect and then appropriate their experiences.

Following his Madrid introduction, Hemingway steps out of the narrative and into direct instruction: he assigns homework. Hemingway critiques what he calls "erectile writing": "It is well known, or not known, whichever you prefer, that due to a certain congestion or other, trees for example look different to a man in that portentous state and a man who is not. All objects look different. They are slightly larger, more mysterious, and vaguely blurred. Try it yourself" (54). Hemingway instructs his students to attempt various metaphoric visual exercises, resulting in a written lecture on mysticism and its detriment to readers. He qualifies the very prose he writes and prefers to read, and he places his readers in the position of students receiving knowledge rather than casual bullfighting spectators. He points out, "This too remember. If a man writes clearly enough any one can see if he fakes. . . . True mysticism should not be confused with incompetence in writing which seeks to mystify where there is no mystery but is really only the necessity to fake to cover the lack of knowledge or the inability to state clearly" (54). Respecting Madrid and its essence leads to respecting writing and its essence, as Hemingway connects the two states (one natural, one aesthetic). Just as Hemingway reacts to the preconceptions inherent in Spanish tourists, he too reacts against the over-mystification and congestion of prose (both in writing and reading), based solely on the preconception readers have for such work. A productive exercise has students bring in a high school paper (usually filled with unessential adjectives and flowery prose) in order to show what students think writing looks like. We then redesign a paragraph or two based on Hemingway's arguments. Hemingway could not have approached such a sharp aesthetic/natural divide had he not hybridized the experience of Madrid with the experience of reading. To make the divide a whole, students' ability to discern fake and true writing (as well as fake and true Spain) is paramount, for now Hemingway has the emphasis right where he wants it: on his students.

Hemingway rewards his readers with yet another assignment. He begins chapter seven: "At this point it is necessary that you see a bullfight" (63). Hemingway emphasizes his pedagogical approach by defining the purpose of guide books (ones read before the action and ones read after the fact). He alters the narrative to direct readers away from the text in order to better understand it in context. His qualification reads:

> So with any book on mountain ski-ing, sexual intercourse, wing shooting, or any other thing which it is impossible to make come true on paper, or at a time on paper, it being always an individual experience, there comes a place in the guide book where you must say do not come back until you have ski-ed, had sexual intercourse, shot quail or grouse, or been to the bullfight so that you will know what we are talking about. So from now on it is inferred that you have been to the bullfight. (63)

This directive serves two pedagogical purposes. First, Hemingway, at page sixty-three, has directed his readers to become doers, rather than casual observers. They must write in order to understand writing. A call for action and experience over passivity calls the students' true intentions into question, and should they oblige Hemingway pays dividends. Second, Hemingway knows that his readers will continue past this point, having seen a bullfight or not. He therefore produces a dialogue (Justice refers to this section as a "morality play" [95]) in order to facilitate the response necessary to continue his text. Understanding Hemingway's duality of purpose (a man of aesthetic force [see a bullfight; write a paper] and man of pedagogical force [continue reading and see how it went]) complicates the text further, which only amplifies an already taxing narrative situation. Hemingway must navigate any literary endeavor as both writer *and* author, and Justice's analysis bears this out. Further, students begin to see the duality in writing, the private composition versus the public presentation. Though both are essential to writing, only one is seen publicly, and the public side shows compromise as a key writing component. Justice argues that the "the inclusion of the Old Lady—her ignorance, her preconceptions, and her judgments—enables Hemingway to represent the medium of exchange between artist and public, an interactive but usually inarticulate medium that necessarily changes the artist, and not for the better" (102). Justice discerns the need Hemingway professed in writing over his obligation as a public author, a need thoroughly necessary in defining his pedagogy. The interaction between artistic functions (author/writer) forces students to reconcile the duality of textual creation and prompts further attention to craft, intention, and eventual reception. Hemingway teaches students that the complex relationship between writer, reader, and author is both crucial to the development of writing and possibly detrimental to its creation. Such discourse shows Hemingway's attention to teaching students the difficulty in writing for public consumption, regardless of genre.

The Old Lady dialogue features distinct lecture points made by Hemingway (as both "author" and "writer") and offers a wide range of compositional knowledge and technique. To best utilize this section, Hemingway allows for questioning (in the form of the Old Lady) and response, a technique Reynolds dubs "an enormous risk: if the device fails, the book will fail with it" (83). Granted, this dialogue facilitates, with singular focus and purpose, the means by which Hemingway positions specific influential discourse throughout his text, culminating in the clearest of his writing methodologies: the iceberg theory. Leading up to it, Hemingway posits several important ideas, including influence, of which he writes "there is no record in the Bible of the number of fake messiahs that came before Our Lord, but the history of the last ten years of bullfighting would record little else" (*Death in the Afternoon* 86). Continuing, Hemingway notes the curious case of Nicanor Villalta, a matador who "invented a type of gyroscopic way of using the muleta, of making his unnatural *natural* passes, his feet tight together.... No one passes the bull closer, no one works closer to the bull, and no one spins as he, the master spins" (87). However, as referenced earlier, the strangeness of Villalta results from his physique ("he has a neck three times as long as that of an average man" [86]) and his style. Hemingway writes that "everything he does he does bravely and everything he does he does in his own way, so that if you see Nicanor Villalta that is not bullfighting either" (87). The case study on Villalta shows both praise and critique, reminding students that while witnessing the matador may be "very strange, very emotional and very, thank God, except for the great courage employed, unique" (86), the important takeaway is not the uniqueness itself, but the position that uniqueness plays in understanding and furthering the art of bullfighting, and metaphorically, the art of writing At this point students are tasked to find a nonfiction piece that seems different, unique, or out of place. Once found, the pieces are contextualized using Hemingway's Villalta metaphor, and their value is either confirmed or denied. Judgment is crucial, as is technique and essence. That essence is real, and Hemingway derives key analytical points, only possible if given the correct metaphorical structure. Matadors such as Villalta provide said structure.

Of course, to make valid the point of structure, it would make sense for Hemingway to guide readers with a personal aesthetic example, just as he guides with bullfighting examples. It would also make sense to precede such an example with a fine theoretical/philosophical statement on these aesthetics, which he does. The direct line to Hemingway's aesthetics is paramount, not only for students to base their own writing on but also for Hemingway himself to gauge direct participation. Introducing and embedding "A Natural History of Death" within the text achieves these aims. The Author argues that "the individual, the great artist when he comes, uses everything that has been discovered or known about his art up to that point ... and then the great artist goes beyond what has been done or known and makes something of his own" (100). Hemingway aligns substance with skill, knowledge with style, and education with active creation. As artist, Hemingway creates an individual personage directed by important influences both revered and rejected. And, similar to the Villalta example, Hemingway brings his students back to the point: where does one find true influence? His Author continues, "They [those who remember the old great writers] are excused from not recognizing at once [the new great writers] because they, in the period of waiting, see so many false ones that they become so cautious that they cannot trust their feelings; only their memory. Memory, of course, is never true" (100). Inaction prohibits influence from taking hold, and to disallow certain influences (good or bad) is only cowardly and cautious, two traits Hemingway rejects. However, Hemingway does not entirely discount memory, only in so far as it alters the basis by which reality functions. Both memory and feeling must coexist in order to facilitate natural human processes. Consequently, though "A Natural History of Death" does not involve bullfighting in any way, it serves as the product of process, which assists with and encourages student involvement, as any teacher knows. With a natural cohesion of substance and style, Hemingway's use of story to both display and teach outshines the story's plot. Its placement, above all else, proves to be the pedagogical move, and students' understanding of this context ushers in Hemingway's major pedagogical point.[1]

Though several points can be made regarding the pedagogical intentions behind *Death in the Afternoon*, perhaps the most overt statement on Hemingway's personal writing style (and the most effective piece of writing instruction for students) exists after the Old Lady and Author have been excised from the book. As Justice notes, to this point "Hemingway has presented his readers with allusion within allegory within analogy within encyclopedia, in nonfiction, fiction, and dramatic genres" (113). Indeed, though several critical points have been made, whether by Hemingway's fictional Author or Hemingway himself, the iceberg theory, widely used and quoted for its cryptic understanding of omission and sustained aesthetic control, dominates the book, and the classroom. Though filled with complicated genre-bending, character abstractions, and complex bullfighting history, the text truly hinges on the understanding and procedure put forth in the following: "If a writer of prose knows enough about what he is writing about he may omit things that he knows and the reader, if the writer is writing truly enough, will have a feeling of those things as strongly as though the writer had stated them. The dignity of movement of an ice-berg is due to only one-eighth of it being above water" (*Death in the Afternoon* 192). The theory deals with several writing issues, though it suffers from several misinterpretations and out-of-context usages. Strictly within the context of the work, Beatriz Penas Ibáñez argues, "The invisibility of the submerged seven-eighths of the iceberg parallels the unreadability of 'most of the matter' not linguistically articulated on the surface of the text" (157). Not only is this a writing theory, but also a reading theory. More than a literary credo, which Hemingway famously discredited in a letter to Perkins,[2] this statement serves the student as much as it serves the artist behind it. As a pedagogical tool, Hemingway's big reveal—nearly three-quarters of the way through his narrative—opens up both the text and the author's artistic production. As if the entire text has built to this point, Hemingway does not shy away from attributing his artistic integrity to what he chooses to leave out. But that is the major point, and Hemingway's pedagogy echoes this point fervently. For a final exercise, students take the same high school paper used earlier and cut as much away as possible in order to really feel what omission does to written prose. Students (much like their teacher) are sometimes leery of cutting precious material, but once enacted, the process becomes an incontrovertible part of their writing identities. Hemingway's approach to writing comes full circle, and students realize that their own confidence now stems from being taught how to write while reading a bullfighting book.

At the end of the process Hemingway emerges as the wise and practical teacher, servicing the interests of students while ingratiating himself to a new kind of writer: one he has created. Ibáñez argues that Hemingway "asks his readers to emulate him by behaving like aficionados to his texts, like involved interpreters daring to fill in the gaps left open in his narratives as well as in the narratives of their lives" (159). This is fitting, especially when one considers the textual marathon Hemingway requires students to run. Though the theory appears as simple as understanding that which has been left out, the theory's true meaning only matters when considering the effects such a theory has on students, not Hemingway himself. The move Hemingway makes eventually sees confidence shift from the writer to the reader, the teacher to the student. He confidently advises readers that "the great thing is to last and get your work done and see and hear and understand; and write when there is something that you know; and not before; and not too damned much after. . . . The thing to do is work and learn to make it" (*Death in the Afternoon* 278). Herein, as his narrative ends, Hemingway encapsulates his natural pedagogy. See, hear, understand, write, work, and learn all point directly at one entity: students. With the complex interplay between the Spanish landscape, bullfighting, authorship, technique, and art, Ernest Hemingway leads close readers toward a substantial conclusion: in writing, experience and creation are two sides of the same coin. Expectation now firmly established, the teacher can sit back and observe, allowing his new writers (his aficionados) to learn and establish their reading and writing processes. After all, is there anything more practical than that?[3]

Notes

1. I teach the placement of "A Natural History of Death" rather than the story itself. As a means to an end, the story's structural fit in the narrative proves more fruitful in explaining Hemingway's intended pedagogical method. Therefore, this essay does not elaborate on the story itself, but rather on the story's textual purpose.

2. Ernest Hemingway to Max Perkins, 28 June 1932: "If they feel disappointed and still want my 'literary Credo' in a book on bull fighting they can run an insert saying 'F-ck the whole goddamned lousy racket'" (Bruccoli 172).

3. An argument can be made for Hemingway's visual pedagogy in *Death in the Afternoon*. The section titled "Illustrations" casts Hemingway as a visual teacher, and his captions showcase another part of his teaching style.

Works Cited

Bruccoli, Matthew J., ed., with Robert W. Trogdon. *The Only Thing That Counts: The Ernest Hemingway/Maxwell Perkins Correspondence.* New York: Scribners, 1996.

Hemingway, Ernest. *Death in the Afternoon.* New York: Scribner's, 1932.

Ibáñez, Beatriz Penas. "'Very Sad but Very Fine': *Death in the Afternoon*'s Imagist Interpretation of the Bullfight-Text." *A Companion to Ernest Hemingway's* Death in the Afternoon. Ed. Miriam B. Mandel. London: Camden House, 2004. 143–64.

Justice, Hilary K. *The Bones of the Others: The Hemingway Text from the Lost Manuscripts to the Posthumous Novels.* Kent, OH: Kent State UP, 2006.

Mandel, Miriam B., ed. Introduction. *A Companion to Hemingway's* Death in the Afternoon. London: Camden House, 2004. 1–17.

———, ed. "Subject and Author: The Literary Backgrounds of *Death in the Afternoon.*" *A Companion to Hemingway's* Death in the Afternoon. London: Camden House, 2004. 79–119.

Messent, Peter. "'The Real Thing'? Representing the Bullfight and Spain in *Death in the Afternoon.*" *A Companion to Hemingway's* Death in the Afternoon. Ed. Miriam B. Mandel. London: Camden House, 2004. 123–42.

Raeburn, John. *Fame Became of Him: Hemingway as Public Writer.* Bloomington: Indiana UP, 1984.

Reynolds, Michael S. *Hemingway: The 1930s.* New York: W. W. Norton & Co., 1997.

Stephens, Robert O. *Hemingway's Nonfiction: The Public Voice.* Chapel Hill: U of North Carolina P, 1968.

Trogdon, Robert W. *The Lousy Racket: Hemingway, Scribners and the Business of Literature.* Kent, OH: Kent State UP, 2007.

Part Five

The Transatlantic Hemingway Text

Flashbacks and the Trials of Hemingway's War Veterans

Healing in the Natural World

Robert McParland

In a war, the landscape loses. War is a disruption of nature. Fought within a specific setting, war affects an ecosystem. It also affects those who fight in it. In this essay, we will look at how we might help students to focus on the inner landscape of war that one finds inside the minds of Ernest Hemingway's characters. Hemingway characters, upon returning home, often seek solace in nature for relief after the war. In the novel *A Farewell to Arms* and in the short stories "Soldier's Home," "Big Two-Hearted River," and "The Snows of Kilimanjaro," we see the effects of war upon characters and their interaction with the natural world. Hemingway implies the value of the outdoors for returning veterans and their process of healing and reengagement with civilian life.

This essay emerges from my own encounters with several veterans who are enrolled at the college where I teach. They are young men and women who are in situations similar to those of Hemingway's characters. They are dedicated people who have returned home from war in Iraq and Afghanistan, and they have arrived at our college, one of the dozens of military friendly schools across America, to pursue new goals. This has raised some questions for us. Can teaching Hemingway stories help these individuals as they return to college after being overseas in the military? Might reading Hemingway with students in high school and college settings sensitize students to the stories of young men and women who have recently returned from service in Iraq or Afghanistan? What do Hemingway's depictions of his characters in ecological settings have to do with the healing, renewal, and revival of a person who has known the landscape of war?

For Ernest Hemingway, war was where men lived fully. The image of war that the camera provides, he said, is clear and true because men going into action do not "act before the camera in the presence of death" (*Spanish Earth* 23). War is an existential condition, we might explain to our students. There is a heightening of ultimate concern, a crucial freedom, in the act of a soldier going into battle.

War is exciting, observes my colleague James Smith, a psychotherapist who has often worked with returning veterans. Smith points out: men with post-traumatic stress disorder (PTSD), who served in Vietnam, have often chosen quiet places to reduce stimuli and have retreated to non-stimulating, rural environments. PTSD, in part, has to do with being keyed up, always on edge and on guard. So, former soldiers, who may be easily excited, may choose these quieter areas and natural settings to tamp down the stimulation. He points out that soldiers returning home have sometimes found home to be dull after the intensity of war. In "Soldier's Home," we see this in Harold Krebs's dismissal of "settling down" and becoming "really a credit to the community" (151). As therapists Daryl S. Paulson and Stanley C. Krippner point out, "Some veterans feel like they have lost everything of value and suffer a total alienation from friends, lovers, family and themselves" (15). Frederic J. Svoboda, likewise, mentions that Vietnam veterans with whom he has spoken have found Krebs's disillusioned homecoming "reflecting accurately their experiences" (170). The place that once was home seems too pedestrian and alienating.

Yet, veterans are often highly motivated students. Despite whatever distress they may be experiencing, they are determined to handle their assignments effectively. Their military training evidently suggests to them that the professor in a classroom ought to take charge. A sense of order in the surroundings seems to be quite important to them. They are often goal oriented, self-motivated, and disciplined. However, as was the case with Harold Krebs, they are readjusting to American society.

Considering this, we might encourage our students to think about their homes and the stories that they share with each other about their experiences. Students can make a chart of the various discourse communities in which they participate: who they speak with and what they talk about. A class lesson might be built around how well we listen to each other when we share our stories. Harold Krebs cannot easily tell his story to people in his community, who are by now tired of stories of war. When he tells someone about his experiences, he embellishes those experiences to get a reaction from people. Krebs wants to be heard, so he makes up stories. However, he soon finds that what has happened to him in the war is distasteful. Whereas he once felt "cool and clear inside," he now finds that valuable quality lost (111).

One of my students was clearly proud of his service. He wore a sweatshirt with lettering that indicated he had been a marine in Iraq. One of his classmates called him a hero. I could see the edginess, the effort, the determination in him, and he confided in me about the changes in his life and his marriage. He participated in the class, did his assignments, earned a good grade, and moved on to other classes. It was clear that he was hurting, like Hemingway's Krebs, and yet, unlike Krebs, he had not given up and he was making his way. He never spoke much about what he had experienced overseas, but it was obvious that this was a special individual.

Narrative is important for Krebs, who needs to tell his story. Storytelling is also valuable for our communities and classrooms. Social recognition of the valuable things that people do on behalf of our communities and our nation is critical to the maintenance of individuals and our communities. Realizing the dedication of military service men and women, a town nearby our college has recognized recent veterans by draping signs with their names across a fence that faces a major traffic intersection. Their names are visible to those walking or driving by. These signs of recognition and appreciation provide reassurances from the community.

Howard Krebs's situation is different from this. Upon returning from war, he goes unrecognized. His personal narrative is diminished, or distorted, because an audience does not hear his true voice. Krebs is bewildered. It is clear that he once liked the simplicity of a military life that focused on survival and fighting an enemy. In such wartime conditions, he was able to trust his instincts and his choices. However, life at home is less defined. Krebs cannot get on with the rest of life. He has experienced trauma. He has been present to too much violence and needs the healing space of a community. While he feels the need to talk about his wartime experience, he is unable to tell his story. The possibility of being listened to has vanished. Interest in the war has eroded with time, and the citizens of his hometown have already heard many war stories. Krebs has to make up stories in order to be listened to. He exaggerates. He incorporates the experiences of other soldiers into his own experiences. The narrator tells us that Krebs's "lies were not sensational at the pool room" (112). True memories become lost. Krebs cannot talk through his memories. He is one of many who have these stories and society has become numb. Tired of these stories, people have stopped listening.

Hemingway is making a point about authenticity here. Krebs needs to become whole again, but he is struggling with being an authentic, truth-telling individual. What we see here in this portrayal of Krebs is that, rather than isolation, there is a need for a reintegration into society. Soldiers need jobs, social connections, and perhaps a college education.

Krebs's mother tells him that his father thinks he has lost his ambition in life. The other people his age are all "settling down" and getting married. Charley Simmons and these others are going to be "a credit to the community," she says (115). Within his mother's comments, Krebs hears criticism. It all seems to say: "so, what is the matter with you?"

It seems that Krebs may need a space apart, like other Hemingway characters. A natural setting would act as a counter for the alienation that Krebs is experiencing. For example, in *Snows of Kilimanjaro,* Harry seeks a zone that is natural and apart, distant and exotic. Nature surrounds Harry, as a grand snow leopard is defined high on a hill against the sky. Likewise, in "Big Two-Hearted River," a story in the collection titled *In Our Time,* Nick Adams, seeks a place away: the peacefulness of a lake, where he can go fishing. There, in a quiet landscape, he finds serene simplicity that is set in contrast with his memories—likely those of a bitterly fought war. Students may find that he wrestles a bit with those memories when he wrestles with a fish on the end of his line.

The natural world is ever a factor in Hemingway's *In Our Time* collection. The presence of Nick Adams weaves through these stories, and World War I, often understated, lingers in the background. There are eleven stories in *In Our Time,* which feature a young male protagonist. He is on "an odyssey of revelation and self-discovery," Wirt Williams points out (33). Four stories fall outside this pattern. In seven stories, the young man is Nick Adams. In "Soldiers Home," we see Krebs. In "Cat in the Rain," we meet George. In "Out of Season" and "A Very Short Story," the young male protagonist is never named. Carlos Baker suggests that these all could have been about "Nick," except for the names given to the characters. Having experienced the violence of war, the absurdity of loss, he goes back to the woods in Michigan. He finds renewal in "Big Two-Hearted River." Williams calls this "reunion with the life force" (37). Hemingway's presentation of Nick's relationship with nature in "Big Two-Hearted River" suggests the psychological reasons that people are drawn to spend time in the natural world.

"He felt he had left everything behind, the need for thinking, the need to write, other needs. It was all back of him" ("Big Two-Hearted River" 164). For Nick, the tent seems "homelike" and he is "settled." To be fishing in this quiet place is simply to be. "He was there, in the good place. He was in his home where he had made it" (167). This happiness is interrupted as he does battle with a fish. In this trout battle, he feels "a little sick, as though it would be better to sit down" (169). He looks forward to "plenty of days" when he can go fishing (177).

Students might think about how we make our homes and how this home of ours relates to the natural world. A tent is a temporary residence—an almost permeable dwelling that is placed within nature by campers. Within it, one is close to the land, while shielded from rain or the cool night air. For a time, it is home. And so it is for Nick, who leaves the world behind. The home (*oikos*) of each student may feel a bit more permanent than this. Even so, that home is within a system of relations, in a specific setting and ecosystem.

Short of taking your class outdoors, you might ask your students to jot down some of their positive experiences of the natural world. After they have read Hemingway's story, you can collect their ideas, having students drop their papers into a bowl or a small box. Then have them go "fishing," drawing from those ideas for a discussion.

You might ask the questions that Kenneth S. Lynn asks: What needs does Nick have to put behind him? Why does he refer to his tent as a home? Why does the episode of battling the fish make him feel sick? (150).

My own answer to Nick's "sick" feeling is that PTSD affects him in this moment of stress as he grapples with the fish. On some level, the sudden jarring battle with the fish elicits those old memories. Lynn relates the story to Hemingway's own biographical context. He points to both the writer's home and his mother as being more decisive than his war experience. I stand with Edmund Wilson's view, however, that this touch of panic is part of the wartorn veteran's experience of memories within the present moment.

Nick, in my view, is a veteran suffering from PTSD, who goes to nature for relief from malaise. It is true, as Lynn points out, that "not a single reference to war appears in the story" (151). This critic extends the trauma to the home-life of the character. One might ask if Nick is not in the same existential situation as Krebs in "Soldier's Home."

Malcolm Cowley in his introduction to *The Portable Hemingway* spoke of a lost generation and insisted that war had shattered their relation to the country of their boyhoods. In Hemingway's story, the implication is that Nick is a war veteran trying to move beyond his emotional wounds. Mark Schorer wrote of Hemingway, "Nothing more important than this wounding was ever to happen to him" (675). The outdoors becomes a space where healing this wound is possible. In this existential condition, the natural world is where one meets with "being," to use the philosopher Martin Heidegger's focus. This is where a person may become aware of a basic connection with life. Hemingway, of course, never says this. Least of all does he ever quote existential philosophers. Yet it is clear that characters like Harry in "The Snows of Kilimanjaro" and Nick Adams are pursuing something true and fundamental in their encounters with the natural world.

Hemingway draws our attention to the phenomenological. He meets the world of objects and the natural setting with a steady gaze. We see Nick viewing the hillside and the river. With him we look down into the water and we see the trout that Nick watches for a long time. Hemingway's writing acts as a way of observation, as a connection of words with careful attention to objects. The author's recreations of landscapes are like series of pictures by Cézanne. In Hemingway's writing, spatial representations are carefully constructed in language. For example, in *The Sun Also Rises* Hemingway encourages readers to see a truck as it moves from the foreground to the hills in the background.

Hemingway's practice of attentiveness to the natural world may have been developed early on in the writer's life. One may recall that Hemingway's father, Clarence Hemingway, was a physician and an amateur naturalist. Dr. Hemingway organized Ernest's eighth-grade class into a club named after Louis Agassiz. They took nature walks along the Des Plaines River. Dr. Hemingway was involved with the Oak Park Third Congregational Church, where he taught a Sunday school class. The scientific orientation of his work as a physician and his interest in naturalist studies developed skills of observation in his son. Susan F. Beegel points out that Ernest Hemingway's father may have "hoped that the habits of an observant natural historian would increase his son's reverence for divine creation" but that his father's nature walks actually "helped him to achieve ultimate disillusion with God" (75). In 1919, Hemingway made a fishing trip to Seney in the Michigan woods about fifteen miles south of Lake Superior at the Big Fox and Little Fox Rivers. He was "trying to do the country like Cezanne" he told Gertrude Stein and Alice Toklas on 15 August 1924 (*A Moveable Feast* 30).

Hemingway's stories can remind students of how to really "see" the world around them, particularly the natural world that is sometimes taken for granted. You might ask them to identify and describe specific sites in the environment near your school. Hemingway has a keen eye for natural phenomena. Students can, likewise, better develop their own awareness. In a few well-chosen details, Hemingway is able to clearly render a landscape, so that we too can "see" it.

Students can be asked to engage in close readings of passages in his texts that offer this careful scrutiny and guide the eye.

"Let no man be ashamed to kneel here in the great outdoors," says Bill Gorton in *The Sun Also Rises* (122). Frederic Henry escapes from war as he dives into the Tagliamento River in a baptism of the natural world. Susan F. Beegel implies that this fact is connected with nature's healing (55). She points out that "Hemingway learned to describe the natural world with a scientist's unwavering gaze, respect for truth, interest in detail, and objective language" (54). She reminds us of how Frederic Henry and Catherine Barkley in *A Farewell to Arms* (1929) escape war into the mountains of Switzerland and Jake Barnes in *The Sun Also Rises* (1926) fishes in the streams of Spain after the Great War (55).

A Farewell to Arms begins with a transposition of nature into human warfare. The flashes of guns are "like summer lightning" (11). The land is turned to the purpose of camouflage: barrels of the guns are covered with green branches, as are the tractors. Small gray motor cars racing through the scene splash mud. War possesses the landscape: "The mountain that was beyond the valley and the hillside where the chestnut forest grew was captured" (5). Past the town, the forest oak trees on the mountain are gone: "The forest had been green in the summer when we had come into the town but now there were the stumps and the broken trunks and the ground torn up" (6). If one looks along the line of the river, "none of the mountains beyond the river had been taken" (8). The landscape is surrounded by guns: "There were many more guns in the country around and the spring had come" (9) begins chapter three. "The fields were green and there were small green shoots on the vines, the trees along the road had small leaves and a breeze came from the sea . . . In the town there were more guns" (9). "The battery in the next garden woke me" (13) begins chapter four. In chapter five the contact with Catherine and Frederic Henry begins in a garden: "It was really very large and beautiful and there were fine trees in the grounds. Miss Barkley was sitting on a bench in the garden" (16).

For Whom the Bell Tolls also underscores human relationship with the natural world. Robert Martin writes: "Through abundant, actually pervasive and detailed descriptions of nature, especially of the pine trees, Hemingway suggests that man is not merely an interloper or casual observer of nature, but rather, he is an integral part of the wild, an active participant. He must, therefore, if he is to grow and mature, be not only a participant in nature, but also a pupil of it as well" (56). Wartime technology—tanks, planes, machine guns—also speaks of the human relationship with nature. The original meaning of the Greek word *techne,* from which our word *technology* derives, meant "to make." However, the sense of this word is that of practicing a craft—one like Hemingway's own disciplined art of writing. Writing has order and structures. For Hemingway, writing was integral. Like the patient act of fishing by his character Nick Adams, writing was closely connected with a disciplined self and with the earth.

Hemingway's characters seek peace and distance from the stimulation of busy environments. Nature, rather than the hospital, is the healing place. Gerry Brenner writes, "Unlike Sinclair Lewis's hospitals, or Thomas Mann's sanatorium, which completes the education of his hero in *Magic Mountain,* Hemingway's hospitals cannot heal the deeper injuries common to the human condition" (131). What can give humankind healing and a sense of order is the natural world. This is so amid "life's utter irrationality" (132). Nature itself, of course, is not controllable and predictable. Nature presents structures of beauty and a placid setting. It may also suggest design. However, nature is not rational and nature may be quite impersonal. At the end of *A Farewell to Arms,* Catherine will not fulfill the cycle of reproduction. Rain will fall inconsolably.

Frederic Henry is disoriented: a character filled with unanswered questions, as Brenner observes (137). This disorientation in his retrospective narration emerges from his PTSD. "I tried to tell about the night and the difference between the night and the day and how the night was better unless the day was very clean and cold and I could not tell it, and I cannot tell it now" (*Farewell to Arms* 13). Indeed, he does "compel empathy" and he is "one of us," as Brenner says (138).

Frederic Henry wants to pin the world down in concrete language and he rejects abstract terms. Critics have often looked at Hemingway's use of the rain, the death in childbirth, and the crafted and often rewritten conclusion of *A Farewell to Arms.* Less attention has been given to the natural world and its disruption. This is so, despite the obvious relationship between the tortured landscape, the waste of war, and Catherine's death that Lionel Trilling called the book's genre tragedy. Yet, even as Trilling is correct in observing how man endures in the face of inhuman circumstances, that man also escapes to nature. Millicent Bell observes that years afterward Henry cannot get rid of the debility and morbidity. Yet, Hemingway characters invariably drift toward settings in the natural world, as if something within them has suggested this.

"The Snows of Kilimanjaro," published in 1936, has a subtext about vitality and meaning. Harry is trying to reaffirm his life on a safari. We read of Harry that "he had sold vitality, in one form or another, all his life and when your affections are not too involved you give much better value for the money. He had found that out but he would never write that, now, either. No, he would not write that, although it was well worth writing" (45). Harry has sold his vitality throughout his life. Being a soldier, or a writer, involves the selling of vitality. Yet, the life force is in nature. Having sold out his vitality, he seems to be attempting to find it again in the natural world.

Of course, Harry is not well, despite being surrounded by all of this vitality. Gangrene has set into his injured leg. Memories return as Harry reflects on death: "Now he would never write the things that he had saved to write until he knew enough to write them well. Well, he would not have to fail at trying to write them either. Maybe you could never write them, and that was why you put them off and delayed the starting" (41).

The epigraph to this story reads: "Kilimanjaro is a snow-covered mountain 19,710 feet high, and is said to be the highest mountain in Africa. Its western summit is called the Masai 'Ngàje Ngài,' the House of God. Close to the western summit there is the dried and frozen carcass of a leopard. No one has explained what the leopard was seeking at that altitude" (39).

One may also ask what the man was seeking. Hemingway's famous code of "grace under pressure" responds to the question of how to live with dignity. Harry represents the man who faces a not entirely hospitable nature. Rather, he lives in an indifferent world marked by violence in which the life of the individual lacks intrinsic meaning. Harry questions his past and struggles with his sense of the meaninglessness of life. At one point, Harry reveals that "for years [death] had obsessed him; but now it meant nothing in itself. It was strange how easy being tired enough made it" (41). Harry spent years of life obsessed with death. He says of death that "now it meant nothing in itself." Death stalks Harry; it is personified, given shape and form (54).

In "The Snow of Kilimanjaro," Hemingway's use of italics offers us Harry's state of mind. We see his reality and we see his imagination. Harry's flashbacks, or memories—events that are occurring only in Harry's mind—are set in italics and the main part of the story is set in standard roman type. One might ask students what they make of this. Does the story say anything about memories and how they are significant in the present?

Psychologists who work with veterans with PTSD point out that "flashbacks indicate the psyche's attempt to heal at the core level" (Tick 215). Harold Krebs, in a spiritual desert, might find meaning in such a place. The fishing that Nick Adams does may be a calming and focusing ritual. Inviting a veteran to participate in a formal ritual, like an *Inipi*, or sweat lodge, is not a casual step, observes Edward Tick. However, a homelier pastime, like the ritual of fishing, might help inspire a sense of calm and introspection. Natural environments are settings that may elicit memories, or meditations—gentle or profound. Nick Adams gazes into the cool waters of a lake. Harry gazes to the mountain. Perhaps, in a safe and natural environment, the recognition of meaning, or healing and renewal, may be possible.

Sharing the stories of Hemingway in classroom settings suggests that men and women who have served in the military may see their own experience reflected in these fictional designs. Reading Hemingway does, in fact, enhance students' appreciation and understanding of the experiences of returning veterans. It also is a way of bringing attention to the potentially restorative effects of spending time in contact with the natural world. Hemingway's portrayal of his characters in natural settings suggests that there are environments where an individual's resources may be refreshed, re-gathered, and restored.

Works Cited

Baker, Carlos. "The Mountain and the Plain." *Critical Essays on Ernest Hemingway's* A Farewell to Arms. Ed. George Monteiro. Boston: G. K. Hall, 1984. 97–103.

Beegel, Susan F. "Eye and Heart: Hemingway's Education as a Naturalist." *A Historical Guide to Ernest Hemingway.* Ed. Linda Wagner-Martin. New York: Oxford UP, 2000. 53–92.

Bell, Millicent. "Pseudoautobiography and Personal Metaphor." *Critical Essays on Ernest Hemingway's* A Farewell to Arms. Ed. George Monteiro. Boston: G. K. Hall, 1984. 145–60.

Brenner, Gerry. "A Hospitalized World," *Critical Essays on Ernest Hemingway's* A Farewell to Arms. Ed. George Monteiro. New York: G. K. Hall, 1994. 130–44.

Cowley, Malcolm. "Hemingway's Wound," *Georgia Review* 38 (Summer 1984): 229–30.

———. Introduction. *The Portable Hemingway.* New York: Viking Press, 1944.

Heidegger, Martin. *Being and Time.* New York: Harper Perennial, 1962.

Hemingway, Ernest. "Big Two-Hearted River," *The Complete Short Stories of Ernest Hemingway: The Finca Vigía Edition.* New York: Scribner's, 1987.

———. *A Farewell to Arms.* New York: Scribner's, 1929.

———. *For Whom the Bell Tolls.* New York: Scribner's, 1943.

———. *In Our Time.* New York: Boni and Liveright, 1925.

———. *A Moveable Feast.* New York: Scribner's, 1964.

———. "Soldier's Home." *The Complete Short Stories of Ernest Hemingway: The Finca Vigía Edition.* New York: Scribner's, 1987.

———. "The Snows of Kilimanjaro." *The Complete Short Stories of Ernest Hemingway: The Finca Vigía Edition.* New York: Scribner's, 1987.

———. *The Spanish Earth.* Cleveland: J. B. Savage Company, 1938.

———. *The Sun Also Rises.* New York: Scribner's, 1926.

Lynn, Kenneth S. "The Troubled Fisherman." *New Critical Approaches to the Short Stories of Ernest Hemingway.* Ed. Jackson J. Benson. Durham: Duke UP, 1990. 149–55.

Martin, Robert. "Hemingway's *For Whom the Bell Tolls:* Fact into Fiction." *The Hemingway Review* 6.1 (Fall 1996): 56.

Paulson, Daryl S., and Stanley C. Krippner. *Haunted by Combat: Understanding PTSD in War Veterans, Reservists and Troops Coming Back from Iraq.* Westport: Greenwood, 2007.

Schorer, Mark. "Ernest Hemingway." *Major Writers of America.* Vol. 2. Ed. Perry Miller. New York: Harcourt Brace Jovanovich, 1962. p. 675.

Smith, Dr. James. Personal interview. December 2012.

Svoboda, Frederic J. "The Great Themes in Hemingway: Love, War, Wilderness, and Loss." *A Historical Guide to Ernest Hemingway.* Ed. Linda Wagner-Martin. Oxford: Oxford UP, 2000. 55–72.

Tick, Edward. *War and the Soul: Healing Our Nation's Veterans from PTSD.* Wheaton, IL: Quest Books, 2005.

Trilling, Lionel. "Hemingway and the Critics." *Partisan Review* 6 (Winter 1939): 52–60.

Williams, Wirt. *The Tragic Art of Ernest Hemingway.* Baton Rouge: Louisiana State UP, 1982.

Wilson, Edmund. *The Portable Edmund Wilson.* Ed. Lewis M. Dabney. New York: Viking, 1983.

Skiing with Papa

Teaching Hemingway in the Backcountry Snow

Scott Knickerbocker

It is difficult to practice good sound thinking when our thoughts are awash with the constant flow of email, social media, online news, and cell phone texts. Researchers have noted the societal consequence of being constantly plugged in, including a phenomenon Linda Stone calls "continuous partial attention," meaning that it has become all but impossible to devote our attention to one thing alone at any given time. As Neil Postman puts it, people have fallen in love with the very technologies "that undo their capacities to think" (xix).

Because we flit constantly between tasks in response to the incessant demands of technology, we are losing the capacity for sustained concentration. In his book *The Shallows: What the Internet Is Doing to Our Brains,* Nicholas Carr describes how human thought has been shaped through the centuries by "tools of the mind" such as the alphabet, maps, the printing press, the clock, and the computer. Incorporating recent discoveries in neuroscience, Carr shows how our brains change in response to our experiences. The technologies we use to find, store, and share information literally reroute our neural pathways. The printed book serves to focus our attention, promoting deep and creative thought. In stark contrast, the Internet encourages the rapid, distracted sampling of small bits of information from many sources. We are becoming ever more adept at scanning and skimming, but what we are losing is our capacity for concentration, contemplation, and reflection.

A few weeks ago I went fly-fishing with a friend on the South Fork of the Boise River in Idaho. As I gazed at the play of light on river ripple, focusing and refocusing my eyes to see rainbow trout surface then resume their shadowy positions below, I recalled this marvelous sentence from Norman Maclean's fly-fishing novella, *A River Runs Through It*: "All there is to thinking is seeing something noticeable which makes you see something you weren't noticing which makes you see something that isn't even visible" (92). Maclean's description of thinking applies to fly-fishing, but it also aptly describes the activity of close reading. When literary critics practice close reading, they enrich our understanding and enjoyment of a text by analyzing the relationship between its form and its content and paying extremely close attention to details in the language, in the process drawing to the surface of the text submerged significance. Close reading demands that we pay attention and go deep; in other words, it is the very opposite of continuous partial attention. Like fly-fishing, a successful close reading is, for me at least, a joyful expenditure of energy that makes us focus our thinking, pay attention with all of our senses, and grow in imagination.

Ernest Hemingway lived his last years and ended his life in the mountain town of Ketchum, Idaho, next to Sun Valley, one of the oldest ski resorts in the United States. An hour's drive north of Ketchum, the craggy Sawtooth Mountains rise above the tiny settlement of Stanley, Idaho (pop. 63), where my wife and I lead an experiential environmental education program every other January called Winter Wilderness Experience, which we designed for a small group of students from The College of Idaho. An interdisciplinary study of the Sawtooth Valley and surrounding mountains, the Winter Wilderness Experience incorporates environmental literature, human geography, winter ecology, public land policy, and backcountry skiing. After many day trips into the snowy backcountry, the four-week program culminates in a three-day ski trip to backcountry yurts in the Sawtooth Mountains. We also take a private tour of Hemingway's Ketchum home. Although Hemingway did not write much about Idaho, he did write compellingly about backcountry telemark skiing in the Alps in the 1920s in short stories such as "Cross Country Snow" and in his memoir *A Moveable Feast*. As part of the literary emphasis, my students read these pieces and do some collaborative close reading in our follow-up discussions. This provides me with the opportunity to consider the place of close reading in the context of experiential, outdoor education.

One of my goals in the Winter Wilderness Experience is to provide not just multidisciplinary education—multiple lenses through which to understand this one region—but truly *inter*disciplinary education in which the content and practices of different disciplines overlap and are integrated. For example, the students' appreciation of Jack London's short story "To Build a Fire," in which the protagonist freezes to death in the Yukon, was shaped partly by what they learned about mammalian heat loss in their winter ecology workshop. Reading Hemingway's backcountry skiing literature enriched the students' experience of their own skiing adventures, and inversely, the students' skiing enriched their appreciation of Hemingway.

But more important than Hemingway providing examples of good writing about skiing for the students to model, and more important than Hemingway's biographical connection to the area, reading Hemingway with my students provided us with an opportunity to practice close reading. This, in turn, provided me with the pedagogical opportunity to ponder the role of close reading in the Winter Wilderness Experience and, more generally, the place of close reading in environmental education. That is, if my ultimate goal in the Winter Wilderness Experience is to foster in the students a sense of place through an integrated, holistic education, what is the role of close reading in achieving this goal? Given the fact that close reading typically happens indoors with eyes glued to a text, can close reading be integrated meaningfully into what is largely *outdoor* environmental education?

Part of my students' academic work includes daily journal writing in response to readings, guest speakers, and our daily adventures. We discuss Hemingway's short story "Cross Country Snow" from his 1925 book *In Our Time*. The story describes friends Nick and George backcountry telemark skiing in the Alps:

> [Nick] looked up the hill. George was coming down in telemark position, kneeling; one leg forward and bent, the other trailing; his sticks hanging like some insect's thin legs, kicking up puffs of snow as they touched the surface and finally the whole kneeling, trailing figure coming around in a beautiful right curve, crouching, the legs shot forward and back, the body leaning out against the swing, the sticks accenting the curve like points of light, all in a wild cloud of snow. (108)

The students and I look closely at the form of Hemingway's language in passages like this—his imagery, figurative language, diction, syntax, and sound effects—to understand how he recreates the experience of telemark skiing (through form) rather than merely writes about it. For instance, the many *-ing* verbs in the passage above emphasize movement and process, and the long sentence both breaks down the overall movement into its various parts, each expressed in a different phrase, and unites all of those parts into one flowing action. The sentence has a cubist effect, in which the different components of the telemark turn are presented all at once rather than sequentially. The first half of the sentence modulates between short and long phrases before settling into a rhythm of phrases of similar length in the latter half of the sentence. This syntactical rhythm connotes the rhythm required in successfully linking telemark turns as one descends the slope. Overall, the sentence balances control and exhilaration in the same way that skiing, which is essentially a controlled fall, requires balance; all of the components of George's elegant and masterful movement occur "in a wild cloud of snow" (108). Hemingway's powerful sentence reproduces that combined sense of wildness and control one feels when skiing.

But how might a close attention to Hemingway's language about skiing be integrated with the outdoor, embodied experience of actual backcountry skiing? After the students do some follow-up critical writing in their journals about Hemingway's skiing passages, I ask them to write extended responses to the question, "What skills necessary for backcountry skiing are also helpful for close reading, and vice versa?" Each of their answers is distinct, yet certain themes emerge.

The most common theme tends to be awareness, of paying close attention, whether one's attention is directed toward a text or one's physical environment. Unlike conventional downhill skiing, which makes use of a chair lift, backcountry skiers "earn their turns," by climbing slopes (with climbing skins—made of seal skin in Hemingway's day—affixed to the bottom of the skis). Ninety percent of one's time skiing the backcountry is spent ascending slopes, and even the free-heel telemark turn downhill is more physically taxing than fixed-heel alpine turns. As one of my students put it,

> If you don't think it's possible to sweat in below freezing temperatures, try backcountry telemarking. You have to earn your turns. There's no chair lift in the backcountry. To reach the top of a slope, you must work hard, but skiing down takes strength too. There's the burn in your quad muscles as you bend your knees and lunge forward. You must hike back up if you want to repeat the dance. Ernest Hemingway remembered what that was like when he wrote about backcountry skiing: "Anything you ran down from, you had to climb up. That gave you legs that were fit to run down with" (*A Moveable Feast* 199).

This not only makes backcountry skiing far more rigorous than lift area skiing; during the long, slow uphill climb, one also has time to make close observations. As a student put it, "The hike up the mountain allows you to closely read the landscape. The aspect, the vegetation types, the snow. You can translate stories as you climb. A snow shoe hare was in a hurry when it crossed the trail here or deer must like to rub on that tree. Its trunk is now smooth with tufts of hair sticking out of the bark." During a field trip to Idaho's Craters of the Moon National Monument, a huge lava flow that stretches from the southern Pioneer Mountains to the Snake River Plain, another student made the following observations as she took in the view, which revealed more and more the higher we climbed up a snow-covered cinder cone:

> The view from the top of the cinder cone is wonderful. A low fog floats like a magic carpet over the Snake River Plain on the southwest horizon. The end of the Lost River mountain range drops off into flatness to the west of us. I continue my panorama. There's the Pioneer Mountains to the north, back to the northeast there is Lava Lake ranch, and with more cinder cones in the foreground. Little vegetation grows here. Leaning, twisted Limber pines are the only ones not completely blanketed by snow. Prickly pear cactus, antelope bitterbrush, big sagebrush lichens, monkey flowers, bitterroot, paintbrush, and syringa are missing from the scene, but in the spring time, they will erupt from the lava rock and splash brilliant colors across the desolate landscape. It's a tough place to survive, with little soil, few nutrients, limited water and shelter, and extreme temperatures, but amazingly the flora supports several fauna including pika, sage grouse, pygmy rabbits, snowshoe hare, elk, and white tail deer. Employees have even seen moose and wolves in Craters of the Moon. Life can survive almost anywhere.

This student not only observed what is visible close by and on the distant horizon but imagined with her mind's eye the plants and animals that live in this harsh landscape.

My students also draw comparisons between the deep attention of close reading and the deep attention required of them while skiing in avalanche terrain. While reading is not a life-threatening activity, backcountry skiers must, like literary critics, read beneath the surface. Specifically, they must *literally* dig below the surface of the snow to analyze the structure of the snowpack and detect avalanche hazards such as a heavy, well-bonded slab of snow on top of sugary, faceted snow. They must look for shooting cracks in the snow and listen carefully for "whoomphing sounds" (when the snow pack suddenly compresses). They must also pay close attention to the environmental context of skiing the backcountry—that is, the terrain (slope angle, aspect, possible terrain traps below), the weather conditions, even the skill level of the skiers in a group. As the students quickly realize, a beautiful, tranquil snowy mountain wilderness can very quickly become dangerous and even deadly if one doesn't probe—literally and figuratively—beneath this surface beauty and heed carefully the many potential red flags in avalanche terrain.

Backcountry skiing therefore fosters humility and receptivity, two qualities requisite in the act of close reading, as this student recognized:

> When I come across a tough phrase and I'm swamped about its meaning, I can't just throw whatever meaning to it that I decide in order to solve the puzzle. I've been taught to respect the integrity of the text. More studious work is required to figure it out . . . to parallel close reading with backcountry skiing, perhaps the story is the slope, the author is the mountain or whatever geological forces shaped it, the reader is the skier, the powder is the author's language and our skies are our understanding of that language. Our ability to telemark ski is our ability to relate to the author's ideas and comprehend their meaning. This is how I would compare backcountry skiing to close reading. The mountain has a story to tell. We who want to telemark ski, endeavor to learn it.

For this student, both mountain and text demand respect if they are to be understood (or survived).

Closely reading a text and closely reading a snowy environment while backcountry skiing combine work and play, as students often note. That is, both activities induce pleasure as a result of a rigorous and concerted effort. As one student put it, "Close reading requires the will to explore new terrain and the drive to skin up and try again. For some works, like short stories or poems, the close reader may make a few laps to curve across the many different aspects of the same area, even returning year after year and still finding hidden meaning. Other works might demand meticulous attention and mental legs that are strong enough to navigate the steep routes of a text." Another student commented, "Backcountry skiing and reading carefully are similar in the sense that while both are a lot of work, the results of such work pay off in the form of fun and a sense of understanding that couldn't have been achieved otherwise." Close reading and backcountry skiing demand that we become more fully sensuous as part of paying attention, and we experience aesthetic pleasure as a result. As David Quammen puts it, telemark skiing just plain "feels beautiful to do" (135).

It is easy to see how aesthetic appreciation of nature's beauty can lead to an ethical concern for one's environment. But why on this damaged earth should we spend any quiet, contemplative time engaged in close reading when so many environmental problems threaten to overwhelm us? The answer lies in the power of close reading—like backcountry skiing—to serve as an antidote to the technology-induced condition of our day: continuous partial attention. In order adequately to understand and address the complex knot of environmental crises now facing us, we need certain qualities endangered by continuous partial attention: the perseverance required to dig deeply and observe closely, the particular kind of creativity inspired by such perseverance, the willingness to be surprised, and the humility to revise our beliefs given the evidence we uncover. Teaching Hemingway's skiing literature in the context of the Winter Wilderness Experience showed me that close reading and backcountry skiing—and the integration of the two—help to foster these qualities.

Works Cited

Carr, Nicholas. *The Shallows: What the Internet Is Doing to Our Brains.* New York: Norton, 2011.

Hemingway, Ernest. *In Our Time.* New York: Boni and Liveright, 1925. New York: Scribner's, 1930.

———. *A Moveable Feast.* New York: Touchstone, 1964.

Maclean, Norman. *A River Runs Through It and Other Stories.* Chicago: U of Chicago P, 1976.

Postman, Neil. *Amusing Ourselves to Death.* New York: Penguin, 1985.

Quammen, David. "Pinhead Secrets." *Wild Thoughts from Wild Places.* New York: Simon & Schuster, 1998.

Stone, Linda. "Continuous Partial Attention." Linda Stone blog. <https://lindastone.net/qa/continuous-partial-attention/>. Accessed 14 Apr. 2017.

Appendix

Teaching Materials

Drawing on decades of teaching experiences, contributors share below a selection of teaching materials that suggest specific classroom approaches to teaching Hemingway with concerns of the natural world in mind. The collection of writing prompts, exam questions, and essay assignments are meant to supplement the preceding essays. While they are specific to each author's essay, they are also adaptable enough to work in myriad classroom settings for secondary, undergraduate, and graduate students.

Adopted from Ellen Andrews Knodt

Ernest Hemingway's stories fit into many literature courses, including a Survey of American Literature, The American Short Story, and Introduction to Literature. Texts for these courses frequently include a Hemingway story in their table of contents; instructors may wish to approach the reading of a story with attention to landscape. Knodt finds that written journal assignments to accompany a reading assignment enhance student involvement in their reading and improve class discussion. Such journal assignments need be only one or two pages and can be informal reader reactions to the story (though she asks students to write in complete sentences and with some detail as evidence for their opinions).

Sample topics for journal assignments:

1. Compare the images of Cézanne's landscapes to the description of landscapes in the Hemingway story. What similarities do you notice between the visual and verbal landscapes?
2. What connections do you see between the depiction of a landscape and a character's emotions or actions in the story?
3. Are there differences in the descriptions of natural landscapes between the beginning of the story and the end of the story? If so, how do these differences affect the meaning in a story?

Adopted from Scott Ortolano

Sample writing prompts

1. In *Hemingway on Fishing,* Nick Lyons explains that Hemingway's fiction and nonfiction about the natural world, and fishing in particular, are critically rich avenues for "understand[ing] a lot about the man and his writing." For this assignment, you will need to choose a selection from Lyons' book that we have not discussed in class (instructors might also assign a specific article or selection from the book or use an entirely different work by Hemingway about the natural world) and explain its significance. What does the essay reveal about Hemingway's relationship with nature in a general context? What are his views of the inhabitants of these natural landscapes and humanity's relationship with and obligations to these creatures and their environments? Additionally, you may consider how the writing itself helps to convey these ideas (in terms of the aesthetic and textual strategies being employed).

2. *Please note that the following prompt is tailored to chapter 4's discussion of Hemingway's "Big Two-Hearted River" and the philosophy of Henri Bergson, but instructors can easily adapt this assignment to any work by Hemingway.*

    For this project, you will use Storify (www.storify.com) or Medium (www.medium.com) to create a multimodal exploration of (1) Hemingway's writing about the natural world, as represented in "Big Two-Hearted River," and (2) Henri Bergson's ideas about existence, as represented in "Introduction to Metaphysics." You will accomplish this by interweaving quotes from Hemingway's story and Bergson's essay with digital content (websites, GIFs, videos, etc.) about the natural world. This digital content could be about a plethora of subtopics, including the environment of the Midwest, rivers as ecosystems or philosophical metaphors, trout or trout fishing, the logging industry, etc. Your essay should relate how the content and form of Hemingway's writing offers readers a deep, often spiritual encounter with the environment and world. The digital content should be used to further illustrate these points, and you need to analyze them as you would any literary passage. Your conclusion should link out to a specific organization or group that is dedicated to advocating for the ecological subject that you focus on.

3. *Please note that the assignment below is tailored to chapter 4's discussion of Hemingway's "Big Two-Hearted River" and the philosophy of Henri Bergson. It could easily be applied to other works by Hemingway that take the form of an open multiplicity and would be especially applicable to courses that engage* In Our Time *or* The Nick Adams Stories. *The ideal place for this assignment is*

a first-year writing course or high school English class, and it could be simplified by removing the Bergson essay and having students use "Big Two-Hearted River" as the sole point of inspiration for their project.

For this project, you will use Storify (www.storify.com) or Medium (www.medium.com) to create a multimodal essay that takes the form of an open multiplicity. Much in the way Hemingway uses concrete images to signify deeper truths about Nick and the world, I would like you to use a number of digital texts (images, GIFs, videos, websites, etc.) to represent various aspects of yourself. Along the way, you should incorporate quotes from "Big Two-Hearted River" and Henri Bergson's "Introduction to Metaphysics" to frame your essay. While you will narrate your project through traditional prose, you should attempt to mimic the iceberg theory and provide readers with just enough to glimpse the surface of your identity. The digital texts themselves will provide the reader with a way of delving further beneath the surface. Thus, you should compose a coherent, flowing, and open expository essay that provides digital representations of what makes you who you are.

Sample exam questions:
1. Provide students with an excerpt of Hemingway's work where his aesthetic of omission is being employed to describe the natural world (the selection should be culled from something that has already been read previously in the semester). Ask students the following response question: Please explain the iceberg theory (or Hemingway's aesthetic of omission), outlining its process and purpose. Once you have done this, use the provided passage to explain how the iceberg theory is at work and what points are being made.
2. How is the influence of Ezra Pound and imagism in general evident in Hemingway's descriptions of the natural world?
3. How have Henri Bergson's ideas shaped Hemingway's fiction, particularly the manner in which he represents human perception, environmental spaces, and time?
4. Provide students with an excerpt from Hemingway about trout moving in the current of a river (passages from "Big Two-Hearted River" are ideal for this question). Ask students the following question: Why are trout such important figures in Hemingway's writing? Use the above passage to explain your answer.
5. Why is fishing so significant for Hemingway? Discuss a story or novel in which fishing plays a central role and explore what makes it such a spiritual exercise and what it teaches readers about existence.

Adapted from Michael Kim Roos

Sample essay prompt from an intermediate composition course

Essay #1: Classical Argument (Hemingway's "Big Two-Hearted River")

In response to our reading and discussion of Hemingway's "Big Two-Hearted River," write a 700–1000 word classical argument paper in which you agree or disagree with one of the following propositions:

1. Evolution by natural selection should be included as part of all high school biology curricula.
2. By the end of the final published version of "Big Two-Hearted," Nick Adams has achieved a state of "enchantment" with nature that will endure for the rest of his life.
3. It is important for those who hunt and fish to do so out of respect for nature and preservation of species.
4. Human beings are a part of the general natural order and subject to the same laws that govern every species.
5. Science, rationalism, and progress have directly led to widespread disenchantment in the modern world.

General guidelines: Have a clear sense of the audience for the paper. Your introduction should provide necessary background and state the claim you intend to support. In constructing your claim, strive to develop audience-based reasons. The body of your argument should summarize and respond to opposing views as well as present reasons and evidence in support of your own position. You need to choose whether to summarize and refute opposing views before or after you have made your own case. Try to end your essay with your strongest arguments. Try also to include appeals to *pathos* and to create a positive, credible *ethos*.

Adapted from Allen C. Jones

Sample essay and discussion questions

1. Choose two scenes in *The Old Man and the Sea* and use our eight questions to compare/contrast the ways in which each scene addresses the central tensions raised by ecocriticism.
2. Take one of the following positions and defend your answer: (A) *The Old Man and the Sea* devalues nature and should not be treated as an ecocritical

text; (B) *The Old Man and the Sea* values nature and should be treated as an ecocritical text.
3. Take one of the following positions and defend your answer: (A) We should assess Hemingway as a man and use this to evaluate his writing; (B) We should focus only on the text and disregard Hemingway's life story.

Experiential exercise on observational writing and metaphor

> Directions: Give students twenty minutes total to go outside, find a spot to sit, and write direct description of something natural. Encourage them to use all five senses, including taste. Share the pieces and the experience when they return.
>
> The Key: Before sending them out (briefly or in a previous class), talk about the difference between abstract and concrete writing, and also between direct observation and interpretation. Briefly: an abstraction is something we cannot sense with the five senses. Interpretation moves us from the object in the outer world into our own minds. Tell them that they must resist interpretation and metaphor. Their goal is to directly describe what they see, touch, feel, taste, smell in nature.
>
> The Goal: Explain to them that the goal of this exercise is to feel the inevitable pull toward interpretation. Even a metaphor is a move toward interpretation that pushes us away from direct observation: a leaf curls like a wave. Suddenly we are observing an ocean, not a leaf. Make it clear that metaphors are very effective and make great writing. The goal of this assignment is *not* necessarily to produce a masterpiece, rather it is to navigate and sense these competing fields as we write. By resisting our natural impulse toward metaphor and interpretation, we experience what we are talking about when we discuss what it means to directly describe nature. Tell students to feel the pull as they write,to resist it, and see what it feels like to repeatedly push back toward the senses. And yes, taste the grass, tree, or mud.

Adapted from Sean Milligan

Lesson plan for teaching the conflicts in "The Snows of Kilimanjaro"

Materials:
- Evans, Oliver. "'The Snows of Kilimanjaro': A Revaluation." *PMLA* 76.5 (1961): 601–7.
- Family Tree template available on Prezi (optional)

Rationale:
A synthesis tree is a way to map a critical controversy in order to have a better understanding of it. Synthesizing sources in this way also helps you to begin to formulate your own position on a controversial issue.

Discussion:
- Students should come to class having read both Hemingway's "The Snows of Kilimanjaro" and Evans's "'The Snows of Kilimanjaro': A Revaluation." The following questions could drive the class discussion:
  - What is the central question driving the controversy in this article?
  - What are the points of similarity among the authors cited by Evans? What are the differences?
  - How could we group these authors based on their similarities and differences?

Prompt:
- Using the "Family Tree" template on Prezi, construct a synthesis tree with the various critics that Evans cites in his essay.
- Write a short (1–2 page) essay in which you articulate your opinion on the effectiveness of the symbolism in "The Snows of Kilimanjaro."

Minimum Requirements:
- A synthesis tree that includes at least 2–3 branches
- A short (1–2 page) response to Evans's essay that articulates an opinion on the effectiveness of the symbolism in Hemingway's story

Adapted from Donald A. Daiker

Assignments for a Two-Week, Six-Class Unit on The Sun Also Rises

For each class, after your reading, write an informal response of 250–300 words to one of the questions or to a topic of your own, provided it focuses on the assigned reading.

Class #1: *The Sun Also Rises*, 1–34 (Book I, Chapters 1–4).
1. What do you think so far of Jake, the novel's narrator and central character?
2. What can you tell, from their meetings in chapters 3 and 4, about the relationship between Jake and Brett?
3. What does it mean that Frances "led him [Robert Cohn] quite a life" (7)?

Class #2: *The Sun Also Rises*, 35–65 (Book I, Chapters 5–7).
1. Do Jake and Brett love each other? Why do you think so? What can you learn from the important bedroom scene in Jake's apartment, pp. 54–56?
2. Some readers think that Hemingway depicts the characters in Book I as a "lost generation." Would you agree?
3. Does Jake have a job? What is it? Does he like it? Does he do it well?
4. Why does Brett not accept Count Mippipopolous's offer to go off with him?

Class #3: *The Sun Also Rises*, 67–151 (Book II, Chapters 8–14).
1. How do the traveling and fishing scenes with Bill and Jake compare to the earlier Paris scenes?
2. Some readers think that chapter 14 is especially important. What does it reveal about Jake's philosophy of life?
3. According to chapter 14, how does Jake define morality?

Class #4: *The Sun Also Rises*, 152–224 (Book II, Chapters 15–18).
1. Why does Jake agree to introduce Brett to Romero?
2. Why is bullfighting so important to Jake and other aficionados?
3. Why is Pedro Romero so special?
4. Why is Jake so depressed at the end of Book II?

Class #5: *The Sun Also Rises*, 225–47 (Book III, Chapter 19).
1. Why does Jake decide to leave Bayonne, France, for San Sebastian, Spain, even though he feels like a "fool" doing so?
2. Why is Jake not surprised to receive Brett's telegrams asking for help?
3. Why does Jake agree to go to Madrid to rescue Brett?

Class #6: *The Sun Also Rises*, carefully reread pp. 225–47.
1. Why is Brett crying when she talks to Jake in her hotel room?
2. How does the bedroom scene in Brett's hotel room compare to the earlier bedroom scene in Jake's Paris apartment (chapter 7)?
3. Is Jake drunk—or just drinking heavily—at the end of the novel?
4. How does the final taxi scene with Brett in Madrid compare to the earlier taxi scene with Brett (chapter 4) in Paris?
5. Some readers think that the novel is circular, with Jake and Brett going around in circles and winding up pretty much where they began. Other readers think that things have changed profoundly. What do you think?

Works Cited

Abbey, Edward. *Desert Solitaire: A Season in the Wilderness.* 1968. New York: Ballantine Books, 1991.

Adams, Carol J. "Ecofeminism and the Eating of Animals." *Ecological Feminist Philosophies.* Ed. Karen J. Warren. Bloomington: Indiana UP, 1996.

Almond, Steve. "Once Upon a Time, There Was a Person Who Said, 'Once Upon a Time.'" *The New York Times Magazine.* 11 Jan. 2013. <https://nyti.ms/2kGXD7T>.

Ariely, Dan. *Predictably Irrational: The Hidden Forces that Shape Our Decisions.* New York: Harper Collins, 2008.

Bacon, John U. "Hemingway's Michigan: Summers in Northern Michigan Helped Shape Nobel Laureate." *Ann Arbor Chronicle.* 27 Aug. 2010. <http://annarborchronicle.com/2010/08/27/column-hemingways-michigan/>.

Baker, Carlos. *Hemingway: A Life Story.* New York: Scribner, 1969.

———. *Hemingway: The Writer as Artist.* Princeton, NJ: Princeton UP, 1963.

———. "The Mountain and the Plain." *Critical Essays on Ernest Hemingway's* A Farewell to Arms. Ed. George Monteiro. Boston: G. K. Hall, 1984. 97–103.

Baker, Sheridan. "Hemingway's Two-Hearted River." *The Short Stories of Ernest Hemingway: Critical Essays.* Ed. Jackson J. Benson. Durham: Duke UP, 1975.

Ballon, Rachel. *Breathing Life into Your Characters.* Cincinnati: Writer's Digest Books, 2011.

Baym, Nina. "Actually, I Felt Sorry for the Lion." *New Critical Approaches to the Stories of Ernest Hemingway.* Ed. Jackson J. Benson. Durham: Duke UP, 1990. 112–20.

Beegel, Susan F. "Eye and Heart: Hemingway's Education as a Naturalist." *A Historical Guide to Ernest Hemingway.* Ed. Linda Wagner-Martin. New York: Oxford UP, 2000. 53–92.

———. "A Guide to the Marine Life in Ernest Hemingway's *The Old Man and the Sea*." *Resources for American Literary Study* 30 (2006): 236–315.

———. "Santiago and the Eternal Feminine: Gendering *La Mar* in *The Old Man and the Sea*." *Bloom's Modern Critical Interpretations: The Old Man and the Sea.* Ed. Harold Bloom. New York: Infobase, 2008.

Bekoff, Marc. *The Emotional Lives of Animals.* Novato, CA: New World Library, 2007.

Bell, Millicent. "Pseudoautobiography and Personal Metaphor." *Critical Essays on Ernest Hemingway's A Farewell to Arms.* Ed. George Monteiro. Boston: G. K. Hall, 1984. 145–60.

Bender, Bert. *The Descent of Love: Darwin and the Theory of Sexual Selection in American Fiction, 1871–1926*. Philadelphia: U of Pennsylvania P, 1996.

———. *Evolution and "the Sex Problem": American Narratives during the Eclipse of Darwinism*. Kent, OH: Kent State UP, 2004.

———. "Margot Macomber's Gimlet." *College Literature* 8.1 (Winter 1981): 12–20.

Bennett, Jane. *The Enchantment of Modern Life: Attachments, Crossings, and Ethics*. Princeton: Princeton UP, 2001.

Bergson, Henri. *Creative Evolution*. 1907. Trans. Arthur Mitchell. 1911. Mineola, NY: Dover Publications, 1998.

———. *The Creative Mind: Introduction to Metaphysics*. 1934. Trans. Mabelle L. Andison. New York: Citadel Press, 2002.

Berman, Ron. "Recurrence in Hemingway and Cézanne." *Hemingway: Eight Decades of Criticism*. Ed. Linda Wagner-Martin. East Lansing: Michigan State UP, 2009.

Bolton, Matthew J. "Memory and Desire: Eliotic Consciousness in Early Hemingway." *Ernest Hemingway and the Geography of Memory*. Ed. Mark Cirino and Mark P. Ott. Kent, OH: Kent State UP, 2010.

Brandt, Kenneth K., and Alicia Mischa Renfroe. "Intent and Culpability: A Legal Review of the Shooting in 'The Short Happy Life of Francis Macomber.'" *The Hemingway Review* 33.2 (2014): 8–29.

Brasch, James D. "Invention from Knowledge: The Hemingway-Cowley Correspondence." *Ernest Hemingway: The Writer in Context*. Ed. James Nagel. Madison: U of Wisconsin P, 1984. 201–36.

Brasch, James D., and Joseph Sigman. *Hemingway's Library: A Composite Record*. New York: Garland Publishing, Inc. 1981.

Brenner, Gerry. "A Hospitalized World," *Critical Essays on Ernest Hemingway's* A Farewell to Arms. Ed. George Monteiro. New York: G. K. Hall, 1994. 130–44.

———. *The Old Man and the Sea: Story of a Common Man*. New York: Twayne, 1991.

Brøgger, Fredrik Chr. "Whose Nature? Differing Narrative Perspectives in Hemingway's 'Big Two-Hearted River.'" *Hemingway and the Natural World*. Ed. Robert Fleming. Moscow: U of Idaho P, 1999.

Brown, Bill. *Reading the West: An Anthology of Dime Westerns*. Boston: Bedford Books, 1997.

Bruccoli, Matthew J., ed., with Robert W. Trogdon. *The Only Thing That Counts: The Ernest Hemingway/Maxwell Perkins Correspondence*. New York: Scribners, 1996.

Buell, Lawrence. *The Environmental Imagination: Thoreau, Nature Writing, and the Formation of American Culture*. Cambridge, MA: Harvard UP, 1995.

———. *The Future of Environmental Criticism: Environmental Crisis and Literary Imagination*. Oxford: Blackwell, 2005.

Burhans, Clinton, Jr. "*The Old Man and the Sea:* Hemingway's Tragic Vision of Man." *American Literature* 31.4 (1960): 446–55.

Calabi, Silvio. "Ernest Hemingway on Safari: The Game and the Guns." *Hemingway and Africa*. Ed. Miriam B. Mandel. Rochester, NY: Camden House, 2011. 85–121.

Carr, Nicholas. *The Shallows: What the Internet Is Doing to Our Brains*. New York: Norton, 2011.

Chawla, Louise. "Ecstatic Places." *Children's Environments Quarterly* 7.4 (Winter 1986): 22–27.

Clark, Suzanne. *Cold Warriors: Manliness on Trial in the Rhetoric of the West*. Carbondale: Southern Illinois UP, 2000.

Coleridge, Samuel Taylor. *The Rime of the Ancient Mariner*. 1798. Illustrated by Gustave Doré. New York: Dover Publications, 1970.

Cowley, Malcolm. "Hemingway's Wound." *Georgia Review* 38 (Summer 1984): 229–30.

———. Introduction. *The Portable Hemingway*. New York: Viking Press, 1944.

Crawford, Matthew B. *The World Beyond Your Head: On Becoming an Individual in an Age of Distraction*. New York: Farrar, Straus and Giroux, 2015.

Cremean, David N. "Man Cannot Live by Dry Fly Flies Alone: Fly Rods, Grasshoppers, and an Adaptive Catholicity in Hemingway's 'Big Two-Hearted River.'" *Hemingway and the Natural World*. Moscow: U of Idaho P, 1999. 31–44.

Daiker, Donald A. "The Affirmative Conclusion of *The Sun Also Rises*." *McNeese Review* 21 (1974): 3–19. Rpt. in *Critical Essays on Ernest Hemingway's* The Sun Also Rises. Ed. James Nagel. New York: G. K. Hall, 1995. 74–88.

———. "Jake Barnes as Teacher and Learner: The Pedagogy of *The Sun Also Rises*." *The Hemingway Review* 27.1 (Fall 2007): 74–88.

Darwin, Charles. *The Autobiography of Charles Darwin*. Rev. ed. New York: W. W. Norton, 1993.

———. *On the Origin of Species: A Facsimile of the First Edition*. Cambridge: Harvard UP, 1964.

DeFalco, Joseph. *The Hero in Hemingway's Short Stories*. Pittsburgh: U of Pittsburgh P, 1963.

Del Gizzo, Suzanne. "Going Home; Hemingway, Primitivisn, and Identity." *Modern Fiction Studies* 49.3 (Fall 2003): 496–523.

Dennett, Daniel C. *Darwin's Dangerous Idea: Evolution and the Meanings of Life*. New York: Simon & Schuster, 1995.

Derrida, Jacques. *Of Grammatology*. 1967. Trans. Gayatri Chakravorty Spivak. Baltimore: Johns Hopkins UP, 1976.

De Waal, Frans. *Primates and Philosophers: How Morality Evolved*. Princeton: Princeton UP, 2006.

Dudley, Marc K. *Hemingway, Race, and Art: Bloodlines and the Color Line*. Kent, OH: Kent State UP, 2012.

Dunbar, Willis Frederick. *Michigan: A History of the Wolverine State*. Grand Rapids, MI: William B. Eerdmans Publishing Company, 1965.

Eliot, T. S. "The Dry Salvages." 1943. *The Complete Poems and Plays: 1909–1950*. New York: Harcourt, Brace, and World, 1971. 130–37.

Ellis, Havelock. *The Dance of Life*. Boston: Houghton Mifflin Company, 1923.

Evans, Oliver. "'The Snows of Kilimanjaro': A Revaluation." *PMLA* 76.5 (1961): 601–7.

Ficken, Carl. "Point of View in the Nick Adams Stories." *The Short Stories of Ernest Hemingway: Critical Essays*. Ed. Jackson J. Benson. Durham: Duke UP, 1975.

Fiedler, Leslie. *Love and Death in the American Novel*. 1960. Normal, IL: Dalkey Archive P, 2003.

Fleischman, Suzanne. *Tense and Narrativity: From Medieval Performance to Modern Fiction.* Austin: U of Texas P, 1990.
Fleming, Robert. "Introduction." *Hemingway and the Natural World.* Ed. Robert Fleming. Moscow: U of Idaho P, 1999.
Flora, Joseph M. *Hemingway's Nick Adams.* Baton Rouge: Louisiana State UP, 1982.
Fludernik, Monika. *Towards a 'Natural' Narratology.* London: Routlege, 1996.
Forsman, Anders, et al. "Rapid Evolution of Fire Melanism in Replicated Populations of Pygmy Grasshoppers." *Evolution: International Journal of Organic Evolution* 65.9 (2011): 2530–40.
Gaillard, Theodore L., Jr. "Hemingway's Debt to Cezanne: New Perspectives." *Twentieth Century Literature* 45.1 (Spring 1999): 65–78.
Gajdusek, Robert. *Hemingway: In His Own Country.* Notre Dame, IN: U of Notre Dame P, 2002.
Glotfelty, Cheryll. Introduction. *The Ecocriticism Reader: Landmarks in Literary Ecology.* Ed. Cheryll Glotfelty and Harold Fromm. Athens: U of Georgia P, 1996.
Godfrey, Laura Gruber. "Hemingway and Cultural Geography: The Landscape of Logging in 'The End of Something.'" *Ernest Hemingway and the Geography of Memory.* Ed. Mark Cirino and Mark P. Ott. Kent, OH: Kent State UP, 2010.
Gordon, Caroline, and Allen Tate. *The House of Fiction: An Anthology of the Short Story with Commentary.* New York: Charles Scribner's Sons, 1950.
Graff, Gerald. *Beyond the Culture Wars: How Teaching the Conflicts Can Revitalize American Education.* New York: Norton, 1992.
———. Foreword. *Falling into Theory: Conflicting Views on Reading Literature.* Ed. David Richter. Boston: Bedford Books, 1994. v–vi.
———. "Organizing the Conflicts in the Curriculum." *The Journal of the Midwest Modern Language Association* 25.1 (1992): 63–76.
Green, James L. "Symbolic Sentences in 'Big Two-Hearted River.'" *Modern Fiction Studies* 14.3 (Autumn 1968) 307–12.
Haldane, J. B. S. "A Mathematical Theory of Natural and Artificial Selection." *Transactions of the Cambridge Philosophical Society* 23 (1924): 19–41.
Hass, Robert Bernard. "(Re)Reading Bergson: Frost, Pound, and the Legacy of Modern Poetry." *Journal of Modern Literature* 29.1 (2005): 55–75.
Hediger, Ryan. "The Elephant in the Writing Room: Sympathy and Weakness in Hemingway's 'Masculine Text,' The Garden of Eden." *The Hemingway Review* 31.1 (Fall 2011): 79–95.
———. "Hunting, Fishing, and the Cramp of Ethics in Ernest Hemingway's *The Old Man and the Sea, Green Hills of Africa,* and *Under Kilimanjaro.*" *The Hemingway Review* 27.2 (Spring 2008): 35–39.
Heidegger, Martin. *Being and Time.* New York: Harper Perennial, 1962.
Helama, Samuli. "Ernest Hemingway's Description of the Mountaintop in 'The Snows of Kilimanjaro' and Climate Change Research." *The Hemingway Review* 34.2 (2015): 118–23.
Hemingway, Ernest. "An African Story." *The Complete Short Stories of Ernest Hemingway: The Finca Vigía Edition.* New York: Scribner, 1987. 545–54.

———. "Big Two-Hearted River." *The Complete Short Stories of Ernest Hemingway: The Finca Vigía Edition*. New York: Scribner, 1987.

———. *By-Line: Ernest Hemingway*. Ed. William White. New York: Scribner, 2002.

———. "Cat in the Rain." *The Complete Short Stories of Ernest Hemingway: The Finca Vigía Edition*. New York: Scribner, 1987. 129–31.

———. *The Complete Short Stories of Ernest Hemingway: Finca Vigía Edition*. New York: Scribner, 1998.

———. *Death in the Afternoon*. New York: Scribner's Sons, 1932.

———. *Ernest Hemingway: Selected Letters, 1917–1961*. Ed. Carlos Baker. New York: Scribner, 1981.

———. *A Farewell To Arms*. New York: Scribner, 1929.

———. *For Whom the Bell Tolls*. New York: Scribner, 1940.

———. *The Garden of Eden*. New York: Scribner, 1986.

———. *Green Hills of Africa*. New York: Scribner, 1935.

———. "Hike Walloon Lake: A Diary June 10–21, 1916." *The American Fly Fisher* 15.1 (Summer 1989): 1–9.

———. *In Our Time*. New York: Scribner, 1925.

———. Introduction. *Men at War: The Best War Stories of All Time*. Ed. Ernest Hemingway. New York: Crown, 1942.

———. *Islands in the Stream*. New York: Scribner, 1970.

———. *The Letters of Ernest Hemingway: Volume 1 (1907–1922)*. Ed. Sandra Spanier and Robert Trogdon. Cambridge: Cambridge UP, 2011.

———. *The Letters of Ernest Hemingway: Volume 2 (1923–1925)*. Ed. Sandra Spanier, Albert J. DeFazio III, and Robert Trogdon. Cambridge: Cambridge UP, 2013.

———. *A Moveable Feast*. New York: Charles Scribner's Sons, 1964.

———. *Nick Adams Stories*. New York: Charles Scribner's Sons, 1972.

———. "Notes on Dangerous Game: The Third Tanganyika Letter." *Hemingway's African Stories: The Stories, Their Sources, Their Critics*. Ed. John M. Howell. New York: Scribner, 1969. 71–73.

———. *The Old Man and the Sea*. 1952. New York: Scribner, 1995.

———. "On Fly Fishing," Item 570. JFK Library. Boston, MA.

———. *Selected Letters: 1917–1961*. Ed. Carlos Baker. London: Granada, 1981.

———. "Shootism Versus Sport: The Second Tanganyika Letter." *Hemingway's African Stories: The Stories, Their Sources, Their Critics*. Ed. John M. Howell. New York: Scribner, 1969. 69–71.

———. "The Short Happy Life of Francis Macomber." *The Complete Short Stories of Ernest Hemingway: The Finca Vigía Edition*. New York: Scribner, 1987. 5–28.

———. "The Snows of Kilimanjaro." *The Complete Short Stories of Ernest Hemingway: The Finca Vigía Edition*. New York: Scribner, 1998.

———. "Soldier's Home." *The Complete Short Stories of Ernest Hemingway: The Finca Vigía Edition*. New York: Scribner, 1987.

———. *The Spanish Earth*. Cleveland: J. B. Savage Company, 1938.

———. "Summer People." *The Complete Short Stories of Ernest Hemingway: The Finca Vigía Edition*. New York: Scribner Paperback, 1987.

———. *The Sun Also Rises*. New York: Scribner, 1926.

———. *The Sun Also Rises: A Facsimile Edition*. 2 vols. Ed. Matthew J. Bruccoli. Detroit: Omnigraphics, Inc., 1990.

———. *True at First Light*. New York: Scribner, 1999.

———. *Under Kilimanjaro*. Ed. Robert W. Lewis and Robert E. Fleming. Kent, OH: Kent State UP, 2005.

"Hemingway in Michigan Pt. 1–3." *YouTube*, uploaded by Bonnie Bucqueroux. 21 Sept. 2008. <www.youtube.com/watch?v=QNiyDN1thkw>.

Hemingway, Jack. *Misadventures of a Fly Fisherman*. New York: McGraw Hill, 1986.

Hendrickson, Paul. *Hemingway's Boat: Everything He Loved in Life, and Lost, 1934–1961*. New York: Alfred A. Knopf, 2011.

Herlihy, Jeffrey. *In Paris or Paname: Hemingway's Expatriate Nationalism*. Amsterdam: Rodopi, 2011.

Heyerdahl, Thor. *Kon-Tiki: Across the Pacific by Raft*. Chicago: Rand McNally, 1950.

Hohn, Donovan. "Everyone Hates Henry." *New Republic*, 21 Oct. 2015.

Hollenberg, Alexander. "The Spacious Foreground: Interpreting Simplicity and Ecocritical Ethics in *The Old Man and the Sea*." *The Hemingway Review* 31.2 (Spring 2012): 27–45.

Howell, John M. "McCaslin and Macomber: From *Green Hills* to *Big Woods*." *The Faulkner Journal* 2.1 (1986): 29–36.

Hutton, Virgil. "The Short Happy Life of Macomber." *The Short Stories of Ernest Hemingway: Critical Essays*. Durham, NC: Duke UP, 1975. 239–50.

Ibáñez, Beatriz Penas. "'Very Sad but Very Fine': *Death in the Afternoon*'s Imagist Interpretation of the Bullfight-Text." *A Companion to Ernest Hemingway's Death in the Afternoon*. Ed. Miriam B. Mandel. London: Camden House, 2004. 143–64.

Justice, Hilary K. *The Bones of the Others: The Hemingway Text from the Lost Manuscripts to the Posthumous Novels*. Kent, OH: Kent State UP, 2006.

Kazin, Alfred. *On Native Grounds: An Interpretation of Modern American Prose Literature*. New York: Reynal & Hitchcock, 1942.

Kidd, David Comer, and Emanuele Castano. "Reading Literary Fiction Improves Theory of Mind." *Science*. 18 Oct. 2013. <http://science.sciencemag.org/content/342/6156/377>.

Knight, Christopher J. *Omissions Are Not Accidents: Modern Apophaticism from Henry James to Jacques Derrida*. Toronto: U of Toronto P, 2010.

Knodt, Ellen Andrews. "Diving Deep: Jake's Moment of Truth at San Sebastian." *The Hemingway Review* 17.1 (Fall 1997): 28–37.

Kolodny, Annette. *The Lay of the Land: Metaphor as Experience and History in American Life and Letters*. Chapel Hill: U of North Carolina P, 1975.

Kroupi, Agori. "The Religious Implications of Fishing and Bullfighting in Hemingway's Work." *The Hemingway Review* 28.1 (2008): 107–21.

Krutch, Joseph Wood. *The Modern Temper: A Study and a Confession*. New York: Harcourt Brace, 1929.

Kunstler, James Howard. *The Geography of Nowhere: The Rise and Decline of America's Man-Made Landscape*. New York: Simon & Schuster, 1993.

Kyvig, David E. *Daily Life in the United States, 1920–1939: Decades of Promise and Pain.* Westport, CT: Greenwood, 2002.

Lamb, Robert Paul. "Fishing for Stories." *Modern Fiction Stories* 37.2 (Summer 1991): 161–81.

———. *The Hemingway Short Story.* Baton Rouge: Louisiana State UP, 2013.

Lears, Jackson. *Fables of Abundance: A Cultural History of Advertising in America.* New York: Basic Books, 1994.

Leopold, Aldo. *A Sand County Almanac.* 1949. New York: Ballantine Books, 1986.

Levine, George. *Darwin Loves You: Natural Selection and the Re-enchantment of the Modern World.* Princeton: Princeton UP, 2006.

Lewis, R. W. B. *The American Adam.* Phoenix Books. Chicago IL: U of Chicago P, 1961.

Litvak, Matthew. "Response of Shoaling Fish to the Threat of Aerial Predation." *Environmental Biology of Fishes* 36 (1993): 183–92.

London, Jack. *The Sea Wolf and Selected Stories.* 1904. New York: Signet Classic, 1964.

Louv, Richard. *Last Child in the Woods: Saving Our Children from Nature Deficit Disorder.* Chapel Hill: Algonquin Books, 2005.

Love, Glen A. "Hemingway's Indian Virtues: An Ecological Reconsideration." *Western American Literature* 22 (1987): 201–14.

———. *Practical Ecocriticism: Literature, Biology, and the Environment.* Charlottesville: U of Virginia P, 2003.

Lynn, Kenneth S. *Hemingway.* New York: Simon and Schuster, 1987.

———. "The Troubled Fisherman," *New Critical Approaches to the Short Stories of Ernest Hemingway.* Ed. Jackson J. Benson. Durham: Duke UP, 1990. 149–55.

Lyons, Nick, ed. *Hemingway on Fishing.* New York: Scribner, 2000.

Maclean, Norman. *A River Runs Through It and Other Stories.* Chicago: U of Chicago P, 1976.

Maier, Kevin. "Hemingway's Ecotourism: *Under Kilimanjaro* and the Ethics of Travel." *Interdisciplinary Studies in Literature and Environment* 18.4 (Autumn 2011): 717–36.

Majerus, M. E. N. *Melanism: Evolution in Action.* Oxford: Oxford UP, 1998.

Mandel, Miriam B., ed. Introduction. *A Companion to Hemingway's* Death in the Afternoon. London: Camden House, 2004. 1–17.

———, ed. "Subject and Author: The Literary Backgrounds of *Death in the Afternoon.*" *A Companion to Hemingway's* Death in the Afternoon. London: Camden House, 2004. 79–119.

Mapes, Ed. "Crossing the Gulf Stream." *Sailing Magazine.* 17 Apr. 2009. <www.sailing-magazine.net/how-to/technique/682-crossing-the-gulf-stream.html.>

Martin, Lawrence H. "Hemingway's Constructed Africa: *Green Hills of Africa* and the Conventions of Colonial Sporting Books." *Hemingway and the Natural World.* Moscow: U of Idaho P, 1999. 87–97.

Martin, Robert. "Hemingway's *For Whom the Bell Tolls:* Fact into Fiction." *The Hemingway Review* 6.1 (Fall 1996): 56.

Marx, Leo. *The Machine in the Garden.* London: Oxford UP, 1964.

Melling, Philip. "'There Were Many Indians in the Story': Hidden History in Hemingway's 'Big Two-Hearted River.'" *The Hemingway Review* 28.2 (2009): 46.

Melville, Herman. *Moby Dick; Or, The Whale*. 1851. New York: Norton, 2003.
Messent, Peter. "'The Real Thing'? Representing the Bullfight and Spain in *Death in the Afternoon*." *A Companion to Hemingway's* Death in the Afternoon. Ed. Miriam B. Mandel. London: Camden House, 2004. 123–42.
Michigan Department of Natural Resources. *Jack Pine Ecosystem*. 4 June 2012. <www.michigan.gov/dnr/0,4570,7-153-10370_22664-60337—,00.html>.
Moddelmog, Debra A. *Reading Desire: In Pursuit of Ernest Hemingway*. Ithaca: Cornell UP, 1999.
———. "The Unifying Consciousness of a Divided Conscience: Nick Adams as Author of *In Our Time*." *American Literature* 60.4 (Dec. 1988): 591–610.
Montgomery, Marion. "The Leopard and the Hyena: Symbol and Meaning in 'The Snows of Kilimanjaro.'" *Hemingway's African Stories: The Stories, Their Sources, Their Critics*. New York: Charles Scribner's Sons, 1969. 145–49.
Morris, Donald R. "Where Do Chickens Come From?" *Baltimore Sun*. 26 Sept. 1996. p. 1.
O'Brien, Sarah Mary. "'I Also Am in Michigan': Pastoralism of Mind in Hemingway's 'Big Two-Hearted River.'" 28.2 (Spring 2009) 66–86.
Ong, Walter J. "The Writer's Audience Is Always a Fiction." *PMLA* 90.1 (1975): 13.
Ott, Mark P. *A Sea of Change: Ernest Hemingway and the Gulf Stream*. Kent, OH: Kent State UP, 2008.
Paulson, Daryl S. and Stanley C. Krippner. *Haunted by Combat: Understanding PTSD in War Veterans, Reservists and Troops Coming Back from Iraq*. Westport: Greenwood, 2007.
Postman, Neil. *Amusing Ourselves to Death*. New York: Penguin, 1985.
Pound, Ezra. "In a Station of the Metro." 1926. *Personae: The Collected Shorter Poems of Ezra Pound*. New York: New Directions, 1950.
———. "A Few Don'ts by an Imagiste." 1913. *Modernism: An Anthology*. Ed. Lawrence Rainey. Malden, MA: Blackwell, 2005.
Quammen, David. "Pinhead Secrets." *Wild Thoughts from Wild Places*. New York: Simon & Schuster, 1998.
———. *The Reluctant Mr. Darwin: An Intimate Portrait of Charles Darwin and the Making of His Theory of Evolution*. New York: Atlas Books, 2006.
Quirk, Tom. *Bergson and American Culture: The Worlds of Willa Cather and Wallace Stevens*. Chapel Hill: U of North Carolina P, 1990.
Raeburn, John. *Fame Became of Him: Hemingway as Public Writer*. Bloomington: Indiana UP, 1984.
Reynolds, Michael S. *Hemingway: The 1930s*. New York: W. W. Norton & Co., 1997.
———. *Hemingway: The Paris Years*. New York: W. W. Norton & Company, 1989.
———. *Hemingway's First War: The Making of* A Farewell to Arms. Princeton, NJ: Princeton UP, 1976.
———. *Hemingway's Reading, 1910–1940*. Princeton, NJ: Princeton UP, 1981.
———. *Young Hemingway*. Oxford: Basil Blackwell. 1986.
Roos, Michael. "Agassiz or Darwin: The Trap of Faith and Science in Hemingway's High School Zoology Class." *The Hemingway Review* 32.2 (Spring 2013): 7–27.
Ross, Elizabeth Irvin. *Write Now! Surprising Ways to Increase Your Creativity*. New York: Barnes and Noble, 2003.

Rovitt, Earl, and Gerry Brenner. *Ernest Hemingway*. Boston: Twayne, 1986.
Savola, David. "'A Very Sinister Book': *The Sun Also Rises* as Critique of Pastoral." *The Hemingway Review* 26.1 (Fall 2006): 25–46.
Scarry, Elaine. *Dreaming by the Book*. New York: Farrar, Straus, Giroux, 1999.
Schorer, Mark. "Ernest Hemingway." *Major Writers of America*. Vol. 2. Ed. Perry Miller. New York: Harcourt Brace Jovanovich, 1962. p. 675.
Schmidt, Susan. "Ecological Renewal Images in 'Big Two-Hearted River': Jack Pines and Fisher King." *The Hemingway Review* 9.2 (1990): 142–45.
Scholes, Robert. *English After the Fall: From Literature to Textuality*. Iowa City: U of Iowa P, 2011.
Seitz, Susan. "A Final (?) Note on the Textual Errors of Ernest Hemingway's 'Summer People.'" *The Hemingway Review* 11.2 (1992): 3.
Shakespeare, Alex. "The Names of Rivers and the Names of Birds: Ezra Pound, Louis Agassiz, and the 'Luminous Detail' in Hemingway's Early Fiction." *Hemingway Review* 30.2 (2011): 36–53.
Shepherd, Allen. "The Lion in the Grass (Alas?): A Note on 'The Short Happy Life of Francis Macomber.'" *Fitzgerald/Hemingway Annual 1972*. Ed. Matthew J. Bruccoli and C. E. Frazer Clark Jr. Dayton, OH: NCR, 1973. 297–99.
Showalter, Elaine. *Teaching Literature*. Malden, MA: Blackwell Publishing, 2003.
Smith, Paul. "Introduction: Hemingway and the Practical Reader." *New Essays on Hemingway's Short Fiction*. Ed. Paul Smith. Cambridge: Cambridge UP, 1998. 1–18.
———. *A Reader's Guide to the Short Stories of Ernest Hemingway*. Boston: G. K. Hall, 1989.
———. "Who Wrote Hemingway's *In Our Time?*" *Hemingway Repossessed*. Ed. Kenneth Rosen. Westport, CT: Praeger, 1994. 143–50.
Spilka, Mark. "Nina Baym's Benevolent Reading of the Macomber Story: An Epistolary Response." *Hemingway: Up in Michigan Perspectives*. East Lansing: Michigan State UP, 1995. 189–201.
Stein, Gertrude. *The Autobiography of Alice B. Toklas*. New York: Vintage Books, 1990.
Steinke, Jim. "Brett and Jake in Spain: Hemingway's Ending for *The Sun Also Rises*." *Spectrum* 27.1–2 (1985): 131–41.
Steinmetz, Jeff, Steven L. Kohler, and Daniel A. Soluk. "Birds Are Overlooked Top Predators in Aquatic Food Webs." *Ecology* 84.5 (2003): 1324–28.
Stephens, Robert O. *Hemingway's Nonfiction: The Public Voice*. Chapel Hill: U of North Carolina P, 1968.
Stevens, Wallace. *Collected Poetry and Prose*. New York: Library of America, 1997.
Stewart, Jack F. "Christian Allusions in 'Big Two-Hearted River.'" *Studies in Short Fiction* 15.2 (1978): 194–96.
Stone, Linda. "Continuous Partial Attention." Linda Stone blog. <https://lindastone.net/qa/continuous-partial-attention/>. Accessed 14 Apr. 2017.
Stoneback, H. R. Interview by Allie Baker. "Pilgrimage, Poetry and Song: An Interview with H. R. Stoneback." *The Hemingway Project*. 21 July 2015. <http://www.thehemingwayproject.com/pilgrimage-poetry-and-song-an-interview-with-h-r-stoneback/>.

———. "Pilgrimage Variations: Hemingway's Sacred Landscapes." *Hemingway: Eight Decades of Criticism*. Ed. Linda Wagner-Martin. East Lansing: Michigan State UP, 2009. 457–76.

———. *Reading Hemingway's* The Sun Also Rises: *Glossary and Commentary*. Kent, OH: Kent State UP, 2007.

———. "'You Sure This Thing Has Trout in It?': Fishing and Fabrication, Omission and 'Vermification' in *The Sun Also Rises*." *Hemingway Repossessed*. Ed. Kenneth Rosen. London: Praeger, 1994.

Strong, Amy L. *Race and Identity in Hemingway's Fiction*. New York: Palgrave MacMillan, 2008.

Summerhayes, Don. "Fish Story: Ways of Telling in 'Big Two-Hearted River.'" *The Hemingway Review* 15.2 (Fall 1995): 20–26.

Svoboda, Frederic J. "The Great Themes in Hemingway: Love, War, Wilderness, and Loss." *A Historical Guide to Ernest Hemingway*. Ed. Linda Wagner-Martin. Oxford: Oxford UP, 2000. 55–72.

———. "Landscapes Real and Imagined: 'Big Two-Hearted River.'" *The Hemingway Review* 16.1 (1996): 33–42.

Tedlock, E. W. "Hemingway's 'The Snows of Kilimanjaro.'" *The Explicator* 8 (1949): item 7.

Thoreau, Henry David. *The Journal 1837–1861*. New York: New York Review of Books, 2009.

———. *A Week on the Concord and Merrimack Rivers*. New York: Literary Classics of the United States, 1985.

Tick, Edward. *War and the Soul: Healing Our Nation's Veterans from PTSD*. Wheaton, IL: Quest Books, 2005.

Trilling, Lionel. "Hemingway and the Critics." *Partisan Review* 6 (Winter 1939): 52–60.

Trogdon, Robert W. *The Lousy Racket: Hemingway, Scribners and the Business of Literature*. Kent, OH: Kent State UP, 2007.

Twain, Mark. *Pudd'nhead Wilson* and *Those Extraordinary Twins*. New York: Gabriel Wells, 1923.

Tyler, Lisa. "'How Beautiful the Virgin Forests Were Before the Loggers Came': An Ecofeminist Reading of Hemingway's 'The End of Something.'" *The Hemingway Review* 27.2 (Spring 2008): 60–73.

Voeller, Carey. "'He Only Looked Sad the Same Way I Felt': The Textual Confessions of Hemingway's Hunters." *The Hemingway Review* 25.1 (Fall 2005): 63–76.

Vopat, Carole Gottlieb. "The End of *The Sun Also Rises*: A New Beginning." *Fitzgerald-Hemingway Annual* (1972): 245–55. Rpt. in *Brett Ashley*. Ed. Harold Bloom. New York: Chelsea House, 1991. 96–104.

Waldhorn, Arthur. *A Reader's Guide to Ernest Hemingway*. New York: Farrar, 1972.

Warren, Karen J. "Feminism and Ecology: Making Connections." *Environmental Ethics* 9 (1987): 3–20.

Watts, Emily Stipes. *Ernest Hemingway and the Arts*. Urbana: U of Illinois P, 1971.

Weber, Max. *From Max Weber: Essays in Sociology*. Ed. H. H. Gerth and C. Wright Mills. Trans. H. H. Gerth and C. Wright Mills. New York: Oxford UP, 1958.

West, Ray B. "Ernest Hemingway: The Failure of Sensibility." *The Sewanee Review* 53.1 (1945): 120–35.

Westling, Louise H. *The Green Breast of the New World: Landscape, Gender and American Fiction.* Athens: U of Georgia P, 1998.

Williams, Terry Tempest. "Keynote Address, Seventh International Hemingway Conference." *Hemingway and the Natural World.* Ed. Robert F. Fleming. Moscow: U of Idaho P, 1999.

Williams, Wirt. *The Tragic Art of Ernest Hemingway.* Baton Rouge: Louisiana State UP, 1982.

Wilson, Edmund. *The Portable Edmund Wilson.* Ed. Lewis M. Dabney. New York: Viking, 1983.

Young, Philip. "'Big World Out There': *The Nick Adams Stories.*" *Novel: A Forum on Fiction* 6.1 (1972): 15.

———. *Ernest Hemingway: A Reconsideration.* University Park: Pennsylvania State UP, 1966.

———. "The Hero and the Code." *Hemingway's African Stories: The Stories, Their Sources, Their Critics.* Ed. John M. Howell. New York: Scribner, 1969. 116–18.

Zach, Natan. "Imagism and Vorticism." *Modernism: 1890–1930.* Ed. Malcolm Bradbury and James McFarlene. 1976. New York: Penguin, 1991.

Selected Bibliography

Armstrong, Philip. *What Animals Mean in the Fiction of Modernity.* London: Routledge, 2008.

Beall, John. "Hemingway as Craftsman: Revising 'Big Two-Hearted River.'" *Hemingway Review* 36.2 (Spring 2017): 79–94.

Buell, Lawrence. *The Environmental Imagination: Thoreau, Nature Writing, and the Formation of American Culture.* Cambridge, MA: Harvard UP, 1995.

———. *The Future of Environmental Criticism: Environmental Crisis and Literary Imagination.* Malden, MA: Blackwell, 2005.

———. *Writing for an Endangered World: Literature, Culture, and Environment in the U.S. and Beyond.* Cambridge, MA: Harvard UP, 2001.

Cave, Ray. Introduction. "The African Journal." Ernest Hemingway. *Sports Illustrated* 35.25 (20 Dec. 1971): 40–67.

Clark, Suzanne. "Roosevelt and Hemingway: Natural History, Manliness, and the Rhetoric of the Strenuous Life." *Hemingway and The Natural World.* Ed. Robert Fleming. Moscow: U of Idaho P, 1999. 55–67.

Del Gizzo, Suzanne. "'Glow-in-the-Dark Authors': Hemingway's Celebrity and Legacy in *Under Kilimanjaro.*" *The Hemingway Review* 29.2 (2010): 7–27.

DeMello, Margo. *Animals and Society: An Introduction to Human-Animal Studies.* New York: Columbia UP, 2012.

———, ed. *Teaching the Animals: Human-Animal Studies Across the Disciplines.* New York: Lantern Books, 2010.

Earle, David M. *All Man! Hemingway, 1950s Men's Magazines, and the Masculine Persona.* Kent, OH: Kent State UP, 2009.

Florczyk, Steven. "Hemingway's 'Tragic Adventure': Angling for Peace in the Natural Landscape of the Fisherman." *North Dakota Quarterly* 68.2–3 (Spring–Summer 2001): 156–65.

Garrard, Greg. *Ecocriticism.* 2nd ed. New York: Routledge, 2011.

Hemingway, Seán, ed. *Hemingway on Hunting.* New York: Scribner, 2003.

Herman, Daniel. *Hunting and the American Imagination.* Washington, DC: Smithsonian Institution Press, 2001.

Herzog, Hal. *Some We Love, Some We Hate, Some We Eat: Why It's So Hard to Think Straight about Animals.* New York: Harper, 2010.

Hiltner, Ken, ed. *Ecocriticism: The Essential Reader.* London: Routledge, 2014.

Murphy, Charlene M. "Hemingway's Gentle Hunters: Contradiction or Duality?" *Hemingway and the Natural World*. Ed. Robert E. Fleming. U of Idaho P, 1999. 165–74.

Oatley, Keith. "In the Minds of Others." *Scientific American Mind* 22.5 (2011): 62–67.

O'Connor, John. "Before the Fame, There Was the Fishing." *New York Times*. 4 Oct. 2015: 10(L).

Oliphant, Ashley. *Hemingway and Bimini: The Birth of Sport Fishing at "The End of the World."* Sarasota, FL: Pineapple Press, 2017.

Ondaatje, Christopher. *Hemingway in Africa: The Last Safari*. Woodstock, NY: Overlook Press, 2004.

Reiger, John F. *American Sportsmen and the Origins of Conservation*. 1975. 3rd ed. Corvallis: Oregon State UP, 2001.

Strychacz, Thomas. *Hemingway's Theaters of Masculinity*. Baton Rouge: Louisiana UP, 2003.

Tackach, James. "Project Healing Waters Fly Fishing and Hemingway's 'Big Two-Hearted River.'" *The Hemingway Review* 35.1 (2015): 102–5.

Weil, Kari. *Thinking Animals: Why Animal Studies Now?* New York: Columbia UP, 2012.

Westling, Louise H. *The Cambridge Companion to Literature and Environment*. New York: Cambridge UP, 2014.

Contributors

Susan F. Beegel holds a PhD in English from Yale University. Recently retired, she served for twenty-two years as editor of *The Hemingway Review*, a publication of the University of Idaho and the Ernest Hemingway Foundation. A former resident of Nantucket Island, where she lived at a biological research station thirty miles at sea, Beegel has published four books and more than fifty articles on various aspects of nineteenth- and twentieth-century American literature, often with a maritime emphasis. She has taught Hemingway's *The Old Man and the Sea* not only in the Williams College-Mystic Seaport program but in many different environments to many different types of students.

Don Daiker, professor emeritus of Miami University in Oxford, Ohio, has published five major essays on *The Sun Also Rises* and a half-dozen essays on the Nick Adams stories in journals like *The Hemingway Review*, *The McNeese Review*, *Texas Studies in Literature and Language*, *North Dakota Quarterly*, *MidAmerica*, and *Middle West Review*. His Hemingway reviews appear in *Studies in Short Fiction*, *Twentieth-Century Literature*, *South Atlantic Review*, and *Resources for American Literary Studies*. He has spoken at international Hemingway conferences in Pamplona, Ronda, Lausanne, and Venice. In a previous life he coauthored or coedited ten books in composition and rhetoric.

Laura Godfrey is assistant chair of the Department of English and Humanities at North Idaho College. She has published widely on American literature and on Hemingway in journals such as *Western American Literature*, *Arizona Quarterly*, *Critique*, and *The Hemingway Review* as well as in the edited collections *Hemingway: Eight Decades of Criticism* and *Ernest Hemingway and the Geography of Memory*. Her book *Hemingway's Geographies* was published in 2016 by Palgrave Macmillan. Dr. Godfrey is currently at work on an edited collection, *Teaching Hemingway in the Digital Age*, for Kent State University Press.

Larry Grimes is professor emeritus of English in the Gresham Chair for Humanities at Bethany College (WV). He is the author of *The Religious Design of Hemingway's Early Fiction* and, with Bickford Sylvester, editor of *Hemingway, Cuba, and the Cuban Works*. Presently, with Peter Hays, he is completing the book Bickford Sylvester began on the *Old Man and the Sea* for the Kent State University Press. A founding member of the Hemingway Society, he currently serves on the Society Board. He has also published essays on crime fiction and film, and continues to publish poems. He resides in Bethany, West Virginia, and near Mancos, Colorado. In both locations he teases trout as often as possible.

Gary Harrington is a professor of English at Salisbury University in Maryland. In addition to essays on Hemingway, he has published on the medieval drama, Shakespeare, Faulkner, Tennessee Williams, Virginia Woolf, and others. In 2002, and again from 2010 to 2012, he held an appointment as Fulbright Distinguished Chair of American Literature in Poland.

Ryan Hediger is associate professor of English at Kent State University (Ohio). He has published essays on a range of subjects, including bicycling (in *Culture on Two Wheels*, University of Nebraska Press), military dogs in the U.S. conflict in Vietnam (*Animal Studies Journal*), and Werner Herzog's film *Grizzly Man* (*Interdisciplinary Studies in Literature and Environment*). His essays on Hemingway, published in *The Hemingway Review* and in essay collections, focus on animals, violence, and ethics. He edited the volume of essays *Animals and War* (Brill 2013), coedited *Animals and Agency* (Brill 2009), and is currently working on a monograph on homesickness.

Jeffrey Herlihy-Mera is a member of the Departmento de Humanidades at Universidad de Puerto Rico, where he has been recognized as Distinguished Researcher. His recent work has appeared in *The Chronicle of Higher Education, The Hemingway Review, Modern Fiction Studies, Voces del Caribe,* and *The Minnesota Review.* Herlihy-Mera has a doctorate from Universitat Pompeu Fabra in Barcelona. He is author of *After American Studies, In Paris or Paname: Hemingway's Expatriate Nationalism,* and coeditor (with Vamsi K. Koneru) of *Paris in American Literatures.*

Allen C. Jones received his MFA from University of New Mexico and his PhD from University of Louisiana at Lafayette. He is presently associate professor of English literature at University of Stavanger, Norway. His scholarly work focuses on creating and theorizing digital interfaces that encourage nonlinear readings of metaphorically dense modernist texts. You can find these interfaces and "games" at allencjones.com. He also publishes traditional essays as well as creative work.

Scott Knickerbocker is associate professor of English and Environmental Studies at The College of Idaho in Caldwell, where he teaches American literature, creative nonfiction, and environmental studies, including off-campus courses in Scotland and the Sawtooth Valley of central Idaho. His book *Ecopoetics: The Language of Nature, the Nature of Language* was published in 2012 by the University of Massachusetts Press. His scholarly articles have appeared in *College Literature, The Kenyon Review, Interdisciplinary Studies in Literature and Environment,* and *The Oxford Handbook of Ecocriticism.* Scott also plays banjo and fiddle in his old-time string band Hokum Hi-Flyers.

CONTRIBUTORS 235

Ellen Andrews Knodt, professor of English, Penn State University-Abington, has been an active member of the Hemingway Society since 1994, presenting papers at each International Conference and serving as a consulting scholar for the Hemingway Letters Project. Her articles and reviews have appeared in *The Hemingway Review, North Dakota Quarterly, Resources for American Literary Study* and in several essay collections on Hemingway, most recently in *War+Ink*, Kent State University Press. She has essays in the Teaching Hemingway series on *The Sun Also Rises* and *A Farewell to Arms*. Dr. Knodt received Penn State's all-University Atherton Award for Excellence in Teaching.

Kevin Maier is associate professor of English and chair of the Department of Humanities at the University of Alaska Southeast. He teaches a wide range of classes in American literature, writing, outdoor studies, and the environmental humanities. His essays on Hemingway have appeared in *The Hemingway Review, ISLE: Interdisciplinary Studies in Literature and Environment,* and the collection *Hemingway in Context*. He is coeditor (with Sarah Jaquette Ray) of an anthology on northern environmental issues titled *Critical Norths: Nature, Space, Theory* (University of Alaska Press 2017).

Robert McParland is professor of English at Felician University. He is the author of *Citizen Steinbeck: Giving Voice to the People* (2016) and *Beyond Gatsby: How Fitzgerald, Hemingway and Writers of the 1920s Shaped American Culture* (2015). His essays on Hemingway include "A Clean Well-Lighted Classroom" and "Hemingway's 'Soldier's Home,': Embellished Stories and Recalling Vietnam for Future Generations."

Sean Milligan is assistant professor of English at Rochester College in Rochester Hills, Michigan, and a doctoral candidate in English at Wayne State University in Detroit. He has presented his work at the Comparative Drama Conference, the Michigan College English Association Conference, and the Cultural Rhetorics Conference.

Scott Ortolano is professor of English at Florida SouthWestern State College. His scholarship explores the cognitive and existential repercussions of consumerism and the future of the humanities. Among other work, he has recently published in *The F. Scott Fitzgerald Review, South Atlantic Review, The Explicator, Women's Studies,* and *Terror in Global Narrative: The Aesthetics and Representation of 9/11 in the Age of Late-Late Capitalism* (Palgrave Macmillan). Dr. Ortolano is currently at work on an edited collection titled *Popular Modernism and Its Legacies: From Pop Literature to Video Games* (Bloomsbury, forthcoming 2017).

Michael Kim Roos is professor emeritus of English at University of Cincinnati Blue Ash College. He has published articles in *The Hemingway Review, The Journal of Popular Culture, Popular Music,* and *Popular Music and Society*. He also has an essay appearing in the forthcoming volume *Hemingway and Italy: 21st Century Perspectives*. He is currently working on a book manuscript for *Reading Hemingway's* A Farewell to Arms, part of the Reading Hemingway series for Kent State University Press. In addition, he has published a book of creative nonfiction, *One Small Town, One Crazy Coach*, with Indiana University Press.

Ross K. Tangedal is assistant professor of English at the University of Wisconsin-Stevens Point. He specializes in twentieth-century American print and publishing culture, bibliography, and textual editing, with emphases on Ernest Hemingway, F. Scott Fitzgerald, and the profession of authorship in America. His work has been published in the *Hemingway Review, F. Scott Fitzgerald Review, Authorship, MidAmerica,* and *Midwestern Miscellany.* He has chapters forthcoming in *Teaching Hemingway and Race* (Kent State University Press) and *The American Midwest in a Scattering Time: How Modernism Met Midwestern Culture* (Hastings College Press), and he is currently at work on a book manuscript titled *A Most Pleasant Business: Authorial Prefaces and American Writers Since 1900.* He is associate editor of *The Letters of Ernest Hemingway* Vol. 6 (Cambridge University Press: projected 2022) and a member of the Hemingway Society's Advisory Council for Younger Scholars.

Rick Van Noy is the author of *A Natural Sense of Wonder: Connecting Kids with Nature Through the Seasons* and *Surveying the Interior: Literary Cartographers and the Sense of Place*, and is working on a book about climate change in the Southeast. He is a professor of English at Radford University and lives in a revived farmhouse with a menagerie of animal dependents in Virginia's New River Valley.

Dan Woods received his PhD from Virginia Tech majoring in Curriculum and Instruction with a focus on English Education. Before pursuing his PhD, he taught middle and high school English in Roanoke City and Montgomery County. He earned his MAEd from Virginia Tech, as well as a BS and MA in English from Radford University. His research interests include teacher education, critical literacy, and social justice. Since August 2011 he has been an assistant professor of English Education at Radford University; currently, he is the coordinator of the English Education Program. Dr. Woods is also member of the Executive Board of the Virginia Association of Teachers of English and editor of the *Virginia English Journal.*

Index

Abbey, Edward, 124
accountability: human, 105; real-world, 107
"Actually, I Felt Sorry for the Lion" (Baym), 141
Adamic brute, image of, 76
Adams, Nick, 1, 3; balance/harmony and, 80, 81, 94; cognitive functions of, 28, 51, 53; consciousness of, 50, 100n3; environment and, 16; epiphany for, 14; fishing and, 15, 16–17, 30–31, 53, 62, 64, 66, 67, 75, 76, 77, 78–83, 84n7, 91–93, 95, 202, 203; geography and, 25, 31; journey of, 93; knowledge/experiences of, 29; landscapes and, 15, 25, 31, 33; memory and, 204; natural world and, 57–58, 60, 63, 67, 89, 90–91, 99, 198, 200; philosophy of, 52; place of, 26, 28, 58, 198; psychological state of, 4, 46, 47, 48, 50, 51, 61, 66–67, 93; PTSD and, 199; recovery by, 48–49, 65, 83; stories of, 3, 11, 20, 21, 22–23, 25, 26, 39, 47–48, 92; two-heartedness of, 67, 81; youthfulness of, 30
Adventures of Huckleberry Finn, The (Twain), 153, 167; discussion of, 154
Aesculapius, 74
aesthetics, 100n4, 123, 157, 158, 184, 185, 188, 211; Hemingway and, 38, 46, 129, 152, 180, 181; nature and, 186
aficion, 6, 134, 164, 171, 181
"Africa Story, The" (Hemingway), reading, 6
Agassiz, Louis, 74, 75, 107, 200
Agassiz Club, 74
Ahab, Santiago and, 96
allegories, 94, 124, 189
Allen, Woody, 97
American Adam, The (Lewis), 77, 83n5, 84n6
American Fly Fisher, The, 75, 83n3
animals, 1, 2, 5; as characters, 106; perspective of, 142; symbolism of, 6; sympathy for, 142–49
anthropocentrism, 95, 104, 112n3
argumentation, 159, 182; teaching, 156
Arnold, Matthew, 153

Ashley, Lady Brett, 18, 163, 164, 175n1; bullfighting and, 176n10; Jake and, 165–75, 175n2, 175n3, 175n4, 176n5; as potentially destructive force, 176n5; Robert and, 165, 169; Romero and, 169, 171
audience, author and, 109
Austin, Mary, 103
author, 189, 190; audience and, 109
Autobiography of Alice B. Toklas, The (Stein), 64

backgrounds, 1, 2, 11, 43, 48, 69, 72, 178, 198, 200, 216; biographical, 58; cultural, 59; maritime, 115; urban/suburban, 36
Baker, Carlos, 124n1, 155–56, 158–59, 198; double vision and, 12; lions and, 110
Baker, Sheridan, 100n2, 100n3
balance, 4, 58, 59, 73, 74, 75, 79, 94, 103, 112, 209; emotional, 15, 16; restoring, 81; spiritual, 80
Barkley, Catherine, 201, 202; animal sympathy and, 144
Barnes, Jake, 6, 18, 201; Bayonne and, 164, 165, 171; Bill and, 163, 169, 176n8; Brett and, 165–75, 175n2, 175n3, 175n4, 176n5; bullfighting and, 176n10; Burguete and, 170; Concha and, 173; emotional geography of, 163; Montoya and, 164; morality and, 176n6; Robert and, 165, 166; Romero and, 166–67; San Sebastian and, 165, 171; self-knowledge of, 168; travels of, *162* (map), 163, 174
Bass, Rick, 73
"Battler, The" (Hemingway), 48
Baym, Nina, 93, 143, 150n6; on Hemingway's summary, 145; on lion, 141; on Margot, 144
Bayonne, 163, 166, 167, 171, 174; Burguete and, 170; described, 165; Jake on, 164; San Sebastian and, 164, 165
Beegel, Susan F., 110, 111, 112n3, 112n4, 200, 201; maritime history and, 4–5

237

238 INDEX

Bell, Millicent, 202
Bergson and American Culture (Quirk), 45
Bergson, Henri, 55n1; Hemingway and, 54, 55n2; life modes and, 51; philosophy of, 3, 46, 47, 49, 53, 55n3; place and, 45; primitivism and, 55n2
Berman, Ron, 21
"Best Rainbow Trout Fishing, The" (Hemingway), 55n5
Beyond the Culture Wars (Graff), 153, 154, 157
"Big Two-Hearted River" (Hemingway), 15, 17, 21, 52, 59, 67, 68, 99, 172, 173, 195, 198; criticism of, 57, 72; discussion of, 54–55, 55n5, 96; dynamics in, 50; evolutionary elements in, 57; existential fulfillment and, 47; fishing and, 1, 17, 76, 77, 79, 94; imagism and, 49; landscapes of, 11, 13, 83n1; metaphors/open language/symbolism of, 46; modernism and, 54; nature and, 3, 89, 198; reading, 3–4, 72–73, 75, 78, 90, 97; renewal in, 198; teaching, 48, 72, 78; Thoreau and, 77, 78; Walden and, 73; writing, 17, 54
billfish, 122; photo of, 122
binaries, 31; human/nature, 109, 110; problematic, 108
biocentrism, 104, 108, 110
body count, Hemingway and, 5, 98
Bolton, Matthew J., 29, 32
Brasch, James D., 74
Brenner, Gerry, 99, 109, 202
Brøgger, Frederik, 15
Brown, Bill, 37
Buell, Lawrence, 103, 104, 112n3
buffalo, hunting, 130, 135–39, 142, 143–44, 147
bullfighting, 65, 164, 167, 168, 174, 175, 176n6, 176n10, 181, 182, 185, 186, 187, 188, 190; Hemingway and, 179–80, 183, 184, 189
Burguete, 163, 167, 169, 174; Bayonne and, 170; San Sebastian and, 165, 171–72, 173
Burhans, Clinton, Jr., 95
By-Line: Ernest Hemingway (Hemingway), 130–31

Calabi, Silvio, 137
Campbell, Mike, 163, 164
Cantwell, Colonel, 1
Carr, Nicholas, 206
Carson, Rachel, 2, 99, 116
Castano, Emanuele, 150n7
"Cat in the Rain" (Hemingway), 198; animal sympathy in, 144

ceremonies, 37, 38; cultural, 39
Cézanne, Paul, 2, 46, 65, 200; landscapes of, 12, 13; writing like, 11, 12
Chawla, Louise, 100n1
Clarahan, Clarence, 75
Clark, Suzanne, 145
climate, 31, 35, 158
close reading, 3, 6, 7, 73, 142, 147, 201, 207–12; as sympathetic understanding, 149
Clyne, Frances, 168
Cobb, Edith, 100n1
Cohn, Robert, 40, 163, 164, 170, 172, 175n1; Brett and, 165, 169; immaturity of, 168; Jake and, 165, 166; physical prowess of, 167; Romero and, 174; San Sebastian and, 173
Coleridge, Samuel Taylor, 115, 124n1
colonialism, 152, 157
Companion to Hemingway's Death in the Afternoon, *A* (Mandel), 178
conflicts, 6, 58, 59, 156, 157, 167; literary, 89; nature and, 97; teaching, 153, 154, 155, 158; universal, 89
consciousness, 50, 100n3; authorial, 29; character-centered, 79; double, 77; narrative, 24, 81, 84n8
cottage-ing, described, 36–39
courage, 139, 142–43, 144, 149n1; as "Grace under pressure," 135
cowardice, 46, 134–35; panic and, 133, 138
Cowley, Malcolm, 1, 83n1, 84n9, 199
Craters of the Moon National Monument, 210
Creative Mind, The (Bergson), 45, 55n3
Cremean, David N., 84n7
criticism, 159, 208; cultural, 149; literary, 83n2, 154–55; professional, 154; psychological, 72; reading, 154–55; theory and, 154
"Cross Country Snow" (Hemingway), 207, 208; teaching, 7
Cuban fishermen, photo of, 121, 122
cubism, 2, 3, 46, 208
cultural, 36; literary and, 32
cultural studies, 149
culture, 37, 38, 39, 42, 58, 181, 183; identity and, 108; literature and, 107; non-Western, 108; regional, 48

Daiker, Donald, 6
Darwin, Charles, 58, 59, 60, 62
Darwin Loves You (Levine), 59
Darwinian theory, 57, 58, 62, 63, 64, 67
death: knowledge of, 182, 183; in natural world, 69n11; pedagogical clarity and, 182;

qualification of, 183; reality of, 66; regeneration and, 64
Death in the Afternoon (Hemingway), 6, 50, 184; bullfighting and, 176n6, 179; iceberg theory and, 25, 55n4; pedagogical intentions behind, 181, 189, 190n3; teaching, 178; themes in, 182; writing about, 178
Del Gizzo, Suzanne, 108
Dennett, Daniel C., 58
Derrida, Jacques, 124
Dillard, Annie, 103
discourse, 179; academic, 154–55, 156–57; free-indirect, 28; phallocentric, 153
distance, romance of, 41–42
"double lens" approach, 75, 76, 77, 79, 80, 83n4
"Dover Beach" (Arnold), 153
Dudley, Marc K., 152, 158, 159
Dunbar, Willis Frederick, 48

ecocriticism, 102, 104–5, 109, 110, 111, 112n3; defining, 103–4; heart of, 108; natural world and, 107
ecofeminism, 104, 109
ecology, 7, 103, 195; deep, 104; marine, 114, 119; spiritual, 116
ecosystems, 42, 93, 95, 195, 199
education, 58, 154, 198; environmental, 280; experiential/interdisciplinary, 5
el mar, la mar and, 117–18
élan vital, 49
Eliot, T. S., 32, 117
Ellis, Havelock, 58
Emerson, Ralph Waldo, 84n6
emotional expression, 12, 16, 183
"End of Something, The" (Hemingway), 21, 29, 47, 48
environment, 52, 66, 99, 102, 106–7, 108, 111, 211, 212; changes in, 62; controlling, 16; fragile, 103; Hemingway and, 1, 2, 4, 32, 202; memory and, 204; natural, 29, 30; nonhuman, 104–5; physical, 33, 103; rural, 196; virtual, 23
Environmental Imagination, The (Buell), 103, 104–5
environmentalism, 99, 104, 107
Ernest Hemingway: A Reconsideration (Young), 50
Ernest Hemingway and the Arts (Watts), 12
"Ernest Hemingway's Description of the Mountaintop in 'The Snows of Kilimanjaro' and Climate Change Research" (Helama), 158

Esquire, Hemingway in, 5, 130
"Esthetique du Mal" (Stevens), 33
ethics, 5, 99, 132; cramp of, 94, 98, 100n4; ecological, 94; hunting, 131, 139, 148; of primitive, 96; proto-environmentalist, 4
Evans, Oliver, 152, 155, 156, 157
"Everyone Hates Henry" (Hohn), 74
evolution, 57, 58; natural selection and, 69n8; psychical, 51
"Eye and Heart: Hemingway's Education as a Naturalist" (Beegel), 5

Falling Into Theory (Richter), 153
Family Tree template, 156
Farewell to Arms, A (Hemingway), 201; conclusion of, 202; landscape and, 18; narrative consciousness and, 24; opening lines of, 23; structure of, 21; war and, 195
fear, 133, 135, 147
"Few Don'ts by an Imagiste, A" (Pound), 49
Ficken, Carl, 30, 92
Fiedler, Leslie, 93
Field Museum of Natural History, 58
Finn, Huckleberry, 37
fishing, 1, 15, 30–31, 61, 65, 80, 89, 91–93, 94, 109, 111, 172, 198–99, 202; assessment of, 16–17; control and, 81; fly, 63, 72, 123, 207; Hemingway and, 39, 54, 75, 78–79, 98, 110; ritual of, 203–4; in swamp, 66, 67, 82, 92–93, 173; true meaning of, 52
Fitzgerald, F. Scott, 43
Fleischmann, Suzanne, 28
Fleming, Robert E., 1, 2, 98
Flora, Joseph, 51, 53
For Whom the Bell Tolls (Hemingway), 201
framing, 104, 106; ecocentric, 110
Francis, Ad, 48

Gaillard, Theodore L., Jr., 12, 13
Gallos, David, 109, 112n5
Garden of Eden, The (Hemingway), 144, 146
gender norms, 141, 148–49
Genette, Gerard, 28, 29
geography: alternating, 167, 167 (fig.), 174; cultural, 25; emotional, 163; Hemingway and, 27, 28, 29, 38; human, 26–27; as memory, 22, 31; narrating, 20; physical, 6, 163; prose and, 163
Geography of Nowhere, The (Kunstler), 32
Glassell, Alfred C., Jr., 122, 125n7; photo of, 123
Glotfelty, Cheryl, 112n2
Godfrey, Laura Gruber, 2–3, 48

Gordon, Caroline, 155, 156, 157
Gorton, Bill, 164, 170, 171, 172; Jake and, 163, 169, 176n7; on outdoors, 201
Goya, Francisco, 183
Graff, Gerald, 6, 153; on academic discourse, 155; criticism and, 154, 159; on teaching, 157
grasshoppers, 15, 61, 62, 63, 67, 68–69n8, 79, 80, 82
Green Breast of the New World, The (Westling), 93
Green Hills of Africa (Hemingway), 73, 136, 137, 149n3, 159; hunting and, 148; teaching, 178; Thoreau and, 74; virility/power and, 146
Grimes, Larry, 3–4
"Guide to the Marine Life in Ernest Hemingway's *The Old Man and the Sea*, A" (Beegel), 112n3, 112n4
Gulf of Mexico, 119, 120
Gulf Stream, 120, 122, 125n5
"Gulf Stream, The" (Homer), 120, *120* (fig.)

Haldane, J. B. S., 69n8
harmony, 66, 73, 74, 76, 78, 79; regaining, 81; spiritual, 46, 80
Harrington, Gary, 5
Harry, 157, 158, 200, 202–3; death and, 203; memories for, 203; nature and, 198, 203, 204; vitality of, 203
Harvey, Guy, 123
Hass, Robert Bernard, 49
Hediger, Ryan, 5–6, 108–9, 112n3, 112n4, 112n6
Heidegger, Martin, 200
Helama, Samuli, 158
Hemingway, Clarence, 74, 83n4, 200
Hemingway, Ernest: death of, 99; fiction of, 11, 25, 26, 35; methods of, 181–82; readings of, 142; visual understanding of, 12; writing environment for, 42
Hemingway, Gregory, 98, 110
Hemingway, Jack, 100n6
Hemingway, Marcelene, 75–76, 83n4
Hemingway: A Reconsideration (Young), 83n1
"Hemingway among the Animals" (Love), 98
Hemingway and the Natural World (Fleming), 2, 98
Hemingway, Clarence, 74, 83n4, 200
Hemingway on Fishing (Lyons), 54
Hemingway, Race, and Art: Bloodlines and the Color Line (Dudley), 158
Hemingway Studies, 35
Hemingway's Boat: Everything He Loved in Life, and Lost, 1934–1961 (Hendrickson), 163

"Hemingway's Indian Virtues: An Ecological Reconsideration" (Love), 5
Hendrickson, Paul, 163
Henry, Frederic, 18, 24, 102, 201, 202
Herlihy-Mera, Jeffry, 3
Heyerdahl, Thor, 116, 117
hiddenness, principle of, 25
"Hike Walloon Lake" (Hemingway), 83n3
"Hills Like White Elephants" (Hemingway), opening paragraph of, 17
Historical Guide to Ernest Hemingway, A (Wagner-Martin), 5
Hohn, Donovan, 74
Hollenberg, Alexander, 106
Homer, Winslow, 121; painting by, 120, *120* (fig.)
House of Fiction, The (Gordon and Tate), 155
House of God, 155, 203
Howell, John M., 130
Hulme, T. E., 49
humans, nature and, 13, 31, 105, 106, 108, 109, 110, 112n4, 147
hunting: buffalo, 130, 135, 136, 137, 138, 139, 142, 143–44, 147; criticism of, 145; culture of, 1, 98; ethical standards for, 131, 139, 148; etiquette for, 94, 144; Hemingway and, 5, 39, 42, 107, 131, 142, 145; lion, 130, 131–32, 133, 134–35, 136, 137, 138, 139, 141, 144, 148; mythologies of, 98; as natural/inevitable, 146; rituals for, 149
Hutton, Virgil, 136

Ibáñez, Beatriz Penas, 189, 190
iceberg theory, 7, 25, 50, 51, 55n4, 55n6, 129, 187, 189
imagism, 49, 50, 54
"In a Station of the Metro" (Pound), 49–50
In Our Time (Hemingway), 13, 15, 20, 29, 47, 48, 64, 72, 73, 208; Hemingway on, 11–12; natural world and, 198; reading, 178–79, 181
"Indian Camp" (Hemingway), 13, 48
individualism, 5, 95, 107
International Game Fish Association, 125n7
interpretation, 13, 14, 50, 72, 108, 130, 141, 143, 145, 152, 153, 157, 182, 217; argumentation and, 159; complex, 154; resisting, 106, 142; as political action, 107
Irati River, 170, 171, 172
Islands in the Stream (Hemingway), 172

James, William, 45
Jones, Allen, 4
Jordan, Robert, 1

Journal (Thoreau), 79
Justice, Hilary K., 183, 184, 186, 187, 189

Kazin, Alfred, 31
Key West, 114, 118, 119
Kidd, David Comer, 150n7
kingfisher, 52–53, 60–61, 67, 68n7, 77
Knickerbocker, Scott, 7
Knodt, Ellen, 2–3
knowledge, 149, 185; questions of, 148; substance and, 188
Kolodny, Annette, 93
Kon-Tiki (Heyerdahl), 116, 118
Krebs, Harold, 196, 197, 198, 199, 203
Krutch, Joseph Wood, 59, 60
Kunstler, James Howard, 32

la mar, el mar and, 117–18
Lamb, Robert Paul, 83n2, 84n9, 112n1
landscapes, 44, 47, 94; appreciation of, 11–12; artistic, 180; body and, 25; character and, 12; cognitive, 48; dry/fertile, 17, 18; emotional/symbolic content of, 18; harsh, 69n8, 93, 210; Hemingway and, 2–3, 11, 12–13, 15, 16, 17–18, 21–22, 24–25, 26, 28, 29, 33, 83n1; human, 31; memory of, 29; narrating, 20, 22; natural, 29, 35, 179, 181, 200; reading, 185, 209–10; ritual, 179–80; Spanish, 181, 190; symbolic, 6, 90; war and, 195
language, 35, 38, 44; choice of, 80; figurative, 208; open, 46
Last Child in the Woods (Louv), 32
"Last Good Country, The" (Hemingway), 47, 55n5
Lears, Jackson, 47
"Leopard and the Hyena: Symbol and Meaning in 'The Snows of Kilimanjaro'" (Montgomery), 156
Leopold, Aldo, 2, 94, 99
Levine, George, 59
Lewis, R. W. B., 77, 83n5, 84n6
Lewis, Sinclair, 202
Life, Hemingway and, 100n7
lion, 98, 109, 110; human and, 147; hunting, 131–32, 133, 134–35, 136, 137, 138, 139, 141, 144, 148; peaceful dream of, 103; perspective of, 142; sympathy for, 145–46, 147
literary: analysis, 22; cultural and, 32
literary theory, 154
literature, 149, 186; culture and, 107; environmental, 2, 90, 207, 210; exposure to, 154; interpreting, 159; physical environment and, 103; safari, 42, 130–31; skiing, 208, 212

"Literature of the Sea" course, 5, 114, 115, 116, 117
Log from the Sea of Cortez, The (Steinbeck and Ricketts), 116
London, Jack, 58, 116–17, 207
Look, Hemingway and, 100n7
Los Desastros de la Guerra (Goya), 183
Louv, Richard, 33
Love, Glen A., 104, 108, 112n2; on body count, 5, 98; individualism/interdependence and, 95; on nature/Hemingway, 107
lumber industry, 47–48, 50, 214
Lynn, Kenneth S., 139, 143, 199
Lyons, Nick, 54

Maclean, Norman, 73, 103, 207
Macomber, Francis: courage of, 139, 142–43, 144, 149n1; cowardice of, 133, 134–35, 138; death of, 130, 139, 141; fear of, 133, 135, 147; hunting by, 129, 131–33, 136, 138, 145, 146; lion and, 131–32, 146–47; Margot and, 129, 138, 141, 143, 144, 145–46, 149n1; personal dramas of, 148; perspective of, 142; Robert and, 130, 132, 133, 135, 136, 137, 138, 139, 143, 146–47, 148; transformation of, 143, 147–48
Macomber, Margot, 130, 137; animal sympathy and, 144; courage and, 144; criticism of, 145; fear of, 135; Francis and, 129, 138, 141, 143, 144, 145–46, 149n1; perspective of, 142, 144
Madrid, 163, 164, 166, 167, 168, 171, 173, 175, 186; described, 174, 184, 185
Magic Mountain (Mann), 202
Majerus, M. E. N., 69n8
"man against nature" theme, 4, 89, 97, 116
Mandel, Miriam B., 178, 181
Mann, Thomas, 202
Manolin, 90, 110, 111, 118
Mapes, Ed, 125n5
maritime classics, 114, 115–16
maritime history, 4–5, 119
marlin, 1, 89, 90, 94, 96, 102, 103, 109, 111, 120, 122, 123; fishing for, 95, 98; as framing device, 106; photo of, *123*
Martin, Lawrence H., 139
Martin, Robert, 131, 201
Marx, Leo, 65
matadors, 1, 180, 187, 188
McAlmon, Robert, 17, 65
McParland, Robert, 6
melanism, 61, 62, 68–69n8
Melling, Philip, 24–25, 83n1
Melville, Herman, 115, 116, 124n2

242 INDEX

memory, 41–42, 188, 197, 198; environment and, 204; geography as, 22, 24; landscape, 24
Men at War (Hemingway), 133, 134
Messent, Peter, 182
metaphor, 46, 80, 188; master, 103, 106; natural, 105
Michigan Department of Natural Resources, 62
Midnight in Paris (Allen), 97
Millán, Ingrid, 39
Milligan, Sean, 6
Moby-Dick (Melville), 114, 115, 117, 124; *Old Man and the Sea* and, 124n2
Moddelmog, Debra, 92–93, 100n7
Modern Fiction Studies, 55n2
Modern Temper, The (Krutch), 59
modernism, 15, 31–32, 46, 54, 107
Montgomery, Marion, 156, 157
Montoya, Jake and, 134, 164
morality, 99, 175n4, 176n6
Mount Kilimanjaro, epigraph of, 203
Moveable Feast, A (Hemingway), 12, 13, 32, 90, 207

narrative, 31, 46, 80, 138, 185, 190; controlling, 179; experiential, 50; experimental, 179; first-person, 92; geographical, 26; Hemingway and, 21, 22, 23–24, 27; omniscient, 139; personal, 197; retrospective, 202; settler-American culture, 37; third-person, 28
National Aeronautic and Space Administration, Visible Earth Collection of, 120
National Oceanographic and Atmospheric Administration (NOAA), 119, 123, 125n4
Native Americans, 37, 38, 40, 43, 48
natural history, 1, 104–5
"Natural History of Death, A," 188, 190n1
natural order, 67, 68, 108
natural selection, 57, 60, 61, 62, 66, 67, 68n7, 69n8
natural world, 36, 41, 58, 60, 63, 89, 93, 99, 111, 123–24, 149, 196; concerns of, 7, 67; Darwinian, 3; ecocriticism and, 107; evolutionary aspects of, 66; focus on, 4, 116; Hemingway and, 1–2, 3, 4, 6, 7, 54, 55, 55n6, 75, 107, 201, 202, 203, 204; importance of, 198, 199–200; nonhuman, 25; relationship to, 2, 6, 64, 90, 99, 100, 201; shock of, 17; teaching about, 119; writers and, 5
nature, 39, 58, 78, 89, 90–91, 104, 111, 124; aesthetics and, 186; complexities of, 106; contact with, 38, 99; as empty space, 106, 108; Hemingway and, 5, 35–36, 41, 42, 99, 107, 201, 202; humans and, 13, 31, 105, 106, 108, 109, 110, 112n4, 147; mastery of, 66; regeneration of, 62, 64, 67; representations of, 103; solace in, 195; thingness of, 79; vacations and, 37; valuing, 106, 108; war and, 195, 201
New York Herald, 164
Nick Adams Stories, The (Young), 17, 26, 64
NOAA. *See* National Oceanographic and Atmospheric Administration (NOAA)
"Notes on Dangerous Game: The Third Tanganyika Letter" (Hemingway), 133, 137, 138

O'Brien, Edmund J., 11–12
O'Brien, Sarah May, 112n1
Ocean Explorer Gallery, 123
oceanography, 114, 119, 125n5
Odgar, 28, 39, 40, 43
Old Lady, 187, 189
Old Man and the Sea, The (Hemingway), 57, 94, 96, 98, 99, 116, 119, 121, 124n1, 172; as allegory, 124; animal sympathy and, 144; audience for, 115; discussion of, 96, 103, 118; doubt and, 111; ecocritical arguments of, 102, 103; individualism/interdependence and, 95; *la mar/el mar* and, 117–18; "man against nature" and, 89; marine life and, 123; maritime history and, 4–5; *Moby-Dick* and, 124n2; nature and, 42, 89, 97; reading, 4, 103; scholarly arguments concerning, 105–6; teaching, 114, 118, 119; understanding, 120
"On Fly Fishing" (Hemingway), 72
"On Writing" (Hemingway), 11, 17, 64
Ong, Walter J., 21, 22, 23
"Organizing the Conflicts in the Curriculum" (Graff), 154
Origin of Species (Darwin), 59
Ortolano, Scott, 3
Otten, Mark, 69n8
"Out of Season" (Hemingway), 198

Pamplona, 163, 164, 165, 167, 168, 169, 170, 171, 173, 175; described, 174
panic, 199; cowardice and, 133, 138
Paris, 163, 164, 165, 167, 168, 169, 170, 171; described, 174
pedagogy, 35–36, 153, 179, 181, 186, 188; death and, 182; defining, 187; natural, 185, 190; visual, 190n3

Percival, Philip "Pop," 131, 133, 139; ethical standards and, 132; hunting and, 136, 137, 138
Perkins, Maxwell, 176n7, 180, 181, 189, 190n2
physical acts, psychological state and, 14
Picasso, Pablo, 116
place, 30, 32, 45, 58, 100n4, 198; ambiguities of, 23, 27; defining, 44; Hemingway and, 1, 2, 22, 25–26, 27, 28, 38; nostalgia for, 38; relationships to, 22
Plimpton, George, 73
politics, 39, 107; cultural, 157, 158; gender, 141; racial, 152
Portable Hemingway, The (Cowley), 1, 199
posthumanism, 149
Postman, Neil, 206
posttraumatic stress disorder (PTSD), 196, 199, 202, 203
Pound, Ezra, 32, 46, 107; imagism and, 49, 50
Practical Ecocriticism (Love), 104, 112n2
PTSD. *See* posttraumatic stress disorder (PTSD)

Quammen, David, 211
Queequeg, 118
Quirk, Tom, 45, 46, 55n1

Race and Identity in Hemingway's Fiction (Strong), 157
Raeburn, John, 179
rationalism, 58, 59, 60
reader: as companion-in-arms, 23; writer and, 187
religion: science and, 58; teleology and, 60
Reynolds, Michael, 14, 22, 74, 180, 187
rhetoric, 6, 39, 145, 155, 158, 179; visual, 2, 3
Richter, David, 153
Rickett, Edward F., 116
"Rime of the Ancient Mariner, The" (Coleridge), 115, 124n1
rituals, 38, 40, 41, 179, 183, 203; hunting, 149; settler, 35, 36, 37
Romero, Pedro, 163, 164, 165, 170; Brett and, 169, 171; bullfighting and, 168, 175, 176n10; Jake and, 166–67; Robert and, 174
Roos, Mike, 3, 58
Roosevelt, Theodore, 37, 58
Rovitt, Earl, 99
Rubens, Peter Paul, 116

San Sebastian, 18, 163–64, 166, 167, 174, 175, 175n1; Bayonne and, 164, 165; Burguete and, 165, 171–72, 173; swimming at, 172, 173
Sand County Almanac (Leopold), 2

Santiago: Ahab and, 96; animal sympathy and, 144; as Christ, 102; cramp of ethics of, 94, 98; fishing and, 1, 42, 95, 99, 111, 119; freedom/happiness of, 95; guilt of, 95; knowledge of, 118; lion and, 109, 110; marlin and, 94, 96, 106, 120; mistake by, 96, 108–9; nature and, 89, 90, 104, 111; regret by, 97, 98, 99; sharks and, 121; skiff of, 121, 122; vacillation by, 110–11; world of, 5, 123–24
Savola, David, 112n1
Scholes, Robert, 54–55
Schorer, Mark, 199
science, 1; rationalism and, 58, 60; religion and, 58
Sea-Wolf, The (London), 116
Shakespeare, Alex, 31, 49
Shallows: What the Internet Is Doing to Our Brains, The (Carr), 206
sharks, 95, 96, 98; menace from, 121; photo of, *121*; quotes about, 116–17
"Shootism Versus Sport: The Second Tanganyika Letter" (Hemingway), 131
"Short Happy Life of Francis Macomber, The" (Hemingway), 139; animal sympathy and, 142–49; discussion of, 129; narrative voice in, 141; publication of, 134; reading, 5, 6, 159; teaching, 142–43
Showalter, Elaine, 153
Sigman, Joseph, 74
Silent Spring (Carson), 2, 99
Simmons, Charley, 198
skiing, backcountry, 207–12
Smith, James, 196
Smith, Paul, 14, 15
"'Snows of Kilimanjaro, The': A Revaluation" (Evans), 152
"Snows of Kilimanjaro, The" (Hemingway), 198, 200, 202, 203; controversy about, 152, 155, 157; racial themes in, 157; symbolism of, 155, 156; teaching, 6, 152–53; war and, 195
"Soldier's Home" (Hemingway), 195, 196, 198, 199
space, 185; empty, 106, 108; natural, 45
Spilka, Mark, 143, 150n6
Stein, Gertrude, 46, 64, 168, 200; Hemingway and, 1, 65–66, 107
Steinbeck, John, 116
Stephens, Robert O., 179
stereotypes, 97, 145; gender, 109; negative, 109; racial, 158; racist, 152
Stevens, Wallace, 33
Stone, Harvey, 168

Stone, Linda, 206
Stoneback, H. R., 13, 112n1, 164, 165
"Straits of Florida and Approaches" (NOAA), 119
Strong, Amy L., 152, 157, 158
"Subject Author" (Mandel), 178
"Summer People" (Hemingway), 26–27, 31, 35; critical view of, 39–41; discourse of, 28; geographical memory and, 24; landscapes and, 3, 25; narrative voice of, 26, 29; place and, 22; reading, 36; teaching, 3; traditions and, 38
Summerhayes, Don, 84n8
Sun Also Rises, The (Hemingway), 40, 134, 201; geography of, 162 (map), 163, 167 (fig.), 174; landscape and, 18; teaching, 6, 167
Svoboda, Frederic J., 38, 68n6, 196; cottagers and, 36–37
swamp, 96; characterization of, 92–93; fishing in, 66, 67, 82, 92–93, 173
symbolism, 12, 15, 46, 52, 67, 157; natural, 155–56
synthesis tree, 156, 157

"Tanganyika Letters" (Hemingway), 131, 133, 137, 138, 139
Tangedal, Ross K., 6
Tate, Allen, 157; on symbolism, 155, 156
Teaching Literature (Showalter), 153
technology, 201, 202, 212; thinking and, 206
Tedlock, E. W., 155, 156, 157
teleology, 59, 60, 67
thingness, 79
This Quarter, 72, 73
Thoreau, Henry David, 31, 83n5, 84n6, 103; Agassiz and, 74; "Big Two-Hearted River" and, 77, 78; Hemingway and, 73–74; human consciousness and, 77; Transcendentalism and, 84n7
"Three-Day Blow, The" (Hemingway), 20, 29, 31; geographical memory of, 24; landscape of, 3, 21, 22, 25
Tick, Edward, 203
"To Build a Fire" (London), 207
Toklas, Alice, 200
Toronto Daily Star, 25
Transcendentalism, 73, 74, 84n7
Treaty of Chicago (1833), 37
Treaty of Saginaw (1820), 37
Trilling, Lionel, 202
Trogdon, Robert, 83n4, 180
trout, 54, 61, 63, 64, 65, 79, 91, 92, 173, 199, 206; fishing for, 17, 67, 75, 80, 81–82, 90;
kingfisher and, 68n7, 77; recollections of, 52; symbolism of, 52
Tutt, J. W., 69n8
Twain, Mark, 135, 167

Under Kilimanjaro (Hemingway), 146; animal sympathy in, 144
Under the Sea-Wind (Carson), 116

vacations, 36, 40, 43, 44; nature and, 37
Van Noy, Rick, 4
"Very Short Story, A" (Hemingway), 198
Viking Portable Hemingway (Cowley), 83n1
Villalta, Nicanor, 187, 188
violence, 97, 182, 197, 198, 203
voice, narrative, 22, 24, 27, 28, 29, 79, 80, 111, 141
Von Blixen, Baron, 133

Walden (Thoreau), 73, 83n5
Walden Pond, 73, 77
war, 195–96; ecosystem and, 195; escaping, 201; landscape and, 195; nature and, 195, 201; violence of, 198
Waste Land, The (Eliot), 32
Watts, Emily Stipes, 12, 13, 14, 16
Weber, Max, 58, 59, 60
West, Ray B., 155, 158–59
Westling, Louise H., 93
wilderness, 38, 60, 65, 74, 103, 115, 211; Hemingway and, 76
Williams, Terry Tempest, 73, 98, 99, 198
Williams, Wirt, 198
Williams College–Mystic Seaport Maritime Studies program, 114, 115, 118, 119
Wilson, Pudd'nhead: on courage, 135
Wilson, Robert, 141, 144; behavior of, 129–30, 131, 132, 136; courage and, 139; ethical standards and, 131; Francis and, 130, 132, 133, 135, 136, 137, 138, 139, 143, 146–47, 148; hunting by, 131, 132, 137; negative assessment of, 130, 131
Windemere, Hemingway and, 37, 38
winter people, literary visions of, 41
Winter Wilderness Experience, 207, 208, 212
Woods, Dan, 4
writing, 182, 190, 202; assignments, 43–44; critical, 208; erectile, 185; nature, 73, 107; style, 189; technique, 181

Young, Philip, 26, 50, 53, 83n1, 84n9, 130; "code hero" hypothesis of, 1

Zach, Natan, 49

www.ingramcontent.com/pod-product-compliance
Lightning Source LLC
Chambersburg PA
CBHW021838220426
43663CB00005B/305